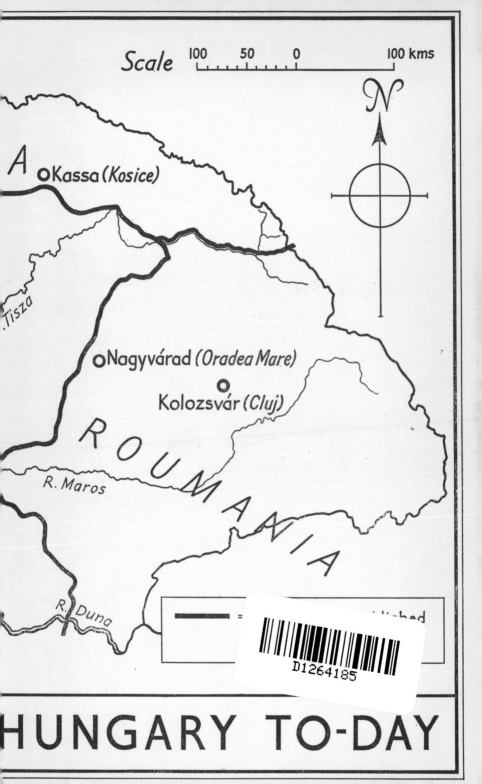

Scale 100 50 0 100 kms

N

A   ●Kassa (Kosice)

.Tisza

●Nagyvárad (Oradea Mare)

●Kolozsvár (Cluj)

R O U M A N I A

R. Maros

R. Duna

D1264185

HUNGARY TO-DAY

HISTORY OF HUNGARY

HISTORY OF HUNGARY

DENIS SINOR

FREDERICK A. PRAEGER, *Publishers*

NEW YORK

BOOKS THAT MATTER

Published in the United States of America in 1959
by Frederick A. Praeger, Inc., Publishers
64 University Place, New York 3, N.Y.

Library of Congress catalog card number 59-15752

To
Muriel and Ivan

INTRODUCTION

IT is unnecessary to expatiate here on the well-known difficulties of condensing into one volume of some 300 pages the whole history of a nation. I should like, however, to point out some of the specific difficulties to be faced in writing this volume and to indicate the exact scope of the undertaking.

There exists no reliable and up-to-date history of Hungary in English, and very few indeed are the works in English, French or German devoted to a fairly extensive period or to a particular aspect of Hungarian history. The effects of this deficiency are considerable. At an epoch when historians are becoming increasingly aware of the interaction of various civilizations, when even the man in the street is painfully conscious that his destiny is linked with, and partially dependent upon, the destinies of men living in other countries than his own, Hungary remains almost a *terra incognita*. Few historians have troubled to learn Hungarian, and to write on Hungary without knowing her language is worse than to write on England without knowing English. For, at the worst, an acceptable history of England could be compiled from the many thousands of French and German books written on England by excellent scholars, whereas there are few foreign works on which the English historian interested in Hungary can rely. Indeed, for the centuries lying between the Middle Ages and the twentieth century, there are none.

The result is deplorable. In English works where reference to Hungary is necessary, not only are the interpretations, as a rule, out of date, primitive and often unwarranted, but the facts themselves are all too often erroneous, and a proper name which is not misspelt is received with a sigh of relief by the reader who knows Hungarian. Misprints can be traced back from work to work, and the German forms in which many Hungarian names occur are pointers to German sources more than a century old, which were probably written with equal lack of first-hand knowledge.

The aim of the present volume is two-fold: to give the general reader a continuous narrative history, and to provide the historian with a reliable handbook to which he could turn in search of general information. Factors of civilization, of social and economic development have been taken into consideration as far as space allowed, but the guiding thread has remained political history. It could not be otherwise in the circumstances, since political history is the skeleton around which all the other histories must be built. This, at least, is my opinion. The desire to help the historian has made me give as many dates as possible, and I have not hesitated to indicate even the day when I felt that such precision might have its advantages.

When I set out to write this book, I thought that it would be a compendium of Hungarian historical research, and I did not aim at originality. In the process of writing I soon discovered that it was impossible for me to subscribe on every point to the traditional or more recent, Marxist, interpretation of Hungarian history. I think this should be mentioned, lest the interpretations found in this book be taken as having the full backing of Hungarian historians. The divergences in points of view are particularly noticeable in the assessment of some outstanding personalities. National heroes are seldom described with full objectivity by their own nationals. In matters of social history my opinion lies usually half-way between pre-war and post-war Hungarian views.

This book, then, probably presents all the shortcomings and some of the advantages of a pioneer work. If it succeeds in calling attention to a serious gap in our historical studies and helps towards better understanding of Hungary, it will not have been useless. Perhaps I shall be able to take up elsewhere some of the questions only touched upon here, but it is more important that some of the younger historians should themselves decide to tackle the not too difficult task of learning Hungarian. They would create the preliminary conditions for a less lunatic handling of Hungarian and also Eastern European affairs than has been customary in the last half-century.

Magdalene College
  Cambridge
  June 1958

CONTENTS

PART ONE

FROM THE EARLIEST TIMES
TO THE ESTABLISHMENT
OF A CHRISTIAN KINGDOM

CHAPTER I

FROM THE BEGINNINGS
TO THE CONQUEST

HUNGARIAN PREHISTORY is the term usually applied to the period which begins with the earliest data of direct or indirect evidence concerning the Hungarian people, and which ends with the conquest by these people of the land thereafter known as Hungary. It is quite certain that towards the end of this period the Hungarian tribes inhabited the regions north of the Black Sea, although, as we shall see, it is not easy to circumscribe their dwellings with greater precision. But when we try to penetrate further back in time we very soon reach a point beyond which there is no direct reference to the Hungarians in our sources, and we have to content ourselves with such evidence as linguistics, archaeology and ethnology can supply.

The great problem of Hungarian Prehistory can be summed up as follows: The Hungarians, who in their present country are surrounded by, and intermingled with, peoples speaking Indo-European languages, mostly Germanic and Slavonic, have themselves a Finno-Ugrian tongue. Since in their earliest historically known dwellings, north of the Black Sea, they lived with probably Turkish-speaking tribes, whom they resembled in their whole appearance and comportment, one must try to find a hypothesis capable of clarifying the historical process by which they kept or acquired a Finno-Ugrian language.

Hungarian, moreover, belongs to the eastern, Ugrian, group of Finno-Ugrian languages, and its nearest relatives are Ostiak and Vogul, spoken today by a few thousand individuals in Western Siberia. Hungarians and the Ugrians of the Ob (a collective name for Voguls and Ostiaks), now separated by thousands of miles, must, at some earlier stage, either have formed one people or had such prolonged contacts that their languages developed considerable similarities. The question arises: where did the contacts between Ugrians and Hungarians take place ? The Ugrians of the Ob are comparative newcomers in their present Siberian country, to which they migrated from some cis-Uralian territory. They formed there the easternmost branch of a greater Finno-Ugrian community, which occupied roughly speaking the same territory as the bulk of the Finno-Ugrian speaking peoples still occupy, namely the central and north-eastern parts of European Russia, probably along the middle parts of the Volga and the lower parts of the Rivers Kama and Oka. As we have no evidence whatsoever that other Finno-Ugrian peoples existed in other parts of the world, we have to surmise that the tribe that was to become the Hungarians detached itself from this greater Finno-Ugrian community, and presumably from its eastern, Ugrian branch. All the theories relating to the date of this separation, which marks virtually the beginnings of Hungarian history, are open to strong criticism, and it is wiser to confess complete ignorance.

From their dwellings in Central Russia, the Hungarians slowly migrated towards the south. The duration of this migration can only be conjectured. It must have taken some time—but it could be anything between say fifty or a few hundred years—because it allowed the Hungarians to borrow a fairly large number of Turkish words, taken, partly at least, from a Turkish dialect (the Chuvash) spoken in the Volga region. The study of these Turkish loan-words sheds valuable light on the cultural influence exerted by the Turks on the Hungarians and it is, therefore, significant that most Hungarian words concerning agriculture and animal breeding are of Turkish origin.

Hungarians appear in contemporary sources (Byzantine, Islamic, Latin) under a great variety of names, but are not as a rule called by the name they use for themselves: Magyar. From this one may, I think, infer that the political importance of the Magyar tribe was relatively small, and that it was therefore incorporated into various successive coalitions. The principal names under which the Hungarians appear—if we may set aside such anachronistic, literary names as Scythians, Sauromates, Getes or Huns—are: *Türk, Bashkir, Sabir, Onogur*. These are all names of probably Turkish-speaking tribes who, in the second half of the first millennium, occupied for periods of varying length some parts of the central and southern regions of Russia. Constantine Porphyrogenitus, whose *De administrando Imperio* is the most important single source on Hungarian Prehistory, consistently calls the Hungarians *Türk;* the name *Onogur* is the source of the names under which the Hungarians are known in the Slavonic and Western worlds: *Ungari, Hungari, Hongrois, Wengri,* etc.

At some time, probably during the ninth century, Hungarians occupied a territory called *Levedia,* adjoining the Black Sea, whose exact geographical position remains subject to controversy. During their stay there the Hungarians became allies of the Khazars. According to Constantine, the close Hungarian-Khazar alliance lasted three years. This figure is hotly contested by almost all scholars dealing with Hungarian Prehistory, but I see no intrinsic reason for rejecting it. In 889, which is the earliest precise date of importance in Hungarian chronology, the Hungarians were attacked and defeated by the Turkish tribe of the Pechenegs, and were forced to move westward into a country commonly called *Etelköz.* The length of the Hungarians' stay in *Levedia* cannot be determined. We have no information whatsoever concerning the date of their arrival there. Once there, however, they definitely enter the orbit of the Byzantine world and assume a rôle of increasing importance. In 839 their roving bands appear in the lower Danube region, between 870–80 they attack various Slavonic tribes, and in 862 an incursion into Pannonia of a 'hitherto unknown people called *Ungri*' is mentioned by the Archbishop Hincmar.

The geographical location of *Etelköz,* like that of *Levedia,* is subject to controversy. The name *Etelköz* itself can be explained since in fact the Hungarian form here used means simply 'the tract between the river(s)', and is similar in construction and meaning to the name 'Mesopotamia'. Constantine gives the names of the five rivers that watered *Etelköz,* but only three of these can be identified with certainty: Dniester, Prut and Seret. The Hungarians' relatively short stay in *Etelköz*—only six years—had immense importance for their political development.

The first Hungarian chief mentioned by name is Levedi—or, according to Hungarian tradition, Elöd—who gave his name to *Levedia.* In the light of later developments, presently to be examined, it is probable that Levedi was a chief of very limited powers, nominated perhaps only under the influence of the Khazars, who must have found irksome the all too loose political organization of their Hungarian allies. Once established in *Etelköz,* and again on Khazar advice, the seven

Hungarian tribes—it is for the first time that we hear of this federal character of the Hungarian nation—decided to elect a chief. The word used by Constantine is *arkhós* and he states clearly that never before had the Hungarians had an *arkhós* at their head. Latin sources use the word *dux*. Although the Khazar King proposed to Levedi that he should himself assume this function, he—according to Constantine—declined this honour, and suggested that either the chief Álmos or his son Árpád be elected.

According to Hungarian tradition, it was Álmos who was elected chief of the seven tribes. Up to then he had been leader of the Magyar tribe, and his election secured the political preponderance of this tribe. The election took place, according to Constantine, in Khazar fashion, with the new chief lifted on a shield; Hungarian tradition speaks of a ceremony of solemn oath-taking during which the blood of the seven chiefs was mixed together in a bowl—and probably drunk by those performing the ceremony.

The reasons which prompted the Hungarian tribes to invest exceptional powers in one man can only be surmised. According to 'Master P.', the great Hungarian historian of the twelfth century, better known as the *Anonymus*—from whose work most of our information concerning this period is derived—the election was held with the conquest of Hungary in mind, for which a leader was needed. This is probably an *a posteriori* explanation. It is possible that the election of Álmos instead of Levedi (Elöd), who had been proposed by the Khazar King, meant an assertion of independence by the Hungarian tribes. It is certain that once established in *Etelköz*, the Hungarians turned their interest to the west. Separated by the Pechenegs from their former Khazar protectors, they were on the look-out for a new master willing to use their services. They soon found a western ruler willing to employ these barbarian newcomers: in 892 King Arnulf of East Francia allied himself with them against Svatopluk, King of Moravia. On this occasion the rôle played by the Hungarian auxiliaries was not particularly important, but it proved of signal consequence for them, as for the whole of Eastern Europe. Having made acquaintance with the riches of Pannonia, they returned on their own account two years later, in 894, and wrought havoc in this flourishing province. It was certainly during these incursions that the idea of settling in Pannonia first occurred to the Hungarians.

Arnulf was not alone in availing himself of the new armed strength proferred to Europe by the arrival of the Hungarians. In 895 Leo VI, Emperor of Byzance, allied himself with them against Simeon, Tzar of the Bulgarians. Hungarian troops, transported by Byzantine ships across the Lower Danube, were led by Árpád's son Levente. Initial success soon turned to defeat; Simeon concluded a separate peace with Byzantium and turned all his strength against the eastern invaders, who, deprived of the help of Byzantine ships, had great difficulty in retreating and reached *Etelköz* only after having sustained heavy losses. There was little in *Etelköz* to hearten the defeated army of Levente. During his absence the Pechenegs, who had previously expelled the Hungarians from Levedia, had made a new attack, probably instigated by Simeon. Deprived of the greater part of his army, which was engaged in Bulgaria, Árpád decided to evacuate *Etelköz* and to attempt the conquest of the Carpathian basin.

The circumstances in which Árpád took over the leadership from his father Álmos are somewhat mysterious. According to Constantine, Árpád was the leader elected by the Hungarians on Khazar advice. According to Hungarian tradition, more likely to be right, the first elected chief was Álmos, and the tone of great respect in which Álmos is spoken of in our sources written under the Árpád dynasty, rules out the possibility of serious dissension between father and son. With pardonable anachronism a later historian speaks of Álmos as a man who, although heathen, almost possessed the gifts of the Holy Ghost, and who, in his own lifetime, conferred the leadership on Árpád. We also have, however, data suggesting that, on the eve of the conquest, Álmos fell victim to a ritual murder, being sacrificed to ensure victory. Whatever the case may be, and whatever the exact date at which Árpád assumed full leadership, it is he who is traditionally regarded as the conqueror.

Information regarding the route by which the Hungarians entered their new country is often contradictory. Árpád himself, having evacuated *Etelköz*, turned north, held Kiev to ransom, and having augmented the ranks of his people with Slavonic and Turkish auxiliaries, entered Pannonia through the pass of Verecke, on the north-eastern part of the Carpathians. Other Hungarian elements came from the east, through the mountains of Transylvania, or the south, probably following the Danube valley. Svatopluk had died in 894 and there was no one to replace this powerful personality. The Hungarian incursion of 894 had deeply shaken the Moravian state and the mostly Slavonic population of the country did not offer serious resistance to the invaders. These were not numerous enough to occupy effectively the whole of what was to become Hungary. Each of the seven tribes—which were joined, in not perfectly clear circumstances by an eighth, probably Turkish tribe, the Kabars—settled on a separate territory, large enough to provide pastures for the horses on which their military strength depended. The bulk of the invaders settled in the so-called Transdanubian territory, i.e. to the west of the Danube, where had lain the Roman province of Pannonia, but the plains between the Danube and the Tisza were also occupied, and so probably were the valleys of most of the affluents of these rivers. The mountainous regions, unsuitable for horse-breeding, were, at first, left unoccupied.

During the ninth and tenth centuries the Hungarians formed a nation of mounted warriors, essentially of the same type, though less powerful, as the Huns and Avars before them. The key of their striking military successes was the ingenious use they made of a very mobile light cavalry, well trained and using the bow from horseback. Their successive raids into Western Europe were operations of exceptional daring, splendidly executed. Their civilization, in what we know of it, differs little from that of other nomadic empires. Though, geographically speaking, of European origin, the Hungarians who settled in the Danube valley were, spiritually and materially, Asiatics, and belonged to the great Central Eurasiatic cultural family whose members lived dispersed from the Danube to China, from Persia and India to the Arctic. The Hungarian bows and arrows 'handled with such art that it is almost impossible to avoid them' (according to the contemporary chronicler Regino) were of exactly the same type as those used in Central Asia, their saddles, made entirely of wood, differed in nothing from those of the Avars. Their stirrups were asymmetrical—the inner side being shorter—to enable the rider to stand up in them and shoot backwards from the galloping horse —a technique greatly admired by contemporary writers.

As nomadic peoples generally do, the Hungarians disliked towns, and even houses, to which they preferred tents. According to Otto von Freisingen, as late as the middle of the twelfth century, summer and autumn were still spent under tents. The lack of permanent dwellings— although the sites on which they pitched their tents were permanent—

determined the nature of their art. They had to find expression for it on the utensils of daily life, on arms and clothing; accordingly its medium was metal and leatherwork, textiles and wood-carvings. They buried their dead and had cemeteries set out according to a strict pattern. Men were buried with bow, arrow and quiver, saddle and other pieces of horse-furniture.

The Hungarians had their own writing, a runic script with connections in Central Asia. Our sources often mention their fondness of songs and tales, but no Hungarian text has come to us from earlier than the middle of the thirteenth century. Such little information as we possess about their religious beliefs shows that these were of a type common among the peoples of Central Eurasia. The Hungarians also shared with these peoples the habit of great religious tolerance, which was later to facilitate their conversion to Christianity.

In 926 a small group of Hungarian raiders visited St Gallen, south of Lake Constance. The annals of the monastery give us the most vivid and detailed account we have of the behaviour of these dreaded warriors. In spite of their rudeness, their wanton but casual cruelty, they emerge as brave, gay, simple men. Some episodes of their visit, as when one of them loses his life removing the cock from the tower of the church, or when others at the request of a simple-minded brother spare the wine-cask, stand out by their simple humanity. According to his own words, never did Brother Heribaldus have a better time than during the Hungarians' stay in his monastery.

Contemporary European sources express horror at the ugliness of the Hungarians. Much of the descriptions given is stereotyped, based, sometimes literally, on earlier descriptions of the Huns or Avars. The same words were later to be applied to the Mongols. The study of anthropological finds cannot yet provide conclusive evidence for the racial composition of the Hungarians. It is, however, quite certain that the Mongoloid type was well represented among them, and that they were, on the whole, of rather short stature, with short legs, bowed through continuous riding. If we take into account their costume, hair-style, odd language and general ferocity, we can hardly wonder that little that flatters is to be found in descriptions given of them by their European contemporaries.

It would, however, be a mistake to see in the Hungarians a people as powerful or as dangerous as the Huns. None of their princes had pretensions similar to those of Attila or, later, the Mongol Khans, and there is no evidence that they were ambitious to found a great empire. The Hungarians, when entering their new country, were after all a people which had been driven out of its dwellings by the Pechenegs twice within a decade. Once established they still had a healthy respect for that people, and some years later Byzantine diplomacy failed to secure their help against the Pechenegs or against Simeon, victor of Levente. It is also probable that their establishment in Transdanubia, rather than in the eastern parts of Hungary, was motivated not only by the greater richness of this territory, but also by the Hungarians' desire to put as much space as possible between them and their former eastern neighbours. In any case, it seemed more profitable to attack the rich and ill-prepared countries of the west than to struggle with the poor but powerful Pechenegs. Their new abodes were at the very threshold of the much-coveted western riches.

Hardly had the Hungarians penetrated into Central and Western Hungary than a group of them raided Italy in the spring of 899. They devastated Lombardy, went as far as the St Bernard Pass and, plundering for a whole year, set ablaze flourishing cities such as Bergamo, Modena, Piacenza and many others. They even tried to take Venice. The final conquest of Pannonia itself was probably achieved by the Hungarians returning from their Italian expedition. By 900 the conquest of Hungary was an accomplished fact.

CHAPTER 2

THE ERA OF 'ADVENTURES'

THE establishment of the Hungarians in King Arnulf's eastern provinces did not diminish their aggressiveness. Arnulf himself, their former ally, died in December 899 (the occupation of Pannonia would probably not have been carried out while he was still alive). In 900 was launched an attack against Bavaria. It was followed, year after year, by other raids, until 904, when the Hungarians lost some of their leaders in a trap set up by the Margrave Liutpold. The following years brought about the complete destruction of what remained of the Moravian Empire, and in 907 the battle of Ennsburg marks the disappearance of Charlemagne's Ostmark. Liutpold himself lost his life. Henceforth Hungarian territory extended to the River Enns. In 908 the Hungarians attacked Saxonia and Thuringia and slew Duke Burchard. In 910 they defeated Lewis the Child near Augsburg. The first success against them was achieved by Arnulf, Duke of Bavaria, who in 913, in the valley of the Inn, destroyed an important Hungarian contingent returning from Burgundy.

There is no point in making here a full catalogue of the constant Hungarian incursions into western lands. Twenty years had to elapse before another major success against them could be achieved. In 924 Henry the Fowler, King of Germany, was lucky enough to capture a Hungarian chief whose troops were plundering his country. In lieu of ransom he obtained from them an armistice for nine years during which time Henry agreed to pay an annual tribute. Henry made good use of this armistice. He reorganized his army and adapted it to the special requirements of warfare with the Hungarians. At the expiry of the armistice, feeling confident in his force, he refused to pay further tribute. A Hungarian army of unusual strength set out to punish him but Henry met it near Merseburg on March 15, 933, and gained a total victory. It was the greatest defeat inflicted so far on the Hungarians by a western army, and it also had the value of showing the way in which a halt could be put to the constant menace of these invaders, to whom popular belief was ready to attach almost magical powers.

The Hungarians, as was their custom, showed little enthusiasm for returning to fight an enemy who had defeated them, and in Henry's lifetime they made no further attacks on Germany. Instead, they already felt strong enough, by 934, to turn their attention towards the Balkans. Tsar Simeon, whom they had carefully avoided ever since Levente's defeat, was dead, and his successor Peter was a less impressive man. The Pecheneg's renown was still great and the Hungarians probably felt honoured to be able to lead an attack against Byzantium in alliance with their arch-enemies. Their troops penetrated as far as Constantinople. There peace was concluded for five years, which was renewed in 938, 943 and 948. Byzantium's immense experience in handling the Barbarians, and its system of fortified towns, helped to ward off the possibility of any serious attack by the Hungarians. These must have felt for the Emperor a respect mixed with fear which the quarrelsome little kings of Western Europe did not command. It is interesting to reflect that it was probably this difference of attitude which prompted the Hungarians to interfere rather with western affairs and which, ultimately, led to their acceptance of the western, non-Byzantine form of Christianity.

This is not the place to depict the chaos into which Europe was plunged in the ninth and tenth centuries. But to understand the rôle the Hungarian incursions were allowed to play, one must remember the self-destroying inner struggles of the dying Carolingian Empire. With its complete dislocation, the last remnants of the Roman Empire in the west were fast disappearing, the distinction between Roman and Barbarian, between Civilized and Uncivilized, was becoming meaningless. In past centuries the chief aim of the average Barbarian had been to gain admittance into the world of the Civilized, and it is certain that the Hungarians, who lacked a leader of the really commanding stamp of, say, Attila, would have been all too glad to curry favour with a really powerful state. But no such state was to be found at the time of their appearance on the western threshold. The waves of invasions that broke from all sides over Europe—the Northmen, the Moslems, the Hungarians—were not due to some sudden increase in the strength of these vastly different peoples, but were the result of the disappearance of any power with the necessary military or moral strength to resist them. It was the power-vacuum which made possible the successful attacks of Barbarians who in earlier times would have been held at bay. In the darkest hundred years of the Dark Ages, roughly 850–950, there was no Aetius to fight at the Catalaunian plains, no Charles Martel to give battle at Poitiers. In the lands where once had been the Avar Empire, destroyed by Charlemagne, there was none to offer resistance to another people of the steppe, the Hungarians.

It cannot be sufficiently emphasized that the Hungarians had neither the power nor the will to undertake methodical conquest in Western Europe. The number of the Hungarians who moved into their new country from *Etelköz* is estimated at 250,000, a round figure including young and old, men and women. None of the western campaigns seems to have been undertaken by the nation as a whole, and there is strong evidence to support the view that the plundering expeditions were purely tribal undertakings. This is why the destruction, through defeat or disease—as in 925 in the Pyrenees—of any marauding bands had little or no effect other than that the survivors, or other bands learning from their lesson, avoided for a while the region where they had been defeated, or waited patiently for the death of the 'strong man' whom they had been taught to fear. There is nothing in these raids to recall the immense 'prestige' campaigns of Attila or Gengis. In spite of all their military dash the Hungarian attacks would not have succeeded without the connivance of western princes.

Ever since their arrival in the Danube valley, Hungarians had been a factor of some importance in the troublesome affairs of the disintegrating Carolingian Empire. The fateful alliance of King Arnulf with the Hungarians was but the first of a series.

The rulers of the Kingdom of Italy and of Bavaria made particularly good use of the Hungarians.

The great Italian raid in 899 ended with a defeat inflicted on King Berengar's troops at the River Brenta. The King had to make great sacrifices to induce the Hungarians to leave his country. From 904 onwards, however, we find the Hungarians allied to Berengar, and this King's successors, Hugh of Arles and Berengar II, followed the same policy. Whether the chief aim in concluding such an alliance with the dreaded invaders was to keep them away by bribes and by granting them the benefit of free passage when they set out against more western countries, or whether it was to make use of their troops in the internal struggles of the kingdom, it is difficult to say. In 919, 921 and 924 Hungarians helped Berengar in his struggle with Rodolph II. Whilst lending him their aid they took the opportunity of thrusting through Apulia, Roma and Naples; and after Berengar's murder in 924 they passed the Alps, penetrated into Burgundy, descended the Rhône valley, fell upon Nîmes and reached the Pyrenees.

At times the Hungarians must have been almost as awkward as allies as they were as enemies. Hugh of Arles, who in 926, hardly two years after he had fought them, accepted them as allies, and who later in 942, 943 and again in 947 made use of Hungarian auxiliaries, found their presence in Central Italy rather cumbersome. For this reason he induced them to pay a visit to Spain and even provided them with a guide. This man was to meet his death at the hands of the Hungarians, who found the road to Cordoba had too little water for their horses and put the blame for this on their unfortunate guide. It would be interesting to know whether during this incursion, or in Southern Italy, there were any contacts between Magyar and Moslem invaders.

More important than their Italian connections were the ties established between the Hungarians and the Bavarians. At the very beginning of the Hungarians' settling in Pannonia, the Bavarians suffered perhaps the most from their constant attacks. We have mentioned how Arnulf, Duke of Bavaria, defeated the Hungarians in the Inn valley. As a result of this discomfiture, the Hungarians seem to have accepted that Bavaria could withstand their raids, and from 915 onwards we find Bavarians and Hungarians allied in more than one undertaking. It is interesting to examine the background of this friendship. Soon after having defeated the Hungarians, Duke Arnulf was himself defeated by King Conrad I, and had to flee. He chose to go to Hungary, where he was very well received. It is not impossible that he there married a Hungarian woman; it is certain that while he was amongst them Arnulf 'the Bad' made friends with the Hungarians. This friendship was to last beyond his own lifetime. During his stay in Hungary, Arnulf persuaded his hosts, together with the Czechs, to lead an attack against Germany. The Magyars, carefully avoiding Bavaria, passed through Bohemia, and bringing destruction into Thuringia and Swabia, penetrated as far as Bremen. In 929 Arnulf, whose relationship with Conrad had in the meantime greatly improved, won from the Hungarians an agreement that henceforth they would not even cross his country. Arnulf's successor Berthold (938–47), though devoted to Conrad, maintained good relations with the Magyars, which were not disturbed when in 943 he successfully warded off a minor attack by Hungarian marauders.

Bavarian-Hungarian relations rapidly deteriorated with the accession to the Dukedom of Bavaria of the Saxon Henry I, son of Henry 'the Fowler', the victor of Merseburg, and brother of Otto the Great. Henry I, an energetic and ambitious man, was the first western prince to change to an offensive policy against the Hungarians. In 950 he did what no one before him had even envisaged; he penetrated into Hungarian territory and returned victorious, laden with booty and prisoners. The tide was about to turn, not only against the Hungarians but also against some of their allies. Thus Berengar II had to recognize the supremacy of Otto, who by now held all the lands bordering on the Magyars' western frontier.

During the half-century that followed the Hungarians' establishment in Pannonia the element of surprise had disappeared from their attacks. Thanks to the shortsightedness and folly of some princes, they had been allowed to intervene in the affairs of the Empire. It can be surmised that even those availing themselves of their services were not quite at ease, and that public opinion—if the anachronistic use of this term may here be forgiven—certainly disapproved the use, for any purpose whatsoever, of Hungarian auxiliaries. Neither Henry I, Duke of Bavaria, nor Otto the Great were men to condone such practices. Otto would perhaps have accepted reluctantly some sort of compromise, but his terms were obviously different from those proposed by the Hungarians. In 954 the latter approached Otto, whose recent successes within the Empire had made them chary of conflict with him, and proposed to him the renewal of old friendship, having probably in mind their relation with Henry of Saxonia before the battle of Merseburg. As a token of friendship, Otto offered them a small present, but refused to do more. The Hungarians attacked. This onslaught was more important than most of their former raids. The great war-lords, Bulcsu and Lél, who had been responsible for most of the Hungarian campaigns, must have sensed that much was at stake. In this they agreed with the Germans, who, forgetting for a while their dissensions, put up an impressive army in which were

represented Franks, Bavarians, Swabians and Czechs. The two armies
met at Lechfeld, near Augsburg, on August 10, 955, and the Hungarians
were completely routed. Their fleeing troops found no mercy from their
pursuers, who were aided by the local population, who had had to suffer
so much from Hungarian incursions. Lél and Bulcsu were made
prisoners and hanged in Regensburg. It was a victory of signal
importance, which brought Hungarian incursions to a halt and led to
complete re-thinking of Hungarian policies. Otto was rightly hailed as
the liberator of Europe and gained complete ascendancy over his
fellow-rulers. The battle of Lechfeld was the last but probably the most
important act of Hungarian interference in western affairs. Through
their defeat they secured for Otto the imperial crown.

CHAPTER 3

THE AGE OF REASON

THE seven Magyars who, according to tradition, were the sole survivors of the disaster at Lechfeld, returned to Hungary with their ears cut off. Despised by their countrymen, they roamed through the land, chanting their shame and the might of the enemy. The people seem to have listened to their warnings, and the era of the 'adventures'—as Hungarian historians call the western incursions—was definitely closed. A few more raids towards the Balkans, conducted almost half-heartedly, had neither the scope nor the effects of the former western campaigns. They lasted, intermittently, up to 970. The half-legendary duel of Botond before the walls of Constantinople can be taken symbolically as the last upsurge of Hungarian bravado, the Hungarian warrior is still capable of staving in the town's metal gate with his axe, but his act bears no fruit. Henceforth Hungary's fate is to depend more on foresight than on recklessness.

We have already mentioned that the foreign raids were mostly tribal undertakings. They were both the sign of and the reason for the weakening of the central power. The dominating personalities of that epoch were the great war-lords, Bulcsu 'the Bloody', Lél, Gyula; Árpád's descendants, theoretically still heads of the Hungarian confederation, enjoyed little popularity, and the influence of the Magyar tribe was no longer preponderant. Constantine says expressly that the first leader of the Hungarians is of Árpád's tribe, but that they also have two other leaders. Bulcsu and Gyula had both been admitted by the Emperor to the dignity of a Roman patrician.

The successive heads of the Magyars, thus overshadowed by the powerful princes of the western tribes of the confederacy, did what they could to consolidate and extend the power of their own tribe. Centrally situated, and not reduced by foreign wars, the Magyars acquired a certain stability, which, in the hands of a clever ruler, could be used as political capital. About 970, on Taksony's death, Géza became head of the Magyar tribe and thus of the whole Hungarian confederacy. Our knowledge of him is comparatively scanty. Historians, even those who lived under the Árpád dynasty, tend to neglect him in favour of his son Stephen, the founder of the Kingdom of Hungary. Géza is, undoubtedly a ruler of what we could call the 'precursor' type, such as Louis XIII, or Friedrich Wilhelm I, whose work made possible the more spectacular reigns of Louis XIV and Frederick the Great respectively.

Géza was aware that the era in which Hungarians could, unpunished, lead pilfering raids into the territories of neighbouring states was over, and he had reasons to fear that Otto might well decide to follow Charlemagne's example, by wiping out the Hungarians as the former did the Avars. Otto was, however, satisfied with the reoccupation of the Ostmark, and did not launch any major attack against the Hungarians; he was too busy with the affairs of the Empire to throw himself into any adventures on his eastern borders, and probably realized that the Hungarians had been checked and were no longer to be feared.

By the time Géza became head of the Hungarian confederacy, the hostility between the Empire and the Hungarians had cooled down. Otto I died in 973 and it was not unreasonable to suppose that the new Emperor, Otto II, whose main interests lay elsewhere, would be willing to establish friendlier relations with the Hungarians. Géza staked his fortune on collaboration with the German Empire, and he won, a fact which had immense consequences not only for the Hungarians but for Eastern Europe as a whole.

In order to pursue a constructive foreign policy, Géza had to strengthen his hand within his own country. Whilst some of the most aggressive Hungarian tribes had bled to death at Lechfeld or elsewhere, the Magyar tribe, as we have already mentioned, had thriven in comparative peace. With slow, methodical expansion, Géza laid hold of the main highways of the country, and thus gained control of its commerce. He also made some changes in the military equipment of his followers. Archaeological finds at sites occupied by the Magyar tribe show a great number of double-edged swords of western type, the weapon which secured victory at Lechfeld over the traditional light sabres of the Hungarians.

Géza realized that no heathen people would be admitted into the

European community, and he put out feelers to see how a wholesale conversion of his people would be received by the western powers. By that time Christianity, both in its eastern and western forms, was well known to the Hungarians. The local populations had already been converted before the arrival of the Hungarians, who had themselves mingled with Christians already in *Levedia* and *Etelköz*. Later, during their campaigns in Western Europe and in the Balkans, the Hungarians were in constant touch with Christian populations, and, more than once, individual attempts were made to convert them. Sigebert of Gembloux relates how towards the middle of the tenth century St Wicbert succeeded in converting some of the Hungarians then roaming his country. Two of the great war-lords, Bulcsu and Gyula, were baptized in Constantinople, but it is difficult to assess the degree of sincerity in these conversions.

As soon as Géza's willingness to admit missionaries into his country became known, many declared themselves ready for the task, and one could almost say that something of a scuffle ensued, not entirely dominated by apostolic zeal. Géza soon saw the favourable results of his new policy and an embassy sent by him to the Emperor early in 973 received a benign welcome from the ex-enemy.

The obnoxious Pilgrim, Bishop of Passau, was particularly eager to number the new proselytes among his own flock. Since it was mainly concerned with increasing Pilgrim's power and influence, his mission to Hungary achieved little, and faded out after a few years. Much greater success was won by St Adalbert, Bishop of Prague, who is, probably rightly, regarded as the chief apostle of the Hungarian conversion. This conversion was only sporadic; even those who had been baptized were reluctant to abandon their pagan customs, and many were those who refused to embrace the new faith. The greatest single achievement of Adalbert's was probably the influence he gained over Géza's son Stephen, whose deep and sincere faith was to be instrumental in the final conversion of his country.

Adalbert probably spent only a short time in Hungary, perhaps only a few months in 995 and 996, but his disciples, fleeing the bloody feud that raged in Bohemia between Slavniks and Przemyslides, came in numbers to Hungary and there gave substance to the movement started by the saintly bishop.

Géza himself saw in conversion only a means of securing the confidence of Hungary's neighbours and chiefly of the Emperor. As for himself, he considered that he was of sufficient importance to allow himself two religions.

Probably on Adalbert's recommendation Géza's show of goodwill secured the hand of the Bavarian Princess Gisela for his son Stephen. The great-granddaughter of the victor of Merseburg, the granddaughter of the conqueror of Lechfeld, who had annihilated the Hungarian army in 955, Gisela was destined to become the first Queen of Hungary. Soon after the marriage, which took place at the end of 996 or the beginning of 997, Géza died.

PART TWO

THE MEDIEVAL KINGDOM
THE DYNASTY OF THE ÁRPÁDS

CHAPTER 4

THE ESTABLISHMENT OF A
CHRISTIAN KINGDOM

GÉZA set his people on the only road which could ensure their survival. It was not an easy road to follow, however, and it was certainly not to the liking of all his countrymen. The changes brought in by Géza were so widespread that they could not strike root in his lifetime. They affected the lives of almost everyone in almost every sphere; they cut through tradition and tribal allegiances, they hurt individuals in their fortunes and ambitions. Géza and his formidable wife Sarolta, probably by making great compromises, kept discontent at bay. This possibility was not open to their son. The further Stephen went, or intended to go, along the road on which his parents had set foot, the more resistance was he likely to find, and a trial of strength became inevitable. Moreover —and this must not be forgotten—Stephen was a saint. Uncompromising on matters of faith, he felt it his duty to further the spread of Christianity by all means at his disposal. His great teacher St Adalbert had sought and found martyrdom. Adalbert's followers, Stephen and his fellow-workers (who were mostly former disciples of St Adalbert), were all imbued with the spirit of Cluniac reform, as was the King's brother-in-law the Emperor Henry II who is reckoned, together with Stephen, among the saints of the Church. Stephen was determined that his country was to become Christian. To achieve this aim he did not hesitate to appeal to foreigners. Severe and energetic, he was also just and clement by the standards of his epoch. His proselytism, though certainly not free from compulsion, does not seem to have made use of violence. It was not Stephen but his opponents who first resorted to force.

The young Stephen—he was certainly under twenty when he

succeeded his father—had a formidable task to face. He first had to contend with Koppány. We do not know Koppány's parentage, but he was a heathen, a kinsman of Géza's, who in the latter's lifetime had been a high dignitary, and who wanted after his death to assume leadership over the Hungarians. As soon as Géza died, Koppány attacked Stephen and was slain. One part of his quartered body was speedily dispatched to Transylvania as a discreet reminder to Gyula that a new chief meant to rule over his country. The reminder went unheeded. Gyula, Stephen's uncle on the maternal side, was himself formally a Christian. The struggle which developed between the two was not religious in character, and though we have little relevant information, it seems likely that it was due rather to a clash of personalities, Gyula being little inclined to obey his young nephew; it was thus a typical conflict between a powerful baron and a king wishing to establish a strong central government. It ended with Gyula's discomfiture and the seizure of his wealthy lands by Stephen. Gyula was taken prisoner, but later escaped and fled to Boleslas, King of Poland, whom he helped in his wars against Stephen.

In the next and last conflict which the new ruler had to settle within his own country Stephen's opponent was Ajtony, formerly a vassal of Gyula's, but in fact independent lord of the regions near the River Maros. Baptized but completely pagan in his habits (he had seven wives) Ajtony was not only a hindrance to the conversion and unification of Hungary; he disturbed Stephen equally by his interference with the salt-transport on the River Maros and his alliance with the Bulgarians. By 1004 Ajtony was vanquished and dead. Henceforth no enemy was to disturb the inner peace of the kingdom during Stephen's long reign.

The use here of the term 'kingdom' is not fortuitous. At Christmas in the year 1000, Stephen was crowned King of Hungary. This is probably the most significant single act in the history of Hungary, and it was the outcome of Géza's and Stephen's foreign policies. It marked the end of an era as well as the final, irrevocable entry of Hungary into the western orbit. By a curious coincidence the turn of the millennium which many believed was to bring the destruction of the world, and the appearance of the mythical tribes of Gog and Magog with whom, some decades earlier, the Hungarians had been identified, saw the crowning with a crown sent by the Pope Sylvester II of the chief of this very people.

Stephen had sought from the Pope recognition as King of Hungary and also (probably) powers to organize the Church in Hungary. It has often been said that by applying to the Pope instead of to one of the Christian emperors, Stephen cleverly secured the independence of his new kingdom from both Byzantium and the German Empire. It is undeniable that his action resulted in complete independence for Hungary from the two great powers of the epoch; the motive for it must be sought, however, in Stephen's whole *Weltanschauung*, which was in concord with the political thoughts of Otto III and of his former mentor, now Sylvester II.

During the reign of Henry II (his brother-in-law), King Stephen's relations with the Emperor continued good; but with the ascent of the violent Conrad II they soon deteriorated. The political ideas of his immediate predecessors, emptied of their religious content, became merely imperialistic. He was perhaps the first champion of the policy of *Drang nach Osten*, and perhaps the first German prince to make alliance with the Russians (in this case with Duke Yaroslav) against Poland. Conrad's policy was successful in Poland, but his wanton attack on Hungary in 1030 proved disastrous. Though helped by the Czechs, he fell victim to the old Hungarian tactics, apparently revived for the occasion by Stephen. The Emperor's army was annihilated and a long strip of German territory, including Vienna, was occupied by the Hungarians. It was the first episode of a struggle which was to last for over nine centuries: the struggle of Hungary to maintain her independence against German ravenousness.

Stephen's reign was, on the whole, a peaceful one. His good relations with Otto III and Henry II allowed him to strengthen his power in the interior. For some years, up to 1018, there was an endemic conflict between Stephen and Boleslas the Brave, King of Poland, probably a consequence of the feud raging between Boleslas and the Emperor, with whom Stephen was allied. At some time during his reign Stephen also had to ward off an attack from the old enemies, the Pechenegs. The only offensive war waged by Stephen was against the Bulgarians, who had reached the apogee of their power under Tsar Samuel. Hostilities against the Bulgarians fell into two phases. In the first phase, Stephen's action against Bulgaria was indirect. Ajtony had established friendly relations with Samuel, relations that could have caused much trouble to Stephen, intent on destroying Ajtony. His attack against the latter was therefore co-ordinated with the campaign of Basil II, 'the Bulgar-killer', against Samuel. In the second phase of Hungarian intervention against Bulgaria, some Hungarian troops aided Basil II in occupying Ochrida in the autumn of 1016, but were soon withdrawn. Their intervention had probably been caused by Stephen's desire to establish good relations with Byzantium. The issue of Basil's Bulgarian campaigns, which was the destruction of that country, was not without consequences for Hungary. For two centuries to come, Byzantium and Hungary were to have a common frontier.

The good relations between Otto III and Byzantium had their share in helping Stephen to establish an independent country; and though his own great merits in achieving this are self-evident, it cannot be denied that in the troubled state of Europe Hungary benefited from an exceptional concourse of circumstances: none of the great powers of the epoch had any interest in preventing the creation of a Christian state in the Danube valley. It was Stephen's good fortune, and that of Hungary, that his ambitions and conceptions were in harmony with those of the two heads of western Christianity. By the time that new men had succeeded them with new conceptions, Stephen was strong enough to resist any attempts at encroachment.

Stephen's achievements were very great and affected all spheres of the country's life. He did not, however, 'create' a state out of nothingness, as was often said. It was also argued that Stephen merely copied German or Slavonic institutions, to the extent that his country was no more than a slavish imitation of a German or Slavonic state. This is certainly not the case. The foundations on which Stephen built were solidly Hungarian and had already been laid by his father. The only decisively new element was Christianity, but even here one must not forget that the adoption of the new religion was not particularly abrupt. On the one hand, acquaintance with Christianity had been widespread among the peoples of Hungary; on the other, the conversion of the whole land was far from being achieved in Stephen's lifetime. From its inception, Hungary was a multilingual, multiracial realm. On a heterogeneous substratum the Hungarians built a powerful state, mixing their own traditions with those of the autochthonous inhabitants. Stephen then deliberately borrowed ideas and institutions from the more developed states of his time, particularly from the Bavarians to whom he happened to be linked by many ties. Nor was there any political consideration in Stephen's western orientation. He became a 'Roman' Catholic because this was the faith professed by his teachers, and the faith of those who had sent them to him. His choice was not due to some cunning political considerations, but was determined by circumstances, political and geographical; for it should not be forgotten—as it often is—that the distance from Transdanubia to Constantinople is considerable.

Stephen showed great activity in administrative, legislative and financial matters. His system of kingship shows no great difference from the autocratic systems then existing in Western Europe. The basis of his power lay in his own broad estates, which were, in fact, the lands belonging to the Magyar tribe. The commonly owned tribal land became the private property of the King, a development whose details remain obscure. We can follow the growth of the chief's power under Géza, but we know practically nothing of the gradual disintegration of the original Hungarian tribal confederacy. Fortified royal places scattered through the King's domain formed the nucleus from which the traditional Hungarian administrative unit, the *megye*, developed.

The King was advised by a number of *seniores* who formed the *senatus* or *consilium*, and who were invited from time to time to assist him in his work. Their choice depended entirely on the King. The King's court was not tied to any one place, but travelled through the land, staying at various residences in the royal domain. The country's permanent administration was very rudimentary, and in fact was equivalent to the administration of the court itself. At its head stood the *comes palatii*, in Hungarian *nádor(-ispán)*. This dignitary, second only to the King, was to play an important rôle in Hungarian history.

Stephen adopted the Carolingian monetary system, and his coins were struck on the model of those of his brother-in-law, Henry II. It is, however, interesting to note that in the division of money he did not follow the Carolingian pattern of 12 *denarii* to the *solidus*, but the Byzantine system of 30 *denarii* to one *pensa*. During his reign Hungarian currency enjoyed great popularity in Eastern Europe, as is proved by the circulation of numerous counterfeits of it, particularly in the Baltic region. Stephen had the advantage of being able to rely for his coinage entirely on the silver production of his own mines. It must not be forgotten that in Hungary, as everywhere in Europe at this period, the amount of money in circulation was very limited, and the country's economy was, on the whole, a natural one.

Stephen showed considerable activity in legislation and we are fortunate enough to possess a reliable twelfth-century manuscript of his

Decretum, the first codification of Hungarian law. There has been much discussion on the origins of this work. As is only to be expected, Stephen's laws are imbued with the Christian spirit and reflect strong western, particularly Bavarian, influences. They are, however, essentially Hungarian, and in some respects are no more than a codification of the already existing customary law. But the *Decretum* is anything but complete or systematic, and deals almost exclusively with contingencies created by the new, Christian kingship of Stephen.

Stephen's country lay at the crossroads of Germanic, Slavonic and Byzantine influences. Different as these might be, they were all Christian, so that there was no real challenge to the religious development of the new kingdom. In all other spheres of human activity there were examples of different types to follow and it does seem as if Stephen, perhaps with the ultimate aim of securing independence, but perhaps without, deliberately chose what seemed to him best in the institutions of his neighbours. But however much he borrowed, and however deep its influence on Hungarian life, it is certain that the national, Hungarian element remained predominant.

In almost every field Stephen's reforms were both good and successful. It was his tragedy that there was no direct heir to his throne. He had several children, most of them seem to have died at an early age. One of his daughters, Agatha, married Edward, son of Edmund Ironside, who sojourned for some time in Hungary. One of his sons, Imre (born probably in 1008) was regarded as heir apparent while he lived. A young man of great religious fervour—he was canonized by the Catholic Church—he died in an accident in 1031.

CHAPTER 5

INTERNAL STRIFE

IMRE'S untimely death, in the absence of any other son, made the problem of the succession very difficult. The oldest living male member of the Árpád family, Vazul or Vászoly, was a pagan and as such did not seem a suitable choice. He might, however, have secured the crown for himself after Stephen's death had he not sought to hasten this event. He made an attempt on the King's life, which failed. Vazul was punished by being blinded and having liquid lead poured into his ears. Though the King's vengeance was justified and, for the epoch, fairly clement, the elimination of Vazul from the political scene, and the banishment of his three sons, deprived Stephen of the possibility of finding an heir acceptable to most of his countrymen. The King's choice fell on Peter Orseolo, son of Otto, Doge of Venice, and of one of Stephen's sisters. On Stephen's death on August 15, 1038, Peter became the second King of Hungary.

It is difficult to extract from our sources a true picture of Peter's character, for these were written under the descendants of Vazul. Stephen's memory had, by that time (the second half of the eleventh century) become unassailable, and so Peter was made the villain of the piece, who by his machinations, together with those of Gisela, Stephen's wife, had brought about the death of Vazul, and who was later driven from his throne by the people, wearied by his cruelties and by his foreign entourage. In fact, although we do not know all the details of the affair, Peter seems to have fallen victim to court intrigues set on foot by Stephen's brother-in-law Samuel Aba, and encouraged by the Queen Mother Gisela, whose financial extravagances compelled Peter to check her activities. Peter, feeling, no doubt, isolated in this strange country, and faced with some sinister Hungarian characters, fled to the court of the Emperor Henry III. After his departure Samuel Aba was crowned King of Hungary (1041–4).

Samuel Aba, a violent, ambitious man, brought to the throne by intrigue and duplicity, had no legal claim whatsoever to the kingship. Probably for this very reason he was eager to prove by conquests that he deserved to rule. He declared war on Henry III, but even in the initial stages of his campaign achieved very little. Henry III launched a counter-attack, penetrated into Hungarian territory and finally accepted a peace offer from Samuel. Samuel's doubtful authority could not sustain a defeat of this sort, the first the Hungarians had suffered for many years. His cruelty had already alienated most of his former supporters when, having found out that a revolt was on foot, he invited the conspirators to his court and had them slain. The lords of the country then decided to call back Peter. Supported by the army of Henry III, Peter returned to Hungary, defeated Samuel and had him beheaded.

Peter's restoration, like most restorations, was short-lived (1044–6). The King, returning from exile, distrusted his people; his entourage consisted almost exclusively of Italians or Germans, who had no interest in things Hungarian, and who were intensely disliked by the population. There were even more grievous reasons for dissatisfaction with Peter's rule. He had recovered his throne with the help of the Emperor and on condition that he recognized Henry as his lord; in return the Emperor granted Hungary to Peter as a personal benefice, and the Hungarian lords were expected to take an oath of allegiance to him. As was only to be expected, Hungarians found this little to their liking and Peter's following dwindled rapidly. The country turned instead to the banished sons of Vazul: Andrew, Béla and Levente.

Andrew and Levente had been living for some years at the court of Yaroslav the Great, Prince of Kiev, where Andrew had been baptized and where he had married Yaroslav's daughter Anastasia. Béla, a brilliant soldier, had settled at the court of Casimir of Poland, whose sister he had married. He too had become a Christian.

Understandably the three brothers followed with close attention the political developments in Hungary and Béla even took part in the fighting against Samuel Aba. When a group of Hungarian lords invited the princes to Hungary, Andrew and Levente, with Russian troops, entered Hungary by the pass of Verecke.

Ever since the death of Stephen there had been cause for much discontent in the country; royal authority was on the decline and the forces of paganism, not yet dead, were on the increase. Peter's partiality to foreigners resulted in a strong nationalist reaction. On the news of the arrival of Vazul's sons, one of whom was known to be heathen, all the reactionary forces, kept at bay by Stephen, broke out and the champions of the 'good old' heathen days had their finest hour. The movement started in the territories lying east of the Tisza, where Christianity had not penetrated as deeply as it had further to the west; and, leaving behind them a trail of destruction and massacre, the insurgents advanced north to welcome the princes. These hordes were not alone in rejoicing in the coming of the new Pretender; members of the King's council, the lords and bishops, were united in wishing a change of ruler, and sent a delegation to welcome Andrew. This delegation, comprising the Bishop St Gerardus, himself an Italian, was massacred by the mob preceding Andrew's army. Andrew and his brother Levente were, at this stage, unable to dispense with the support of the reactionary, pagan elements of the population, though they obviously disapproved of their practices. In the meanwhile, Peter, fleeing towards the Austrian border, was made prisoner. Andrew intended to come to terms with the man who was still King of Hungary, but Peter's captors, enraged by his courageous resistance, gouged out his eyes. The unfortunate man died of his wounds and was buried by Andrew with the honours due to a king. It was fortunate that Levente spontaneously abandoned any claims to share in the government of the country; he died soon after and Andrew I (1047-60) could count on the support of the entire population.

Though unwilling to antagonize his heathen subjects, Andrew I was Christian and had no desire to put back the clock and to revert to old Hungarian customs. A rather weak soldier, the new King was a man of compromises, and this quality proved useful in his lifelong struggle with the Emperor Henry III.

Henry III was a formidable enemy to have and Andrew did his best to appease him for the death of his vassal Peter, and recognized Henry as his lord. But at Peter's death the Emperor held himself entitled to entrust Hungary to a vassal of his own choosing, and a trial of strength became inevitable between him and Andrew who, realizing his own weakness as a soldier, appealed to his brother, the valiant Béla. Béla, accompanied by his family, left Poland and was recognized by Andrew as heir to the throne, and during Andrew's lifetime as a 'prince', ruler

of one-third of the country. Béla brilliantly fulfilled his duties as leader
of the Hungarian army. On two occasions, in 1051 and 1052, he was
victorious over German armies on Hungarian territory. Neither party
was able to obtain a decisive victory, and in the years that followed, just
as in the time of the 'adventures', Hungarians were found intervening
in the internal struggles of the Empire. When Henry died in 1056, it was
clear that he had failed to reduce Hungary to vassalage, and that his
failure was due to the brilliant generalship of Béla. The German peril
was thus warded off, but by then Béla's increasing popularity had come
to imperil the stability of the kingdom.

Béla had been invited by Andrew I on the express understanding that
he would eventually succeed his brother on the throne. But, later, a son,
Salomon, was born to Andrew, in whose favour he wished to secure the
throne. Although Béla publicly renounced his right to the succession,
his brother remained suspicious, perhaps not entirely without reason,
and in the end attempted Béla's life. The prince fled to Poland, whence
in the autumn of 1060 he returned with Polish auxiliaries to enforce
his rights and wreak vengeance on his brother.

With the death of Henry III, relations between the Empire and
Hungary had rapidly improved. As so often at this period of European
history, when wars were waged for no other reason than the whim of
the aggressor, the death of one party, in this case of the Emperor, easily
brought about the establishment of normal relations. Two years after
Henry's death, his daughter, then aged eleven, was betrothed to
Andrew's son Salomon, aged six. This betrothal, concluded with great
solemnity (the widow of Henry III and the young Henry IV themselves
accompanying the bride to the Hungarian border), must have filled
Andrew with great satisfaction. The act meant peace with the Empire,
and the assurance that his son and successor would be allied with the
greatest power of the time. It is psychologically understandable that in
the general euphory the promise concerning the succession which he
had made to his brother Béla was the only discordant note. As we have
seen, it was enough to spoil the whole harmony.

When Béla and his Polish allies appeared on the Hungarian border, it
was clear that Andrew's alliance with the Germans had roused serious
misgivings among the people. Peter's disastrous submission to German
rule was still present in the minds of those who now flocked to join Béla.
It must not be forgotten that Béla was something of a national hero, the

man who had repeatedly routed the armies of Henry III. Béla was not only a good soldier, he was also a man of high integrity, with a marked understanding of social problems. For years he had been an honest and efficient servant of the King and country, who had been slighted on more than one occasion. Opposed to the sick King—Andrew had just suffered a stroke—who was surrounded by German knights, Béla appeared as a national leader. The prince's forces were victorious, and the King, severely injured in an accident as he fled, died soon after. His tomb can still be seen in what was the monastery of Tihany: it is the oldest tomb preserved of any Hungarian king.

During his short reign (1060–3), Béla I lived up to the expectations of the nation, though the still existing pagan elements suffered at his accession a decisive setback. These had joined Béla in numbers in his fight against the hated westerners, and there was danger of a repetition of the events that had marked the return from exile of Andrew and Levente. This new pagan revolt was nipped in the bud by Béla, its leaders were killed, and the mob was dispersed. By acting swiftly and with determination Béla left no doubt about the way in which he conceived government. The next few years were for the new King years of preparation for the inevitable trial of strength with Andrew's son Salomon, backed by the forces of the Empire. Béla honestly sought a compromise and would perhaps have been prepared to withdraw into his former status as prince. The advisers of the young Henry IV and of Salomon thought it better to attack. Whether Béla could have withstood their onslaught remains an open question, for, as he was preparing for the first encounter, he was grievously hurt in an accident in which one is tempted to see foul play. Shortly after, the King died, one of the most attractive figures of the Hungarian Middle Ages. 'He kept his country at peace . . . [records the chronicler] he did not allow that with the detestable greed of avariciousness merchants and money-changers should from the simple-minded and the peasants gather superfluous richness. . . . He raised his head above the neighbouring lands: the poor were made rich, and the rich glorious.'

As Béla's son Géza laid no claim to succeed his father, Salomon became, unopposed, King of Hungary.

During the reign of Salomon (1063–74) personal struggles continued to determine the country's destiny. The situation between the cousins Salomon and Géza was somewhat similar to that in which their fathers

Andrew and Béla had found themselves. In the year following Salomon's accession an agreement was reached between him and Géza, whereby the latter while recognizing Salomon as King of Hungary and his liege-lord, succeeded his father Béla in the dignity of 'Prince Royal'. This, it will be remembered, implied effective rule over approximately one-third of the country. Géza had much of his father's character, a straight-forward honest man; his younger brother Ladislas had all the martial brilliance of Béla. Salomon himself was a brave man, by education a true German knight. It was in a measure fortunate that at this time the country should have been led by men able and willing to fight, for a new danger, this time not from the west but from the east, appeared on the horizon.

For the first time since their establishment in Hungary, the Magyars had to face serious incursions by nomadic Turkish peoples; the Pechenegs and the Comans. Though the attacks did not mean a serious threat to the country as a whole, they involved some hard fighting, such as the battle of Cserhalom in 1070. Salomon, Géza and Ladislas all had their share in these combats, but it was Ladislas who seems to have captured most the imagination of the people. Incursions into Hungarian territory by Pecheneg auxiliaries of the Emperor of Byzantium provoked a Hungarian counter-attack which culminated in the capture of Belgrade, surrendered by the Byzantine commander to Géza—not to Salomon. We are not quite sure of the reasons that prompted this gesture, but it seems certain that it irritated Salomon who then, according to our sources, tried to cheat Géza at the distribution of the spoil. History seems to repeat itself, sons to re-enact the deeds of their fathers. Salomon, jealous and suspicious, decided to attack, but, like his father, had to retreat. The victorious Géza had himself crowned in 1074, while Salomon, encircled by Ladislas's men in Pozsony in Western Hungary, made desperate efforts to obtain the Emperor's help. Technically a usurper—the Pope, for instance, never recognized him as King of Hungary—Géza I had none of the feelings of inferiority common to his kind. He ruled with moderation, content to leave Salomon in Pozsony and to hope that time would solve the problem, which it did, and fairly soon, with the unexpected death of Géza himself in 1077. During his short reign contacts between Byzantium and Hungary multiplied, as witness the lower part of what is known as the Holy Crown of Hungary, which was sent to Géza by Michael VII, Ducas.

Since Stephen's reign contacts between the two neighbouring states had been rather sporadic; but the siege of Belgrade does not seem to have affected their relations for long, and at it Byzantine sympathy for Géza was already marked. The fact is worth mentioning here because the tranquillity of Hungary's common border with Byzantium had the most beneficial effects on the new state.

Since the death of Stephen, some forty years before, Hungary had been anything but fortunate with her monarchs. Six kings, seven reigns, three kings murdered, one killed in battle against a pretender to the throne, one dethroned, one perhaps the victim of foul play: not a favourable balance by any standards. After Géza's death a period of internal consolidation began with the comparatively long reigns of Ladislas I and Coloman I.

When Géza I died, Hungary's lawful King, Salomon, was still alive. The country's choice fell not on him, however, but on Géza's brilliant brother, Ladislas. This choice was most fortunate, for few reigns can match Ladislas's in Hungarian history.

CHAPTER 6

CONSOLIDATION

LADISLAS I (1077–95) was crowned in the year of Canossa. The struggle between Empire and Papacy was bound to affect external relations during his reign and, by paralysing Henry IV, gave Hungary a chance to consolidate her internal affairs. During Ladislas's reign the inner peace of the country was fairly undisturbed. Salomon made one abortive attempt to recover his throne through an alliance with the Turkish Comans, but Ladislas had no great difficulty in thwarting the project. After this we lose sight of the pretender, whose figure does not lack some tragic grandeur.

In the investiture contest Ladislas stood unreservedly at the Pope's side. His attitude was dictated both by political and religious considerations. Hungary had no interest in the establishment of an unlimited Imperial power on her borders, and, therefore, saw no reason to support Henry's anti-papal policy. Religious feeling also weighed heavily in favour of taking the side of the Pope. Ladislas was a devout Catholic—he was canonized later—a man in many respects similar to Gregory VII, a fiery champion of good causes, a true defender of the faith. Oddly enough, it was precisely because of his sympathetic attitude towards Rome and his fidelity to the principle of papal supremacy in religious matters, that Ladislas could, for many years, fill vacant benefices undisturbed. In doing so, however, he did not deny the Pope's exclusive right to make ecclesiastical appointments, but referred to an otherwise unconfirmed privilege accorded to St Stephen. Thus, while in practice maintaining lay investiture, Ladislas did not set himself at variance with official papal policy.

For some years Hungary's internal affairs prevented her from expanding her frontiers. During Ladislas's reign the consolidation of the royal power, the absence of danger on the western border and, also, the military qualities of the King provided circumstances favourable for conquest. The first King of Croatia, Zvoinimir, was Ladislas's brother-in-law. After his death a struggle started for the succession, which gave Ladislas a golden opportunity to claim the throne. In 1091 he conquered Croatia and thus secured for Hungary a passage to the Adriatic Sea. The annexation of Croatia to Hungary was an act with incalculable consequences for both countries. For Hungary it meant the incorporation of an alien body which could never be fully assimilated and which, particularly in the nineteenth and twentieth centuries, caused acute crises. Nor were the immediate consequences of Croatia's annexation favourable either. The late King had been a vassal of the Pope, who viewed with serious misgivings the high-handed way in which Ladislas had seized the country and filled its ecclesiastical posts with his own men. Ladislas entrusted the newly acquired territories to his nephew Álmos, and hoped that he would eventually be recognized as King of Croatia. The Pope, however, was little inclined to accept the *fait accompli*, and the ambitious Álmos, embittered, turned to the Emperor. With Salomon dead the principal bone of contention between Ladislas and Henry IV had disappeared, and so, at the end of his reign, Ladislas found himself further from papal policy than he had ever been before. Neither Urban II nor Ladislas were men of weak character and the dissensions of the King's closing years resulted largely from the clash between two vigorous personalities. Neither was inclined, however, to jeopardize irrevocably the prospects of further collaboration.

Ladislas died in 1095 and his nephew Coloman, the son of Géza and elder brother of Álmos, followed him on the throne (1095–1116). Coloman was a man who seemed to lack many of the qualities expected at that epoch in a king. He was a frail man, by temperament a scholar: his epithet in Hungarian history can be rendered in English as 'the book-lover'. Yet though weak in body—in his last years he suffered from unbearable headaches—Coloman had a powerful mind, a burning intelligence and a great determination to rule for the greatest benefit of his people.

In the field of foreign policy, Coloman displayed a remarkable unity of purpose, a sound judgment of men and events, and a great sense of dignity. The problems he had to face were numerous and often of a complex nature. Soon after his accession the first pseudo-crusaders, led by Walter Poissy and Peter the Hermit, asked for and obtained permission to cross Hungary. Thanks to Coloman's firm and efficient organization, no serious friction occurred until the armies reached Hungary's southern border. Another band, led by Gotschalk and Folker of Orleans, had to be dispersed by Coloman soon after their arrival in his country. The more dangerous band of the ill-famed Emico was refused transit. When they tried to force their way through Hungary, Coloman resisted successfully and routed them. It speaks in favour of Coloman's honesty of purpose that, in spite of the experiences he had had, he did not oppose the transit of the crusaders under the leadership of Godfrey of Bouillon. An agreement was worked out between him and Coloman, and Godfrey's brother Baudouin, together with his family, was handed over as hostage to the King. The crusaders crossed Hungary without any serious incident and Coloman's reputation was greatly enhanced.

Coloman's handling of this delicate matter is but one instance of his deliberate policy of maintaining the best possible relations with the Papacy. In the controversial question of lay investiture, after a certain time, during which Coloman never questioned the basic correctness of the Pope's point of view, the King, in 1106, solemnly declared that henceforth he renounced the right to make investitures. In Hungary this vexed question had never wholly left the religious sphere to which it truly belonged, and the solution was satisfactory to both sides. Coloman's rather surprising marriage with Buzilla, daughter of Duke Roger Borsa of Sicily, was yet another tie with the papacy, and the first Hungarian attempt to establish contacts with a power lying, as it were, at the back of the Empire.

The Norman alliance presented also some advantages for Coloman's Croat and Dalmatian policy. In this field, as in many others, the King followed Ladislas's aims and, in spite of the constant though not always open hostility of Venice, endeavoured to seize the Dalmatian towns. The actual conquest was delayed until 1105, though for some years previously Coloman had been using the title of King of Croatia and Dalmatia. Though apparently successful, the conquest of these countries brought little advantage to Hungary, and—among other disadvantages —caused a deterioration of relations with Hungary's two most powerful southern neighbours: Byzantium and Venice.

Ladislas and Coloman were both excellent administrators and notable lawgivers. Ladislas's penal code marks an important step in the development of Hungarian law and reflects well the economic and social conditions of the country. His laws to punish theft are of an almost savage severity and show that the troubled years preceding his reign had left their mark on public behaviour. His laws concerning ecclesiastical matters throw an interesting sidelight on the great problems of the epoch. His attitude toward clerical celibacy, for instance, underwent a gradual stiffening over the years and was in full accord with that of Pope Gregory VII. He also, and for the first time in the history of Hungarian law, enforced the principle of the indissolubility of marriage.

Whilst in these matters Ladislas tried to improve on St Stephen's legacy by adapting it to the needs of his own time, Coloman was much more of an innovator. He enacted a new code and made considerable reforms in legal procedure. Coloman moderated Ladislas's draconian laws and enacted his law on witches, famous throughout Hungarian history: *de strigis vero, quae non sunt, nulla questio fiat*, 'of witches, who do not exist, no mention should be made'.

Coloman took important steps to regularize the law of succession concerning land. Henceforth landed estates were grouped in three distinct categories: *patrimonium*, i.e. inalienable land either owned by right of *prima occupatio* by the descendants of the conquerors or bestowed by St Stephen; *beneficium*, i.e. land bestowed by later kings; land acquired through purchase. Only an owner of estates belonging to the last category could dispose of his property freely. Estates belonging to the first category were considered as communal, whereas estates conferred by kings other than St Stephen could be inherited only by the direct male descendants of the first owner or of his brother. In the absence of such heirs, ownership of the estate reverted to the King. Since hereditary rights to land played an important part in the development of Hungary's social pattern, their codification by Coloman constituted a step to which we shall have to refer again later.

Coloman's reign was by any standards a successful one. It bore, within it, however, the deadly germ of family discords, which were to spoil the results of his labours. His younger brother Álmos could never forget that, though Coloman had the title to the throne, in Ladislas's mind he, Álmos, was to have been King of Hungary. All through his brother's reign Álmos remained a constant source of trouble, and after the birth to him of a son, his ambition pushed him to new intrigues.

Coloman's attitude towards his brother was, on the whole, one of indulgence until the time when he too had a son born to him. Coloman's family life was an unhappy one. He lost his first wife very early and his second wife, Russian born, was taken in adultery. As Coloman's own laws made divorce impossible, he had to repudiate her and send her back to Russia, together with her son Boris, born out of wedlock, who was later to become a dangerous pretender to the throne. Wishing to secure the succession for his own son, born from his first marriage, Coloman was more and more exasperated by Álmos's constant intrigues and finally decided to take a desperate step: he caused both Álmos and his son to be blinded. This act, which was unjustified even by the harsh customs of the time, lay heavily on Coloman's conscience, and was severely judged by contemporaries at home and abroad.

Unfortunately Coloman's act had not even the justification of many political crimes, namely success. His son, Stephen II (1116–31), who ascended the throne at the age of fifteen, was a man totally unworthy of this dignity. He had all the violence and cruelty, and none of the intelligence and cunning of his Norman ancestors. Surrounded by his bodyguard, recruited from among the foreign populations of Hungary, he led a reckless life and, though courageous, brought Hungary into a number of conflicts as useless as they were unsuccessful. He was the first Hungarian king to show undue favour towards the Turkish tribes, particularly the Pechenegs, established in Hungary. When he died without a son, the country welcomed to the throne Álmos's son, Béla II the Blind (1131–41). The new King, though terribly hampered by his infirmity, proved a beneficent ruler. On his accession he wrought terrible vengeance on all those whom he thought responsible for his own and his father's mutilation, but he was sufficiently popular in the country to thwart all the projects of Boris, the illegitimate son of Coloman's second wife, to secure the throne for himself. Béla II was married to the daughter of the Serbian *supan* and maintained excellent relations with the Balkan states. He also enjoyed the sympathy of the Byzantine court and so, under his reign, a steady and unspectacular southward expansion of Hungary took place.

Béla II died, as did so many kings of the Árpád dynasty, at an early age. He was succeeded by his son, Géza II, barely eleven years old (1141–61). His maternal uncle, the *ban* Belos, assumed the Regency. Both he and, in his maturity, Géza II, were men capable of facing the challenge presented first by the transit through Hungary of the Second Crusade, then by a new imperialistic policy of Byzantium.

The members of the Second Crusade presented themselves at the Hungarian border in two successive waves. A German army led by Conrad III was of a rather predatory character, and could only be kept within bounds by a munificent distribution of gifts and bribes. The second contingent, led by King Louis VII of France, caused no trouble, in spite of the fact that the Pretender, Boris, seized the opportunity to enter Hungary in its ranks, concealed as a crusader. The two great historians of the Second Crusade, Otto of Freisingen and Eudes Deogilo, attached to Louis VII, were among those who crossed Hungary. We owe to them valuable descriptions of contemporary Hungary.

For some years the relations between Byzantium and Hungary had been deteriorating. Quite understandably, the emperors were not prepared to watch Hungary's penetration into the Balkans without taking some action. The asylum which Hungarian pretenders like Álmos had found in Byzantium was in itself an indication of the Byzantium desire not to leave unchallenged the rise on the northern borders of a new expansionist power. Active hostilities, however, began only with the accession of Manuel I Comnenus (1143), grandson of St Ladislas. In twenty-two years, starting in 1150, Manuel made not less than ten major attacks on Hungary. These attacks, though they succeeded in checking further Hungarian advances, were, on the whole, successfully resisted by Hungary. In the meanwhile the great struggle between Frederick Barbarossa and Pope Alexander III had begun. Though the possibility of Manuel and Frederick Barbarossa concluding an alliance and, in consequence, encircling Hungary, could not be discarded, Géza followed the by then traditional Hungarian pro-papal policy. His sudden death—he too died at the age of thirty-two—deprived Hungary of a most capable monarch and left the throne to his son, the fourteen-year-old Stephen III (1161–72). Manuel found the moment opportune to secure for himself a decisive influence in Hungarian affairs. He therefore supported Ladislas II (1162–3) and, after his death, Stephen IV (1163–5), younger brothers of the late King Géza, as anti-kings. Stephen III, however, succeeded in making prisoner his uncle, Stephen IV, who then, abandoning his claims, returned to Constantinople. Faced with the failures of his own protégés, Manuel changed tactics. Having no son of his own, he made an offer to Stephen III, according to which Stephen's younger brother, Béla, was to go to the Byzantine court and eventually succeed the Emperor. As Béla was heir to the Hungarian throne as well, Manuel's hope was to secure a personal union between Byzantium and Hungary and thus, for all practical purposes, incorporate Hungary into the Byzantine Empire. The arrangement was also to serve more immediate purposes. As soon as his offer had been accepted, Manuel put forward his claim to the customary one-third of the country bestowed on 'the Prince', heir to the throne. The death of Stephen III solved the problem in God's time. In the meanwhile, in 1169, a son had been born to Manuel and so Béla ceased to be the heir apparent to Byzantium. His position, however, remained stable at the Byzantine court, and on Stephen's death he went to Hungary, with Manuel's full support, to occupy the throne.

The reign of Béla III (1172–96) is a glorious period in Hungary's history. Béla not only had the qualities of an outstanding ruler, he also had an immense experience in European politics gained at Manuel's court. His family relations also assured him a high place in the hierarchy of European monarchs. At the death of his first wife, Anne Chatillon, who was French, he asked for and obtained the hand of Manuel's sister, Theodora Comnenus. The marriage, however, was never consummated because ecclesiastic authorities refused to lift the religious vows which Theodora had previously taken. Béla then married Marguerite Capet, daughter of Louis VII, King of France. His own daughter, Margaret, later became the wife of Isaac II Angelus.

The Third Crusade, led by the Emperor, Frederick Barbarossa, crossed Hungary during the reign of Béla III. From the descriptions left to us by the historians of these Crusades, we gain a splendid picture of the richness and magnificence of Béla's court and of the help he gave to the Crusaders. The difficulties arising between Frederick and Isaac were overcome and a disaster averted, thanks to the intervention of Béla III at the Byzantine court. Béla himself, though he did not take the Cross, encouraged his subjects to join the Crusade. In Manuel's lifetime, Béla, who seems to have had a genuine affection for the Emperor, abstained from any hostile act against Byzantium. After his death, however, Béla continued the active Balkan policy of his predecessors and, already in 1181, he reconquered Dalmatia. It is not impossible that at Manuel's death Béla toyed with the idea of himself becoming the Emperor of Byzantium. He had after all been educated for this dignity. His armed intervention in the struggle following Manuel's death can be, and has been, interpreted in this light. But his friendly relations with Isaac Angelus show that, if he ever had such ideas, he abandoned them in time. Béla also expanded the frontiers of his country towards the north. He intervened in the affairs of the Principality of Halicz, whose duke, Vladimir, had been driven out by his rebellious subjects and who came to seek Béla's help. Béla's troops crossed the Carpathians and occupied Vladimir's country. Béla, however, did not hand over the conquered territory to Vladimir, but kept it for himself, and entrusted it to his younger son, Andrew. Béla was the first Hungarian king to use the title 'King of Galicia'.

Although it was in the field of foreign policy that Béla could boast the greatest achievements, his chief merit lies undoubtedly in the consolidation of Hungary. On his arrival from Byzantium, Béla had had to overcome the distrust of his countrymen, who, like the powerful and ascetic Lucas, Archbishop of Esztergom, feared in him a foreigner alienated from his country by Byzantine influence and opposed to the Catholic faith by his Orthodox upbringing. Béla soon overcame this initial hostility and kept the inner peace of his kingdom throughout his reign. In Constantinople he had become accustomed to a higher degree of civilization, which, on his return to Hungary, he tried to implant there also. In Manuel's court he came under considerable French influence, which was later reinforced through his successive French wives. Though some sporadic French influence is met earlier in Hungarian cultural life, it increased throughout Béla's reign, until it became the greatest single foreign influence of the epoch on Hungarian culture. Béla invited the Cistercian order to Hungary and granted great privileges to them; and there, as in other countries, they introduced improved methods of estate management, and brought into cultivation the former wastes of Transdanubia. It was also in his reign that the Order of Premonstratensians was established in Hungary. Béla III was probably the first Hungarian king to dispose of a real chancellery. The hand used in the writing of his documents closely resembles contemporary French handwriting and Hungarian proper names occurring in the Latin text are often spelt in accordance with French orthography. This suggests, either the presence of Frenchmen in Béla's chancellery, or else that Hungarian priests visited France for the purpose of study. Considerable

French influence can be detected in the *Gesta Hungarorum*, written by Béla's notary, the so-called *Anonymus*.

Ever since the establishment of kingship in Hungary the right to mint coins had remained a royal privilege. Since Stephen's death, his excellent coinage had been debased through successive issues and a biennial, and later annual, issuing of new coinage had become the rule. The value of each issue was less than that of the previous one, and, moreover, each subsequent change was burdened by the *lucrum camerae* which, at the time of Béla II, amounted to fifty per cent. This meant that each previous, better, issue was worth after one year only half the value of the subsequent more debased issue. The deterioration of Hungarian coinage was particularly marked during the reign of Béla II, and only Géza II halted this disastrous course. But it was only under Béla III that money acquired some of its lost value. He also introduced custom duty on any merchandise imported into Hungary, and fixed its value at one-eighth.

CHAPTER 7

THE RISE OF THE BARONS

IT is difficult to determine whether the lustre of Béla III's reign was due to improved economic conditions or to his successful policies. As no new factors, economic or social, seem to have appeared during his reign, and as almost one-third of his income came from the royal estates, exploited in the conventional manner, one is tempted to see in the general prosperity of the kingdom the joint effects of his personal influence and his luck. Though after his death there were no marked changes in production, Hungary's political development then reached a turning-point of exceptional import.

Béla III, probably as a result of his Byzantine upbringing, did not follow the, by then, well established Hungarian custom of appointing his elder son heir to the throne, and his younger son 'Prince', with effective rule over one-third of the country. The elder son Imre (1196–1204) was to rule the country alone, whereas his younger brother Andrew had to be content with the considerable wealth left him by his father, and—a legacy of doubtful value—with the obligation undertaken by his father to take the Cross. Strife with the embittered Andrew, who considered himself as wronged and deprived of his rightful heritage, marred the whole of Imre's reign. Though he resisted successfully Andrew's attempts to obtain by force what he had not otherwise received, Imre could only do so by the greatest possible efforts and with strong papal support. Celestine III, and, later, the formidable Innocent III, supported Imre on moral grounds as well as on those of expediency. Practically ever since Coloman's reign papal influence had grown steadily in Hungary. In return for his support of the King, Innocent III exacted Imre's intervention in the Balkans, where he had to proceed against the Bogomil heresy, and he also kept pressing the harassed King to take the Cross. Whatever sacrifices Imre made to obtain and maintain the Pope's help, they were not enough to avert the loss of Zara, then a Hungarian possession, to the bandits of the Fourth Crusade (1202). Though the town soon returned to Hungary, the event caused Imre much bitterness.

When Imre died—he was but thirty years old—he left his throne to his five-year-old son, Ladislas III (1204-5). Andrew was not the man to stand aside of his own free will in the struggle for power. This time he had behind him the support of the people who—in conformity with old practice—preferred to see at the head of the State the adult brother of the late King rather than a child. Andrew, immediately on Imre's death, seized power; the young child had to flee, but his death, soon after, put an end to the conflict.

After so many short-lived kings of the Árpád dynasty, Andrew II reigned for thirty full years (1205-35), a lapse of time long enough to jeopardize most of the achievements of his predecessors.

There is very little one can say in favour of this vain, light-headed, unprincipled monarch, incapable of grasping the tenets of efficient government, pursuing aims unattainable, with means most inadequate. He was highly ambitious, and the bitterness that had grown in his heart during his brother's reign turned, on his accession, into an intense longing for spectacular achievements. He wanted to outdo Imre, whom he despised and envied at the same time. He needed the admiration of his friends, women, the glory of conquest, the satisfaction of renown. Reaching for all, he got none—and none of his predecessors had to endure so many humiliations as he.

Foreign policy was foremost in Andrew II's mind, and in pursuit of his unrealistic plans he paid no regard to the country's economic resources. His desire to be considered original in his ideas made him abandon the policy of southward expansion which had been pursued since St Ladislas, on the whole fairly successfully.

The fourteen wars of aggression led by Andrew in the first fifteen years of his reign constitute an astonishing achievement, when one bears in mind that they remained wholly unsuccessful, and that Andrew maintained fairly peaceful relations throughout with the emperors of east and west. The country's strength was wasted in abortive attempts to bring Halicz under Hungarian rule. The conquest of this Russian principality had already been achieved once by Béla III, and for three years, in his childhood, Andrew figured as its prince. Driven by his ambition to surpass the achievements of his father (who was intelligent enough to withdraw from an untenable situation), and spurred, no doubt, by dim memories of his boyhood when he was 'ruler' of that country, Andrew—with a remarkable lack of diplomatic skill—tried to prove by the occupation of Halicz that he was a man capable of conquest. It was Hungary's misfortune that he was of quite a different strain.

Andrew's part in the Fifth Crusade was not more fortunate than were his northern campaigns. Having postponed for twenty-two years the vow, originally taken by his father, to lead a Crusade, in 1217 he decided to join the Fifth Crusade. By that time Hungary's finances were so much weakened by the King's spendthrift management that large-scale borrowings had to be made from Jews and, even worse, in order to pay Venice for the transport costs incurred by the troops the town of Zara had to be sold to the Republic. The Fifth Crusade—in which his rank assured precedence to Andrew—achieved nothing, and had more the character of a promenade than that of a campaign. No serious engagement took place and Andrew—having spent some time enjoying himself at the court of his cousin Bohemond II, Prince of Antioch—decided in January 1218 to return. His decision aroused something of a scandal and rendered abortive such hidden schemes as Andrew might have had in connection with his expedition; for this man, incapable of conquering, or forcing the issue with, the tiny principality of Halicz, had set his mind on becoming Emperor of Byzantium. In 1215 he had married Yolande of Courtenay, daughter of Peter, who in 1217 became Emperor of Byzantium. At Peter's death his wife Yolande assumed the Regency, and Andrew's hope was that he might be elected to the succession. It must be said that thanks to his family connections he could produce claims as good as anyone else's, or, more particularly, as good as those of his equally incapable brother-in-law, Robert, who became Emperor in 1218. It gives the measure of Andrew's maladroitness that, with such ambitions, he did not try to secure for himself the advantages which some military success against the Moslems would undoubtedly have brought. There is in his character a certain amount of straightforward cowardice, which may partially explain his extraordinary behaviour during this odd Crusade. In any case, with his reputation at a low ebb, he failed to secure for himself the throne of Byzantium. The campaign, which entailed for Hungary the loss of Zara and brought the country to the brink of bankruptcy, achieved nothing.

Andrew's foreign policy was matched by his equally inefficient handling of internal affairs. The undue influence gained by foreigners, belonging mostly to the entourage of his wives, had been for some time a thorn in the flesh of the Hungarian nobles. Their discontent had led, in 1213, to the murder of Gertrude of Meran, his first wife, one of the few instances of political assassination in Hungarian history. Matters had not improved with his second wife, Yolande of Courtenay; former German influence had simply receded and been replaced by French. In 1211 Andrew invited the Teutonic knights to settle on the eastern borders of Transylvania and to form a bulwark against the penetration of nomadic peoples and heretic ideas alike. With their efficient ruthlessness—which later was to make history on the shores of the Baltic—the knights tried to carve out a state of their own, until, in 1225, they were finally cast out of Hungary.

More grievous than the unrest caused by favours shown to foreigners, was the financial crisis in which the country found itself. Causes for this can be found on both sides of the balance sheet. On the expenditure side, the heaviest items are the ruinous military campaigns and the luxuries of the royal household. On the credit side we find a great loss of revenue from the royal estates. This was due to the King's reckless donations, determined, in their turn, by his need for military services.

Ever since the foundations of the monarchy, royal estates had been the basis of the King's wealth, and hence of his power. Such grants of land as had been made—and most of the kings were chary of doing this—entailed feudal obligations for the recipient. Moreover—whatever the practical chances of this were—the fiefs were liable to return one day to the King. It was in the nature of things that, with the passing of time, the royal estates should diminish, as the granting of a fief was the most obvious means of recognizing services rendered to the King. As by the end of the twelfth century the possession of an estate entailed very few obligations, but, apart from any material advantages, assured the holder a higher stake in the social hierarchy, the desire to acquire land remained the principal aim in the life of the individual. In order to enlist the support of as many men as possible, first for his struggle against Imre, then for his campaigns abroad, Andrew felt compelled to make great gifts of land. He proceeded unrestrained, with a carelessness bordering upon lunacy; it once happened that he bestowed the same estate twice! The King even introduced an innovation of some moment: breaking away from previous practice, Andrew made his grants *iure perpetuo*, i.e. the beneficiary of the royal present received the land in full ownership with no obligations attached to it. In practice Andrew's activity amounted to giving away the kingdom.

The decline of the King's income from his domains was not compensated from other sources. Hungary was at this time a purely agricultural state, land being the principal, if not the sole source of real income. Income derived from mining precious metals and from salt was negligible compared to the yield from the land, and benefit from foreign trade, though growing, did not amount to much. As production could not be speeded, the wealth of the country was a constant, and only its distribution was liable to change. Mining had always been a royal monopoly, and so were the different toll and custom duties, and the more important right to mint coins. Andrew made the maximum use of this latter source of income and at the rate of several issues a year he debased his coinage to the extent of making it unacceptable. He even went so far as to farm out the mint without actually renouncing his right of coinage. The King proceeded in similar fashion with his income from salt, tolls, collection of taxes and his private estates. In Hungary, as elsewhere, such a system led to abuses and, hence, to a growing dissatisfaction among the population. In Hungary, as elsewhere, it did not put an end to the ruler's financial troubles.

The reign of Andrew saw the disintegration of the country's social system. The indiscriminate grants of land widened the gap between various sections of the community; indeed they created new classes. The formerly fairly homogeneous 'free' section of the community split, and the poorer elements could not assert themselves in face of the barons who enjoyed immense new fortunes. The collapse of the King's authority, his inability to enforce law and to maintain order led to an anarchical state, in which, in a frenzy of universal grabbing, every man's main aim was to carve out for himself as large a slice of land as possible. In this rush for possession the big landowners had an initial advantage which the holders of smaller estates or the landless free men had no chance of overtaking.

The feudal system had never struck as deep roots in Hungary as in Western Europe; the descendants of the conquerors remained *eo ipso*

free men, and the many foreigners settled in the country were assimilated
to them in status. In view of the acute changes which threatened their
very existence, free men united in opposition to the King and oligarchy.
In 1222 they compelled the King, much too weak to quell what
threatened to become an insurrection, to sign the so-called Golden Bull,
which was to become one of the principal instruments in the development of the Hungarian constitution.

It is tempting to draw parallels between the Golden Bull and Magna
Carta, but the comparison should not be pushed too far. Though equally
important for the respective constitutional developments of England
and Hungary, the only thing in common between them is that they were
intended to limit the powers of the Crown. But, whereas the Magna
Carta was extracted from King John by the barons, the Golden Bull was
achieved by pressure exerted by ordinary free men, and was directed
more against the barons than against the King. It marks, as it were, the
coming into existence of a new class, the nobility, comprising all the
free men not included among the great barons. The labouring men had,
as before, no word to say, and the Golden Bull, by asserting the rights of
a new class to which they did not belong, had, in fact, contributed to
their increasing isolation and cut them off even more decisively from
the body politic.

The Golden Bull is concerned mainly to defend the privileges of the
ordinary free men directly dependent on the King, the so-called
servientes regis, against the encroachments of the barons. The
dispositions of the Bull are highly technical, and were intended to put
an end to malpractices. Obviously no one in the thirteenth century
could foresee the effects the Bull was to have on Hungary's constitutional
development. The Bull forbade the accumulation of high offices, and
debarred foreigners from obtaining them. The King was forbidden to
bestow land on foreigners, and those who had already obtained estates
were forced to sell them. Guarantees were given to ensure that the
servientes regis should—except on some minor charges—not be brought
to trial elsewhere than before the King. The Bull fixed the military
obligations of the *servientes regis* who—thenceforth—would not have to
follow the King abroad at their own expense; a stipulation probably
made because of the hardships caused by Andrew's ceaseless foreign
wars.

The Bull also altered, in favour of the *servientes*, Coloman's dispositions concerning benefices. They were allowed to dispose freely of their land and only in case of their dying intestate and without rightful heirs was the benefice to return to the King.

The final clause of the Bull recognized the right of resistance to the King were he to break the dispositions contained therein. Perhaps unfortunately the means thus devised to enforce the Bull were too general—compared to the English committee of twenty-five barons—to be truly effective. It was probably for this reason that, together with many other dispositions of the Bull, the final clause remained a dead letter.

Andrew himself showed scant respect for the Bull and changed little, if anything, of his former habits. This time the Church threw in her lot with that of his rebellious subjects. The head of the Hungarian clergy, the French Archbishop of Esztergom, Robert, used his influence and obtained, in 1231, the renewal, with slight variations, of the Golden Bull. When the King still failed to put its clauses into effect, Robert placed the country under interdict, a measure that had only been used once before in Hungarian history. The second version of the Bull had already shown the growth of papal influence in Hungarian affairs; Robert's intervention in purely secular matters, though it was in favour of the people against the King, set a dangerous precedent and led, two years later (in 1233), to the signing of an agreement between the Holy See and Andrew. This strange document, called, after the place where it had been signed, the Agreement of Bereg, reads like a travesty of the Golden Bull. It is a deplorable document, displaying a total disregard for the country's interests and an almost incredible greed. The 'spiritual' side, if one may be allowed to use this word in such a context, is represented by some stringent regulations affecting the Jews, Ismaelites and other non-Christian inhabitants of Hungary. Otherwise the agreement is nothing but an arid but most precise enumeration of the exorbitant payments the King (virtually bankrupt!) was expected to make to the Church. The fact that the King did not respect this sordid agreement more than his own previous edicts does not mitigate the Church's responsibility in the drafting of it. Papal fulminations were not enough to make Andrew fulfil his obligations. To do that he would have needed money, and money there was none. Archbishop Robert himself realized that and did not resort to the supreme weapon of interdict. Thus the last years of Andrew's reign were no less tumultuous than the earlier ones. The old King, growing less ambitious and more apathetic, sought refuge in his private life from the troubles of the century. Shortly before his death, in 1234, he married for the third time, taking Beatrix of Este, daughter of the Margrave of Ancona, to wife.

As a soldier as well as a politician, Andrew fell short; but there is a reproach even more grievous, which the historian feels entitled to make. The thousand years of Hungarian history produced a fair number of poor statesmen but very few dastards; it was Andrew's sad privilege to belong to both categories.

CHAPTER 8

BÉLA IV AND THE MONGOL INVASION

THE situation at Andrew's death was a fairly desperate one and his son Béla IV (1235–70) had to contend with uncommon difficulties.

Béla's childhood had been a difficult one. At an early age he saw his mother, Gertrude, assassinated—a rather ugly butchery. Though he was crowned at the age of eight—in his father's lifetime—and received at the age of sixteen the territories due to the 'Prince', he was on anything but friendly terms with his father. He was a serious, rather humourless person, strongly disapproving of his father's happy-go-lucky ways, probably resenting the manner in which Andrew had got over Gertrude's assassination (without really punishing those responsible for it), and was living happily with his second wife. By temperament Andrew was an innovator and Béla a conservative, even a reactionary. It is not then surprising that father and son could not see eye to eye in political matters, and that Andrew viewed with displeasure the grouping around his son of those—and they were many—who were dissatisfied with his conduct of the country. Had the rôles been reversed—Andrew the son and Béla the King—Andrew would certainly have revolted and Béla would certainly have used the strongest possible measures against him. As things were, however, Béla kept on lecturing his father in a somewhat pedantic fashion and Andrew continued as he always had done. He probably considered his son a bore. In spite of attempts to replace the inefficient King by Béla, things never came to open revolt.

Béla's model was his grandfather, Béla III, and he did what he could to re-establish things as they were in his reign. It is regrettable that Béla IV should have used his uncommon administrative gifts, and his zeal, to accomplish the impossible task of putting back the clock. The Golden Bull, whatever its imperfections, carried in it the seed of constitutional development. Béla, by his very virtues, stifled the growth of new ideas and lent a fresh lease of life to the basically outmoded, patrimonial type of kingdom.

While his father was still alive, Béla did what he could to enforce those decisions of the Golden Bull which concerned the recovery of estates granted to undeserving persons. On his accession to the throne he pursued this task with unrelenting fervour, causing thereby much bitterness among the barons. Not content with improving on what in his view had been wrong during his father's reign, Béla set out to punish those responsible for it. Among other punishments meted out, Dénes, Andrew's treasurer and first adviser in financial matters, paid for his mistakes with the loss of his eyes; an interpretation of ministerial responsibility which might sometimes commend itself. In order to re-establish royal authority, Béla did not shrink from almost provocative measures, such as burning the chairs of his councillors so that none should sit in the presence of the King.

It is probable that Béla, given sufficient time, would have overcome the difficulties, which form an integral part of every process of purification. Though he had made many enemies he had also many devoted followers, glad to see him cleansing the Augean stable of Andrew's reign. Unfortunately for everyone concerned, all his early achievements were to be swept away by the Mongol cataclysm.

The Mongols invaded Hungary in 1241, but their attack was anything but unexpected. We know of a journey undertaken by a Dominican Friar, Julian, in 1236–7, to find out more about the Mongols. Julian brought back with him a Mongol ultimatum addressed to Béla, in which mention was made of previous Mongol embassies sent to the King of Hungary. The reason for Mongol grievances was also plainly stated: the asylum given by Béla to the Comans, fleeing before the Mongols.

As this Turkish-speaking people played a not insignificant rôle in Hungarian history and as is little known to western historians, a few words on them may not be out of place here.

From the middle of the eleventh century, Southern Russia, i.e. the steppe lying north of the Black Sea, was taken possession of by the Turkish tribes of the Kipchak. This people, or rather this confederation of tribes, appears in different sources under different names, the connection of which is not clearly established. Their Hungarian name is *kún* and contemporary Latin sources call them *Cumani*, *Comani*, or

Cuni, Chuni. In their new abodes the Comans were brought into contact with Byzantium, the Slavonic principalities of Russia, and also with Hungary. The first contacts between the Byzantines and the Comans were made in 1086, when the Pechenegs, breaking through into Thracia, had the Comans as allies. A few years later, in 1091, Alexis Comnene played off the Coman forces against the menacing coalition of the Pechenegs and the Turkish Emir of Smyrna. The first Coman intervention in Hungarian history is connected with the name of Salomon, who married the daughter of the Coman Prince Kutesk and who, with the aid of the Comans, attacked his cousin St Ladislas in 1085. This attack was beaten off and the Comans driven from the country. We meet them again in 1219, when Coman auxiliaries joined Mistislav, Prince of Novgorod, in his struggle against Andrew—an episode in the fighting over Halicz. Coman forces were lingering all along the eastern arch of the Carpathians. The Teutonic Knights settled by Andrew in the south-eastern parts of Transylvania, the so-called Barcaság, were constantly troubled by them and had to build wooden forts and entrenchments to ward off their incursions. The Coman menace to Hungary was never very dangerous, and in many instances they themselves were the victims of Hungarian expansion. This was noticeable not only in politics but also in the religious sphere. The conversion of the Comans was one of St Dominic's favourite aims, so Hungarian Dominicans were very eager in this task. Paulus Hungarus, their first Provincial, suffered martyrdom at the hands of the Comans. In 1227, Robert, Archbishop of Esztergom, baptized the Coman Prince Barc, together with his son and about fifteen thousand of his people. The following year the Dominican Theodor was established as first Bishop of Comania. The spread of Christianity and the strengthening of the political ties binding the Comans to Hungary went hand in hand. Simultaneously with the conversion of Barc and his people, Béla, then 'Prince', who must have played an important part in the conversion, received the allegiance of the neophytes. Soon after his accession Béla took the title of King of Comania.

The few facts chosen here, from a considerable amount of material, are intended to help place the Comans in the political framework of Eastern Europe. They also show that, on the eve of the Mongol invasion, close ties had already been established between the Comans and the Hungarians.

Barc had very good reasons to seek the protection of the King of Hungary. The Comans were among the first European peoples to face the Mongol onslaught. In the disastrous battle of the River Khalkha (1223) a joint army of the Russian princes and the Comans had suffered defeat, but the Mongols did not follow up their victory and returned to Russia. Barc, fearing a new Mongol attack, put himself under Hungarian protection, and the chief Coman Prince Kuthen—father-in-law of Mistislav—followed his example in 1239. He sent ambassadors to Béla asking for asylum for himself and his whole people, comprising about 40,000 soldiers. In return he offered to become a Catholic, together with his people. Encouraged by the Dominicans, who saw in this immigration the opening of a new and promising field of proselytism and the fulfilment of their old hopes concerning the conversion of the Comans, Béla accepted the offer. He received Kuthen in person at the frontiers of Hungary and agreed to be his godfather. Measures were taken to settle the immigrating Comans and to integrate them in the Hungarian community.

Béla's decision proved fatal for Hungary, but it would be belated wisdom to criticize him on that ground. For centuries Hungary had been a natural link between European civilization and the nomadic peoples of the South Russia steppe. It had been a constant and, on the whole, successful policy of the kings of the Árpád dynasty to settle within their own borders small groups of nomadic peoples whose attacks against Hungary had previously been repulsed. The Roman Empire and Byzantium had the same policy and the assimilation of the Barbarians was in constant progress all along the frontiers. But apart from these precedents, Béla's decision could also be justified on more specific grounds, both religious and political. We have shown the importance that had been attached to the conversion of the Comans, and the reception of Kuthen and his people into the Church could rightly be considered as the crowning of these efforts. The reception of the Comans could also be justified politically. On the eve of a possible Mongol attack it was a statesmanlike act to accept the alliance of a people disposing of a large and efficient army, and the sight of a people coming of its own accord to recognize the suzerainty of the King of Hungary was bound to enhance Béla's own prestige.

In fact everything turned out unfavourably. The integration of the Comans into Hungarian life could not be accomplished in the short period that elapsed between their arrival and the Mongol attack. By the thirteenth century Hungary had become an agricultural country and the nomadic habits of yore were all forgotten. The mentality of the Comans seemed as foreign to the Hungarians as had their own customs, three centuries earlier, to the western peoples. The herds of the Comans, accustomed to the endless Russian steppe, needed space that Hungary could not put at their disposal. Either the pastures accorded to them were insufficient or, what is more likely, the Comans were unable to keep themselves and their animals within any given boundaries. Their herds did considerable damage to the farmlands. The great number of the Comans was also an obstacle to their speedy assimilation. One has further to bear in mind the difficulties that inevitably arise when peoples of different languages (the Comans, as we have said, were Turkish-speaking) and of different civilizations have to live together. Complaints were voiced that Coman men were paying too much attention to Hungarian women, whereas it seems that the ugliness of Coman women debarred Hungarians from seeking compensation in kind. Many thousand Comans were being baptized, but their entering the Church was not without material considerations. In short, the arrival of these nomads into Hungary, far from being an asset, augmented greatly the odds Béla already had to face.

We have seen that Béla's pro-Coman attitude was of long standing. His assuming the title of King of the Comans involved in his eyes obligations, and he was trying to protect his new subjects against the Mongols. This attitude led him not only to offer shelter to Coman refugees, but also to intervene protectively in their favour.

For over two centuries Hungary had been one of the strongest military powers in Europe. Following a somewhat aggressive and imperialistic policy towards the neighbouring Slavonic peoples in the Balkans and to the north of the Carpathians, Hungary had been able to defeat repeated attempts by the German and Byzantine emperors to intervene in her internal affairs.

The Hungarian army was an imposing force and it is certain that it would have been able to oppose with success any of the contemporary European powers.

Béla was a serious and conscientious ruler, aware of the dangers that the Mongol advance meant to his country. He tried through spies and informants to obtain facts about the oncoming enemy. He also tried to secure the help of other nations. The Coman alliance was certainly regarded as an important military asset. Béla could also reckon with the help of the Polish princes to whom he was closely related. Boleslas, Prince of Sandomir (on the Vistula), had married Béla's daughter Kunigunda, and the powerful Henry II of Silesia was Béla's first cousin. The King also endeavoured to rouse Western Europe to a sense of danger.

From Frederick II Béla could not expect any help. The Emperor was too much involved in his life-and-death struggle with the Papacy to divert any of his forces. As he himself later declared, he had heard of the Mongol advance, but thought the danger negligible, partly because of the immense distances that separated the Mongols from the Empire, and partly because he was confident that the Eastern European powers would be able to withstand the Mongol assault. In any case Frederick II had no particular reason to wish to help Béla IV, who had remained neutral in Frederick's struggle against the Pope. In 1236–7, when Frederick had visited Vienna, he had been approached by a small group of discontented Hungarian lords who had offered him the crown of Hungary, a proposition which Frederick did not firmly reject. This conspiracy was discovered and left a certain bitterness between Frederick and Béla. The former regretted his failure to possess himself of Hungary without sacrifices, the latter was indignant at Frederick's attitude. At the same time the Pope was so much absorbed in his struggle with the Emperor that he completely failed to realize the imminence and the strength of the impending Mongol attack. And so it happened that in mid-February, 1241, a crusade was being preached in Hungary, not against the Tartars as one would have expected, but against the Emperor!

The preparations made by Béla to meet the Mongol peril were not exclusively diplomatic. When, around Christmas 1240, the Mongol forces were said to be approaching the Hungarian borders, Béla himself undertook a tour of inspection of the fortifications built along the line of the Carpathians. In all the mountain passes barricades were erected and the *nádor* Denes was set in charge of these defences. Béla also ordered the mobilization of all forces and summoned the dignitaries of his country to meet him in Buda on February 17, 1241. The mustering of the forces went fairly smoothly and was completed by February 14th, when Béla arrived in Buda. The assembly of the lords was well attended;

all the high dignitaries of State and Church were present, and Kuthen, accompanied by other important Comans, also took part in the deliberations. Béla's policy was perfectly straightforward: since the enemy stood at the frontiers, all forces should be mobilized to repulse the impending attack. To the lords, however, this seemed a splendid opportunity to extort from the King all manner of advantages. They were obviously pleased to see the strongly autocratic Béla in need of their help, and were not willing to accord it without recompense. They also took the opportunity to attack Kuthen, whom they reproached for his former alliance with some of the Russian princes hostile to Hungary. Béla was a bad negotiator; he sternly refused to yield to blackmail by the lords, but failed to gain their support, and was also unable to prevent Kuthen's imprisonment. The sterile negotiations were brutally interrupted by the arrival on March 10th, of a messenger announcing that the Mongols had launched their attack against the Carpathian passes. Four days later the *nádor* Denes himself arrived in Buda, exhausted and desperate, bringing the sad news that his troops had been annihilated and the passage through the mountains forced by the Mongols.

Béla immediately dissolved the assembly, which had lost so much valuable time in vain disputes, and proceeded to mobilize all the forces at his disposal, including those of the Comans. He also wrote to Duke Frederick of Austria, asking for his help, and sent the Queen, Maria, accompanied by the Bishop of Vác and others, to the Austrian border. This measure shows clearly that Béla was aware of the exceptional danger the Mongols meant to his country.

The Mongol army massed against Hungary was divided into three army corps placed along the north-eastern arch of the Carpathians. The right flank, facing west, stood approximately on the River San and was under the command of Orda, seconded by Qadan and Baydar, sons of Chagatay. The central army corps under Batu—Commander-in-Chief of all the western forces of the Mongols—took up a position on the Dniester in Halicz. Batu's younger brother, Sheyban, was attached to this army. Büdjek, son of Tolui, was in charge of the left flank, standing further down the Dniester and facing south.

The great attack started on the right wing and was aimed at the destruction of Béla's Polish allies. Sandomir fell on February 13th. Afterwards, Orda's army corps divided into three parts operating independently from one another. The first, under Orda's personal command, turned to the north and attacked Prussia, the centre pushed westwards in the direction of Breslau, whereas on the left wing the advance followed the Vistula. Krakow fell on March 22nd and ten days later, on April 2nd, the three armies joined before Breslau. Their first attack against the fortress having failed, the Mongols did not lose time with a regular siege, but by-passed the town and pushed forward. Seven days later (April 9th), at Liegnitz, they fought their decisive battle of annihilation against Henry, Duke of Silesia, helped by a considerable force of Templars.

After his victory Orda's army penetrated into Hungary from the north-west, descended the valley of the Vág and proceeded along the Danube towards Pest. The left wing of the Mongol army attacked from the east and invaded Transylvania. The main force, under the command of Batu, attacked through the pass of Verecke—through which the Hungarians themselves had entered the country—swept away the defences erected there and moved forward towards Pest, which obviously was intended as a meeting-place of the three Mongol armies.

In the meanwhile Béla tried to gather around Pest as many men as he could muster. His lieutenants, eager to take up the struggle, indulged in individual skirmishings with the advance-guards of the Mongols. Frederick of Austria was fairly successful in one of these raids and brought in a few prisoners, among whom a number of Comans were found. As it was a standard Mongol practice to compel defeated peoples to fight for them, and as Comans must have been fairly numerous in the heterogeneous Mongol army, there was no reason for surprise. The Hungarians, however, already hostile to the Comans, sensed treachery, stormed Kuthen's residence and put him and his entourage to the sword. The Comans, gathered in strength to meet the Mongols, were roused at this news, turned southwards and causing great devastations, left Hungary.

No one, with the possible exception of Béla himself, realized the magnitude of the danger threatening, and the barons mocked at the King for his seriousness in the matter. Everyone was eager to meet the Mongols as soon as possible, and Béla had to give in. He advanced from Pest in a north-easterly direction, and finally met Batu on April 11th, at the River Sajó, in the neighbourhood of the village Mohi. It was not even a battle, but rather a massacre. In the face of the deadly efficiency of Mongol strategy, the Hungarians could do nothing: Béla's army was totally destroyed, and the King himself only escaped with his life through the extreme devotion and courage of a handful of men.

Hungarian resistance was thus broken even before the Mongol armies had made their junction. The whole territory lying east or north of the Danube became subject to Mongol rule. It is difficult to estimate the loss in life and property caused by the Mongol occupation: according to contemporary sources it was appalling.

Whilst the Mongols were devastating Transylvania and advancing to the Danube, Béla, in his flight to the west, reached the Austrian border and stopped in Pozsony, on the left bank of this river. While he was there, an invitation reached him from Frederick, Duke of Austria, to cross the river and become his guest. In spite of some unpleasant experiences which Béla had had with the duke during his skirmishing with the Mongols, he accepted the invitation. 'But alas! the poor King' —says a contemporary chronicler—'was like a fish, who in trying to escape from being frozen in the icebox jumps into the fire to be roasted.' Clearly Frederick had made up his mind to take advantage of Béla's distress. Once he had hold of the King's person, the duke made very heavy demands. He exacted and obtained three Hungarian departments, and demanded a very large sum of money. The fugitive King, being unable to produce it, had to leave with him, as a pledge, all the silver and gold vessels which he had managed to save in his flight.

Frederick's hostility did not stop there. Not content with the *megyes* which Béla had handed over to him under duress, he attacked Hungary, proceeded down the right bank of the Danube, and occupied Györ. Subsequently this town, together with its garrison, was burned to the ground by the Hungarians who lived in its neighbourhood, and it is clear that happenings of this sort did nothing to restore the now badly shaken friendship between Austrians and Hungarians. The duke's systematic despoiling of Hungarian fugitives also caused great bitterness in Hungary.

Béla did not enjoy Frederick's 'hospitality' for very long. In the middle of May 1241 we find him in Croatia, in Zagreb, from where he tried to reorganize what remained of his country, and to forestall possible Mongol attacks across the Danube. He also wrote a letter addressed to the Pope, to the Emperor Frederick II and to Louis IX, charging his ambassador Stephen, Bishop of Vác, with it.

In this letter he asked the Pope to give orders for the preaching of a crusade, and entreated the Emperor to muster the forces of the German Empire.

Hungary's collapse came as a shock to Frederick II, who blamed Béla for its occurrence. He, too, tried to make capital out of the disaster. A splendid opportunity was offered to him by Béla himself. The King was ready to recognize the suzerainty of the Emperor, on condition that Frederick provided quick and efficient help against the Mongols. The Emperor, though pleased by this offer of homage and making use of its moral effect in his correspondence with the Roman Senate, was neither willing nor able to send forces sufficient for such a task. He was content to ask his son, King Conrad, to raise an army, and he advised Béla, while waiting for an imperial victory in Italy, to join with Conrad in an attempt to liberate Hungary. The Emperor also made representations to Louis IX and to Henry III of England urging them to help Conrad. The news of a crusade against the Mongols preached, it should be remembered, in the Emperor's name, caused some agitation in Germany. Troops and money were raised but the enthusiasm proved short-lived, and at the news that the Tartars had stopped at the Danube the armies again dispersed.

It is difficult to know whether Frederick was prompted by conviction or by necessity when he acted in this way. He must have had a fairly accurate picture of the Mongols, and there is no doubt that at least some moral pressure was exerted to make him help Hungary. What is perfectly clear is that Frederick used the imminence of the Mongol peril to urge the union of all Christian princes under his own leadership.

The Pope was hardly more helpful than the Emperor. Grandiloquent sentences, promises of help after the defeat of the Emperor, the announcement of a crusade—that was all that the hard-pressed Pope could offer. The death of Gregory on August 22nd and the subsequent interregnum reduced to nothing the part the Papacy could play at this juncture with regard to the Mongols.

St Louis represented but a minor power in comparison with the Pope or the Emperor. He was also too distant to be able to provide efficient help against the Mongols.

Europe, even after the disaster that had befallen Béla, was unable to show a united front and, even less, to help Hungary at grips with the Mongols. These kept to the line of the Danube all through the summer of 1241, and the German forces raised by Conrad, lured into a false feeling of security, disbanded. Béla was more perspicacious. He took it for granted that the Mongols would try to cross the Danube, and acted accordingly, seeking to build up an effective resistance. As there could be no hope of resisting a Mongol onslaught in the open field, Béla, whose policy proved right, paid particular attention to the building of fortifications which, provided they had efficient ballistae at their disposal, stood a good chance against Mongol attacks. On Christmas Day, 1241, the Mongols crossed the frozen Danube. Buda fell almost immediately and Mongols, presumably under Batu's personal command, proceeded up the right bank of the river and laid siege to Esztergom, then the most important Hungarian town. The defenders had to abandon first the outer and then the inner town, but the citadel, under command of the Spanish Burgrave, Simeon, resisted successfully.

More important, from our point of view, was the advance of the Mongol General Qadan, who proceeded in a south-westerly direction towards Croatia, with the obvious purpose of seizing the King's person. Warning of the oncoming peril reached Béla early enough to allow him to escape towards the Adriatic coast, where he took refuge on the island of Rab (Arbe). Mongol attempts to cross the small channel that separates the island from the mainland were unsuccessful. Béla fled further south, to Spalato, and thence to the island of Trogir. In March 1242 small detachments of Mongols reached this region, but the scarcity of grass in these barren mountains prevented the use of great numbers of cavalry there.

It is difficult to follow the vicissitudes of this campaign, rich in minor skirmishes, and resembling a game of hide-and-seek among the small islands and ports of the Adriatic. Béla proved the winner, since, at the end of March, Qadan abandoned his pursuit, proceeded down the coast to Albania, penetrated into the interior of the Balkans, and in Bulgaria joined forces with Batu, who had come there directly from Hungary. The two chiefs held a council and then turned to the east. Other Mongol armies left Hungary through the mountain passes of Transylvania. By the end of May 1242 the evacuation of Hungary was complete.

The Mongol retreat from Europe was sudden, unexpected and perfectly organized. It was caused by news of the death of the Great Khan Ögödei reaching Batu. European claims—voiced by some contemporaries—that their withdrawal was due to some defeat, or even to the

Mongols' fear of the Emperor, must be dismissed as preposterous boasts. Small Mongol detachments operating more or less on their own may occasionally have been beaten, but the Mongol army as such remained untouched and even invincible by the then existing European forces. The study of the invasion of Russia, Poland, Bohemia and Hungary shows that in well-fortified places resistance was possible, but that none of the field armies of the epoch would have been able to make a victorious stand against the Tartars.

Even looking back over more than seven centuries we must rejoice that no attack was made on Western Europe. Such an assault, with its trail of utter destruction, would have had incalculable effects on the growth of European civilization. Hungary for the first, but by no means the last, time in her history served as a buffer between Western Europe and an eastern invader. For the first time she received a lesson which she was never to learn, namely that it was vain for her to expect any help from the west.

The news of the Mongols' withdrawal was received in Europe with a sigh of relief, and the many who had not lifted a finger to help now felt themselves justified and tried to forget the displeasing affair. There were two exceptions, namely the Church, which, since the election of Innocent IV in June 1243, maintained an interest in Mongol affairs, and Béla IV, who had to face the immense task of reconstructing his devastated country. It was now that Béla was to show the full measure of his capacities. He set to work with a method and a relentlessness that compel our admiration. Hungarian history calls him rightly 'the second founder of the country'.

The Mongol invasion had the impact and effect of a natural disaster, an earthquake or hurricane. But it was reasonable to expect a repetition of it and there seemed just a chance of sustaining a new attack if—and there lay the crux of the matter—the country's defences could be reorganized. The campaign had shown that fortified places stood a good chance against the Mongols. The task of erecting fortresses was not one which could be tackled centrally. Béla had to entrust it to the barons who were able, on their big estates, to mobilize the necessary manpower. The King also granted considerable privileges to settlements to enable them to build defences, and it was this policy which first led, in Hungarian history, to the formation of towns in the western sense. By nature and tradition Hungarians were not inclined to urban life, and

Béla therefore granted great privileges to German and Italian settlers willing to populate the new towns. To compensate for the terrible loss of life caused by the Mongols, other foreign settlers were invited to the depopulated areas. Thus the Comans were once again installed in their former territories between the Danube and the Tisza, the north-eastern parts of the country received some Slavonic, Polish and Russian settlers, whereas Roumanians entered in greater numbers the southern part of Transylvania. Hungary's multinational character owes its being to the Mongol massacres.

The conditions in which the country found itself on the morrow of the invasion made imperative the re-establishment of internal peace. Some of the antagonisms between the King and barons seemed indeed to have receded into the background; but the necessity of building fortresses compelled the King to make grants of lands to the lords, and therefore to abandon his previous policy in this respect. Béla further made the fatal mistake of entrusting the government of Transylvania to his son Stephen. In fact a dual kingship developed, with two royal courts and with a feud between father and son which culminated in an armed conflict (1264–5). Béla was defeated, and though a reconciliation soon followed, the damage done to royal authority was considerable. Towards the end of his reign Béla IV moved further and further away from the principles that had governed his policy towards the oligarchy. Both he and his son were compelled to secure the help of the lords by large donations of land. The patrimonial form of kingship which Béla had set out to restore in its full vigour foundered in the Mongol invasion. It was simply not adapted to the times.

In spite of these internal difficulties, Hungary made a truly remarkable recovery and slowly regained its former weight in East European politics. Already in 1245 Béla had to face an attack by Frederick, Duke of Austria, who was seeking to lay hold of the territories that Béla had had to concede to him when taking refuge from the Mongols. The duke's army got the upper hand, but the duke himself fell on the field of battle. As a result Styria was attached to Hungary for a few years. A conflict arose over Austria with the Czech King Otakar II but—as happened so often during Béla's reign—military reverses were put right by diplomatic skill. This skill was put to a severe test when an offer of alliance was made by the Mongols in 1259 and repeated in 1264. Though knowing full well that in the event of a renewed Mongol attack no help would be forthcoming from the west, Béla was reluctant to ally himself with the Mongols against the west. It was the first occasion on which Hungary out of solidarity with western civilization took the risk of antagonizing powerful eastern neighbours. Béla's temporizing policy proved successful; political developments within the Mongol empire put an end to its expansion towards the west, and Hungary was spared a new invasion.

Béla made clever use of matrimonial policy. Among the matches he made, those of his son Stephen with a Coman princess, Elisabeth, and the double marriage of Stephen's two children with two children of Charles I, King of Sicily, Count of Anjou and Provence, stand out as having far-reaching consequences for the history of Hungary.

Béla's long life, spent entirely in the service of his country, was not without great disappointments and sorrows. Though a poor soldier, he succeeded in strengthening Hungary's position among her neighbours and in rebuilding the land after the Mongol devastations. His was, in many respects, a rich life; with his death perished the last great king of the Árpád dynasty.

CHAPTER 9

THE END OF THE ÁRPÁDS

BÉLA'S violent and overstrung son Stephen V (1270–2), who had for many years shared the government with his father, had little opportunity to rule over an undivided country, for he fell victim to feminine intrigues. First the treachery of his sister Anne involved him in a war with Otakar II, which, though it could have been avoided, had the advantage of leading to a reasonable settlement of some territorial problems. But his wife, Elisabeth, dealt him a blow which was to cause his death. Jealous of growing French influence, she let her son Ladislas be kidnapped. The ten-year-old child was abducted on his way to Sicily, where he was to visit his father-in-law, Charles I. Stephen V succumbed to the emotional stress created by this incident, leaving his country to his young son, Ladislas IV, who was to be called the Coman (1272–90).

The death of her husband, and Ladislas's youth, gave Elisabeth a long-awaited opportunity to rule. This Coman woman, ambitious, violent, barely civilized, had resented the minor part devolving upon her in the court and land. She now seized the reins of government and, as Queen Regent, ruled according to her caprice. Elisabeth's lust for power was not backed by any political gifts. Ever under the influence of one of her frequently changing favourites, she plunged the country into chaos. As he grew up, Ladislas came more and more under the evil influences prevailing at his mother's court. He lived in an atmosphere of immorality and of mutual distrust, and had no more confidence in his mother than in his wife, Isabelle of Anjou. He looked for escape and found it in his mother's clan, among the Comans. There, in the company of his beautiful Coman mistress, surrounded by his Coman friends, he led their life, dressing in their fashion, and would probably have forgotten all duties of his kingly state had not the troubles threatening the land become so acute that they reached even the escapist King in his retreat.

At the beginning of Ladislas's reign it had seemed that the greatest danger to Hungary would be from Otakar who, encouraged by a group of Hungarian lords, was taking an increasing interest in the country's internal affairs. In the conflict that later arose between the Czech King and Rudolf of Habsburg the Hungarians sided with the latter. Young Ladislas, with a large mixed force of Comans and Hungarians, intervened decisively in the battle of Marchfeld (1278) in which Otakar lost his life. He thus acted as midwife at the birth of the Habsburg power which was to be such an overwhelming factor in Hungarian history.

Ladislas had no desire to make capital out of this victory; he returned to Hungary and foundered in debauch. The kingless country drifted at the mercy of greedy oligarchs and was torn by three factions, each opposed to the other. Of these three factions only one had anything approaching a national policy. The first group, the Comans, formed a solid alien mass, non-Christian, without any constructive policy. They relied on their friendship with the King to assure the continuance of their national entity and were, on the whole, the ready executors of his short-sighted schemes (such as the capture of the papal legate Philip, who, in 1275, came to produce some order out of the chaos prevailing in the country). The second faction was also alien, consisting of German families which had recently settled in the country, and which felt no solidarity with the population at large. Their aim was to fish in the troubled waters, and they displayed a separationist tendency which might eventually have led to the loss of some of the western and northern parts of Hungary. The family of the Köszegis can be considered as best representing this group. The third faction, whose main representatives were perhaps the families Csák and Aba, though no more scrupulous than the other two, had at least some sense of duty towards the country as a whole; they were also firmly enough rooted in the Christian faith to deplore the heathen practices which were rapidly gaining ground all over the country. In 1284 they repelled Kipchak and Tartar hordes called in from Russia by the King himself, and, on two occasions, even seized hold of the King's person. On the first they kept him in custody together with his wife 'so that they should procreate a child'. His second imprisonment followed the Tartar attack in Hungary and the sequestration of his wife in a cloister. Ladislas, probably feeling persecuted by everyone, lost more and more control over his passions. He seems almost to have forgotten his royal rights and to have felt as any of the oligarchs struggling for power. His self-degradation found a tragic dénouement. In June 1290 he was murdered amidst his beloved Comans, by the Comans themselves.

Though, as an individual, this harassed, unfortunate man may deserve some compassion, there is nothing to be said in his favour as a ruler. At a time when kings of the stature of St Louis, Charles of Anjou and Edward I were ruling in Europe, Ladislas brought his country to the verge of complete disintegration. Never before had the prestige of Hungary sunk so low, never before had the foundations of the kingdom been so shaken. Western countries had undergone grievous disturbances, and the miseries of England under the reign of Stephen have no parallel in Hungary. The problem that arose under Ladislas IV was of another nature; it was the choice between two worlds, East and West. Béla IV, in spite of his disappointments from western powers, had had the moral strength to refuse the Mongol offer of alliance. Ten years after his death, his grandson called in Tartars to combat Hungarians, and felt himself at home only in company of the nomad heathen Comans. Barbarism and inhumanity could reach unfathomable depths in the west, but they were, as it were, home produced. They sprang not from the denial of moral values, but from their neglect. Hungary, the last country in history to seek and gain admittance to the western community, situated at the border of western civilization, has often been directly challenged by ideas and ways of living which are fundamentally different. Hungarian Christianity has been a perpetual renewal of baptismal promises. Ladislas's reign shows how great could be the temptation to side with the east. On the face of it, Coman barbarism was not worse than its western counterpart, and it would have needed a perspicacity signally lacking in Ladislas to see the difference in deeper values. It was the historian Simon of Kéza, working at Ladislas's court, who first evolved the entirely gratuitous theory of the Hunnish origin of the Hungarians; it pleased Ladislas to be considered as a successor of Attila, and passing centuries have not destroyed the emotional appeal of this tale.

Deplorable as they were, the internal conditions of the country at this time favoured the development of constitutional ideas and thus brought

Hungarian institutions more into harmony with those of other countries. Under a weak king such as Ladislas, who, for the most part, simply refused to govern, the executive power fell into the hands of high dignitaries who, in a constantly increasing measure, tended to impose their will upon the King. During Ladislas's reign a kind of two-party system developed, with Köszegi versus the Aba-Csák group, and the King calling upon members of one or other of these two groups to conduct the affairs of state. Such 'changes of government' were due either to the desire to seek an alternative to a government incapable of redressing a desperate situation, or else simply to the success of one group in ousting the other, with complete disregard of the possible merits of its activity. The weakening of the royal power did not lead in Hungary to a greater measure of democracy; it simply entailed the shifting of power from the hands of the kings into those of a small group of oligarchs.

Ladislas IV died childless and the succession was hotly disputed by a number of pretenders. The most serious among them were Charles Martel of Anjou and Rudolf of Habsburg who, on a very weak basis, put forward a claim on behalf of his son Albert. The rightful heir to the throne was Andrew, grandson of Andrew II, and son of Stephen, who had been born after the death of his father, of the King's third wife Beatrix. Not without difficulties, and opposed by the Pope, Nicholas IV, he finally succeeded in obtaining the crown.

The new King, Andrew III (1290–1301), was an honest, capable man. His reign was to be a difficult one, menaced from within and without. The Anjou pretender, Charles Martel, supported by the Pope, kept fomenting trouble, and even his death in 1295 did not put an end to pro-Anjou propaganda in Hungary. The powerful Ivan Köszegi was won over by it, and following an armed conflict he even for a while kept the King prisoner. To curb the power of the Köszegis, whose huge estates, wedged between Austria and Hungary, tended towards a virtual independence, Andrew married as his second wife Agnes, wife of Albert of Habsburg, himself a pretender to the Hungarian throne. The Köszegi family was not the only one bent on carving out for itself a piece of Hungary. In the north-western parts of the country the Csák family acted in a similar fashion.

The great ills of the time of Andrew II reappeared again, and in a virulent form, during the reign of his grandson. Once again the nobles, incapable of taking any direct action against the great barons, sought help from the King himself. Since 1277 it had been customary for the nobles to gather on St Stephen's Day—by tradition the day of the Royal Assizes—and to submit their recommendations to the King and his councillors. The nobles thus assumed, quite spontaneously, an advisory function which was soon to grow into a Diet. In 1290 Andrew III himself convened the nobles, on whose help he had to rely in his struggle with the barons. It was then decided that it should be the duty of every nobleman—whether a 'baron' or a 'common noble'—to appear, once a year, at a Diet, and that their advice should be sought in the filling of some high posts. From 1298 the nobles and the clergy were represented by two members each in the Royal Council, which hitherto had been composed solely of barons, who, owing to their fortune, were *eo ipso* considered the most important men of the realm.

Monarchy, no longer able to defend itself against the increasing power of the barons, sought and found help in the lesser nobility, equally anxious to check its growth. This alliance could not muster, under Andrew III, forces sufficiently strong to secure victory. Oddly enough only a strong absolutist monarchy would have been able to improve the constitutional government. For Hungary was unlike England in that parliament was not there imposed by the barons, but was a means devised jointly by the King and the lesser nobles to check the barons, who *de facto*, and as sole members of the King's council also *de jure*, had ruled the country to its detriment and their own benefit.

Andrew III, with an unspectacular but efficient policy, was slowly turning the tide of the barons' power, when on January 14, 1301, quite unexpectedly, he died. The 'last golden twig on the stem of the Árpáds' had been broken off. In him, before its final extinction, this great family had brought forth yet another honest and devoted ruler.

Few dynasties produced more able monarchs than that of the Árpáds. They ruled over the Hungarians for over four centuries, and for almost exactly three hundred years they gave kings to the Christian realm. Their line produced splendid soldiers, excellent administrators, and saints. Often violent, and living passionately, most of their kings have a tragic grandeur, an Asiatic streak of sombre dignity. They were aware that their subjects looked upon them as men chosen by Providence to rule; never was there any revolt against the dynasty. True, the Árpáds considered the country as their private property, but for this very reason, they watched over it with tender care, and only slowly, with the gradual infiltration of western ideas of more democratic government, did things change, let us admit, for the worse. Otto of Freisingen notes with amazement the authority enjoyed by the King: 'The King's will is the supreme argument.' But this dictatorial system had a feature of its own: it was loved by its subjects. The Hungarian King was not a *primus inter pares*, he was the heritor of a mystic gift, carried in the blood of the Árpáds, who had turned a poor vanquished nomadic tribe, driven from its country, into a nation, prosperous and respected.

PART THREE

THE ZENITH OF HUNGARIAN POWER
THE ELECTED KINGS

CHAPTER 10

THE ANJOU KINGS

WITH the extinction of the House of Árpád Hungary faced an unprecedented situation. For over four centuries the dynasty had been reigning over a nation that owed it its very existence. That nation was now free to elect a king of its own choice. So great, however, was the authority of the late dynasty that the election of a king unrelated to the Árpáds was out of the question. The choice had to fall on one not only deserving the confidence of the nation, but also possessing the virtues inherent only in the blood of Árpád's descendants.

The most important candidate for the vacant throne was Charles Robert, son of Charles Martel of Anjou, whose attempts to secure the Kingdom of Hungary for himself we have already mentioned. He was the favourite candidate of the Pope, a very doubtful advantage in the eyes of nobles not over-fond of papal interventions in the political life of the country. Indeed, at the national assembly held in Pest in 1308 the Papal Nuncio, Cardinal Gentilis Montefiore, nearly jeopardized the election of his protégé by presenting him as the nominee of the Pope.

The other most important candidate was Wenceslas, son of Wenceslas II, King of Bohemia, and grandson of Béla IV. His staunchest supporters came, not unnaturally, from among the mighty lords of the north-western provinces of Hungary, with whom he obviously had been able to establish closer contact.

They were better prepared than the supporters of other candidates, and already in 1301 they succeeded in crowning Wenceslas—or Ladislas as he was then called—with St Stephen's crown. Charles Robert made a vain attempt to dislodge him from the fortress of Buda, although his resistance prompted the Pope to excommunicate both him and the defenders of Buda. His own carelessness and his liking for wine were, however, of greater danger and led to his early death. Before, in 1305, at the request of his father, he had returned to Bohemia, taking with him the Holy Crown.

Wenceslas's friends now proclaimed as King, Otto, Prince of Bavaria —also a grandson of Béla IV—and having recovered the crown, crowned him in great haste. He enjoyed very little support and after having been arrested by Ladislas, Voivode of Transylvania, in whose house he had presented himself as a suitor, he returned in 1308 to his country. The most important opponents thus eliminated, at the national assembly held at Pest Charles Robert succeeded in securing for himself the unanimous support of the estates. In 1310 he was crowned with the Holy Crown, which had meanwhile been recovered.

The reigns of Charles Robert and of his son Louis belong to the most glorious epochs of Hungarian history. The auspices under which the Anjou kings began their rule were, however, far from being favourable. The last decades of the Árpáds, and the ensuing feuds had given extraordinary powers to the oligarchs, the 'little kings' as they were called in Hungarian history. Their destruction, or at least their neutralization, was a prerequisite of any efficient government. If Charles Robert was determined to bring order to Hungarian affairs, he was also most reluctant to relinquish any morsel of the power he forged for himself by military, political and economic means. His conception was a feudal one, and although his main antagonists were the powerful lords, Charles Robert contented himself with personal changes, with the creation of a new aristocracy faithful to him, without encouraging a change of system. Determined as he was to break the power of recalcitrant lords, he had no intention of checking them by strengthening the lower strata of society. The huge confiscated estates of rebellious oligarchs were redistributed almost in their entirety to members of the lesser nobility. The royal domains covered only about twenty per cent of the country's territory. Charles Robert thus created a new aristocracy, virtually almost as dangerous as were the 'little kings', but whose bonds of gratitude towards him proved strong enough to prevent them from becoming a menace to the crown, at least during the reign of the Anjous.

The reforms introduced by Charles Robert affected practically every sphere of public life. During the anarchic period preceding and following the extinction of the Árpáds, the country's military power had declined, and, not unnaturally, the ambitious Anjou King, whose interest in foreign affairs was a natural result of his background, wanted to forge himself a military force capable of carrying out his decisions. Not content with compelling all the nobles themselves to serve in his army, Charles Robert made them set up small armed units, the so-called *banderia*, whose soldiers were recruited among the serfs. The size of each unit depended on the size of the noble's land, and if the number of soldiers in a given *banderium* reached the figure of fifty, it was entitled to have its own banner.

The system, though considerably increasing the military power the King could dispose of, had, at the same time, the disadvantage of creating a great number of private armies on whose fidelity to the King depended to a very great extent his might. It was the Anjou kings' good fortune that in their lifetimes they did not have to contend with restlessness among the lords commanding these *banderia*.

Perhaps more important than any military reforms were the economic measures introduced by Charles Robert. Having decided not to keep the confiscated estates for himself, he had to find ways and means of strengthening his own hand by the fostering of industry and trade. The main step was the reorganization of Hungary's mining industry. Whilst maintaining the old privileges of mining prospectors, who were allowed to open new shafts on any territory, irrespective of the landlord's consent, Charles Robert, in order to secure the co-operation of the owners on whose territory the mines were working, decided that, of the rent paid by the miners to the King from each mine, henceforward one-third was to go to the lord of the domain. He also introduced a royal monopoly on gold and silver, thus creating a base for his monetary policy. At the beginning of the century some thirty-five types of currency were in circulation in Hungary. The minting of golden florins, on the Florentine model, and of smaller silver coins produced a monetary stability which in its turn had the most salutary effects on commerce. To arrive at a full appreciation of the measures taken by Charles Robert in favour of the mining industry, it should be borne in mind that at that time Hungary provided more than one-third of Europe's total gold production.

A not inhuman but efficient fiscal policy was also instrumental in the creation of the economic prosperity that characterized Charles Robert's reign.

The sound conditions within the country permitted the King to pursue his rather ambitious plans in foreign affairs. These were centred on two main objectives, namely the securing for his family the succession to the thrones of Naples and of Poland. The simple fact that Charles Robert could reasonably hope for success in lands geographically so distant from one another gives already the measure of his achievements in the consolidation of Hungary.

He married his younger son Andrew, then aged seven, to Johanna, aged six, granddaughter of Robert, King of Naples, and heir apparent to the throne. In 1333, during a visit to Naples, the two kings, uncle and nephew, agreed that at Robert's death the crown of Naples should go to Andrew. The child was then left at the Neapolitan court to become familiar with his future surroundings.

Charles Robert had himself married Elisabeth, daughter of Vladislas, King of Poland. By helping Poland in various wars against the Lithuanians and Tartars, he gained some influence in its internal affairs; and at Vladislas' death he exerted himself successfully to secure the throne for his brother-in-law Casimir. In 1335, at a meeting held at Charles Robert's court in Visegrád with Casimir and John, King of Bohemia, the King of Hungary succeeded in making John renounce his claims to the Polish throne. In recognition of his services, the Polish nobles, in 1339, recognized Charles Robert's son Louis as heir to the throne.

The meeting of the three kings in Visegrád was, as it were, an apotheosis for Charles Robert, presenting him in the rôle of arbiter of a number of litigious questions in Eastern Europe. On the same occasion Charles Robert concluded an agreement on the use of a trade route passing through Czech territory to the west, and providing an alternative to the traditional route through Vienna. The heavy duties levied by that town had been for some time a great impediment to Hungary's foreign trade.

On the whole, Charles Robert's reign was a peaceful one. His smaller campaigns, such as those against Serbia and the Dalmatian towns, seem of little purport to the modern eye. They are rather military exercises, a display of the readiness of the King to assert himself as the most powerful potentate of Eastern Europe. A small campaign against Michael, Voivode of Bessarabia, however, nearly turned out a disaster, and the King almost lost his life.

Viewed in historical perspective, Charles Robert's reign was one of preparation for the long reign of his son Louis I (1342–82). He made ready the ground on which was to blossom this most spectacular but already sterile flower of the Hungarian late Middle Ages. The relation of the two kings is somewhat similar to that of Frederick the Great and his father. The son's achievements were, to a great extent, due to the solid foundations laid by a father of less spectacular qualities.

Louis I—Hungarian historians surnamed him the Great—was a French knight, transplanted to Hungarian soil; deeply religious, a lover of justice, a patron of arts, a promoter of knowledge. It was his tragedy that he could not reckon among his achievements one, the desire for which lives in most men's hearts, namely the begetting of a son. His fondness for *gloire* set him on roads that led nowhere, and he bequeathed to his successors a burden they could hardly have carried even had they been stronger than they were.

Louis's foreign policy was decidedly imperialistic, and can be dealt with under four headings: (1) the occupation of the kingdom of Naples, (2) the wars with Venice, (3) wars in the Balkans, (4) the acquisition of the Polish crown.

Soon after his accession to the throne, Louis had to turn his attention to the developments which had taken place in Naples after the death of King Robert. Under the influence of circles not very eager to see a Hungarian prince on the throne, the old king—breaking his agreement with Charles Robert—had left his kingdom to his granddaughter Johanna. Having obtained the consent of her liege lord Pope Clement VI, Johanna let herself be crowned, and frowned upon her husband, Andrew. First Louis sent his mother Elisabeth to Naples in 1343, and she proposed to bring her son Andrew back to Hungary. She was dissuaded from doing so and returned alone. After her departure from Naples, the courtly intrigues against Andrew continued and culminated in his assassination in Aversa in 1345. There can be little doubt that the deed was done with the full consent of Johanna.

Louis's strong protests, and his demands that justice be done, were met, by the Pope living at Avignon, with very moderate enthusiasm, which prompted the King of Hungary to take into his own hands the punishment of the culprits. In 1347 he set out for Naples. Johanna fled to Avignon and Louis had to content himself with beheading Charles of Durazzo, presumed leader of the conspirators; and with capturing four princes, whom he then sent to Visegrád. His attempts to secure recognition of this conquest from the Pope remained unsuccessful. Leaving the German *condottiere* Ulrich Wolfart in command, Louis then returned to Hungary. Soon after his departure, Johanna returned to her kingdom, Wolfart capitulated, and Louis set out for the second time to make his will prevail in Neapolitan affairs. Louis again proved his military brilliance, and in spite of some difficulties soon occupied Naples (1350). As, once again, Clement VI refused to legalize the conquest, the campaign achieved nothing permanent. Only at the end of his reign had Louis the satisfaction of having the crown of Naples offered to him, by Pope Urban VI. But by then he was too old to shoulder this additional burden, and he renounced his claim in favour of his adopted son, the son-in-law of the late Charles of Durazzo, who then, as Charles III, reigned over Naples from 1381 to 1386, and for two months, in 1387, over Hungary. Unable to refrain from further intrigues, Johanna met the end of her tumultuous life in 1382, when she was strangled on the order of Charles III.

Louis's French and Italian connections, his whole background, brought him nearer to Western European politics than any other Hungarian king before the Habsburgs. We shall examine later the influence which his Italian ventures had on Hungarian civilization. It is clear, however—and Louis himself must have been aware of this fact— that Hungary's geographical position hardly allowed her to play any permanent rôle in the Mediterranean countries. The interest displayed by the Anjous of Hungary in that area was the fruit of a kind of home-sickness, of a habit, perhaps even a sense of duty towards Naples and the Italian states in general. It must be counted among the great virtues of these kings that, though indulging in these dynastic ventures, they paid no less attention to the part of the world where the country's more permanent interest lay, namely to Eastern Europe.

During the reign of Steven Dushan (1331–55) Serbia had risen to a position of considerable importance. Albania, Macedonia, Thessaly and Epirus were conquered and Dushan advanced as far as the shores of the bay of Corinth. Leaving the title of the King of the Serbs to his son Urosh, he had himself crowned 'Emperor of Greeks and Serbs' (1346). Louis, in order to ensure for himself permanent authority in the Balkans, had married Elisabeth, daughter of Steven Kotromanich, Ban of Bosnia. A conflict between Dushan and Louis became inevitable, and

Venice did her best to strengthen the Serbs, who, acting in the rear of Louis's forces, were very useful allies. In 1354-5 Louis led victorious but, on the whole, useless campaigns against Dushan, and during the reigns of Urosh (1355-65) and Vukashin (1365-71) he frequently intervened in the almost anarchic Balkan affairs. These were further complicated by the spread of the Bogomil heresy, which had found a protector in Steven Tvartko, the new Ban of Bosnia. Louis was deeply involved in Bulgarian and Valachian affairs, and it seems that he did not fully grasp the importance of the Turkish power now appearing on the European horizon.

Murad I (1359-89) was the first sultan to achieve considerable successes on the Balkan peninsula. By 1361 he had occupied Edirne (Hadrianapolis), and ten years later—though still at the River Maritza— he defeated Vukasin, who lost his life in the battle. A few years later, probably in 1366, Hungarian and Turkish troops, for the first time in history, clashed. The Hungarian Chapel in the Cathedral at Aachen bears witness to the victory then achieved. But this victory was of small importance and did not check Turkish expansion in the Balkans.

Meanwhile John Paleologue (1341-91) was making desperate efforts to call the attention of the west to the magnitude of the Turkish menace. At his request Pope Gregory XI proclaimed a crusade (1373). Although Louis should have been the head of such forces that might assemble to answer the Pope's appeal, he was too much involved in his Italian and Polish affairs to take upon himself such a responsibility. He delayed his intervention until 1377, when he beat the joint armies of Murad I and Sisman, Tsar of Bulgaria. At this time—just as for almost a century and a half afterwards—the King of Hungary could match the military strength of the Sultan. Unfortunately for Hungary, however, the Turkish menace was not treated as the main issue in foreign policy. Louis's negligence bore bitter fruit for the Balkan states, who were the first victims of Turkish imperialism.

The political anarchy, the bitter religious strife, made the Peninsula very vulnerable but also very dangerous for any would-be conqueror. We have seen the difficulties Louis had to face there. The missionary fervour of the Anjous alienated great portions of the population and Louis's multifarious interests prevented him from giving the population the effective help against the Turks which would have been a compensation for his interference with their religious and national lives. The local princes then, having to choose between two powers, the Turks and the Hungarians, neither of which presented to them very tempting prospects, developed a pendulum policy, a policy compounded of petty intrigues and small dynastic interests, which was to remain for many centuries the principal characteristic of political life in the Balkans. Some of the Balkan princes, ignoring the warning of the Scriptures, tried to serve two masters, accepting feudal bonds with the Turks as well as with Louis—a policy laden with danger, in which Louis with considerable short-sightedness, seemed to acquiesce.

In fact Louis had to pay the price of the dispersal of his own forces. For these Poland was yet another burden. On November 17, 1370, Louis was crowned King of Poland in Cracow. This was the fulfilment of a plan conceived, as we have seen already, by his father. The main supporter of the plan was the ambitious Elisabeth, the Queen Mother, Polish by birth, into whose hand Louis put the reins of government in Poland. He himself had little interest in his new subjects, whose language he never learned. Elisabeth failed to secure the sympathy of her former countrymen, and it cost Louis much energy to sustain her rule. Though lending lustre to Louis's reign, the Polish crown was in fact yet another drain on his insufficient resources.

Sound economic policy and clever measures adopted by Charles, and by Louis himself, to improve the social structure of the state, enabled Louis to pursue an imperialistic policy. On his death he left behind a country resplendent in *gloire* but not strong enough to live up to what is expected from a really strong state.

The inner peace that characterizes the rule of the first Anjous was due more to the personal excellence of the rulers than to the quality of their system of government. In fact they were not innovators, but simply worked the state machine created by the Árpáds efficiently. It is very likely that the Anjous' conservatism was partly motivated by a clever political consideration: as foreigners they wanted to avoid hurting Hungarian susceptibilities, and they tried, therefore, not to impose foreign ideas or institutions on the country. However, it was not only clever expediency, but also a sincere desire to adapt themselves to their adopted country and to embrace its spiritual heritage which moved Charles and Louis. Catholicism was a strong bond between the country and its foreign dynasty. Louis's devotion to the great Árpádian knight-king St Ladislas was certainly sincere, though it undoubtedly served also to emphasize his will to continue the Hungarian traditions. The same intention motivated in 1381 the transfer from Venice to Hungary of the body of St Paul the Hermit, patron of one of the very few religious orders founded in Hungary, which was strongly supported by the Anjou kings. Foreign, particularly Italian, influence had in the past been more than once resented by Hungarians, and the Anjous were anxious not to repeat the mistakes of Peter or Andrew II. Ties of blood no longer secured for the Anjous—as they did for the Árpáds—an absolute and contested privilege of ruling. *Legitimitas*, the right to rule by virtue of consanguinity, gave way slowly to *idoneitas*, the right to be king through personal aptitude. It is not without reason that the mystic conception of the Holy Crown as the real source of kingship finds its first fairly clear expression in Anjou times. If Stephen's crown is the source of power, it follows that he who wears it with the consent of the estates acquires the dignity of the true King, joins *legitimitas* to *idoneitas* and enters the spiritual lineage of the Árpáds.

The weakening of the importance of descent—a development by no means new, but which automatically gained momentum with the accession of the Anjous—led during their reign to the official doctrine that all nobles, whatever their origins, should have the same duties and privileges. This principle of the *una et eadem libertas*, formulated in one of a number of most important laws promulgated by Louis in December 1351, spelt the end of any distinction between former conquerors and newcomers, Hungarians and foreigners, melting them together in one huge group characterized by the possession of estates, whether obtained at the conquest of the country or bestowed at any time through royal favour. As in this way the possession of land acquired an importance not purely material, it was logical to codify the already existing usage that any such property was inalienable, the actual owner having no right of disposal (a marked change from the dispositions of the Golden Bull). Inherited land must go to the rightful heirs and if none can be found it must be returned to the King. This law, giving formal recognition to the principle called *ösiség* (*aviticitas*), aimed at pleasing the nobles by doing away with the old feudal practice by which the fief returned to the lord (king) in the absence of direct male descendants, and by granting to the lesser nobility the same rights enjoyed by the great lords from whom, in a recent past, they had suffered so much. In fact, although Louis was generally moved by principles of equity—his dispositions to improve the judicial system attest this amply—the laws promulgated in 1351 did untold harm to the country, and were for half a millennium the main legal obstacle to a healthy natural development of the country's life. The inalienability of a noble's estate put a brake on economic competition, stifled initiative and in general—as we shall see—had the most disastrous economic consequences. Another measure, apparently of no great consequence, must here be mentioned. It was the establishment of a new tax called 'the ninth'. By a seemingly innocuous law a uniform charge—one-ninth of all production, payable to the landlord—was put on all members of the lower classes who had the use of land. The uniformity of this charge, accompanied as it was by strict orders that the tax should be levied effectively, appeared to make it serve simultaneously the interests of lords and serfs. The former were thus assured of a constant income enabling them to fulfil their military obligations; they were also safe from the competition of more powerful nobles attracting peasants by the promise of lower taxes to come to work on their estates. Undoubtedly Louis's aim was to strengthen the middle strata of the nobility, on which his military strength greatly depended, and which was able to check—if economically strong enough—the power of the great lords. The imposition of a compulsory 'ninth' meant to the majority of serfs a safeguard against exploitation by their landlords, and in most cases a reduction of their charges.

It happened, however, that precisely this uniformity of a charge, set on a large but hitherto not entirely homogeneous section of Hungarian society, resulted in the creation of a new class, that of the so-called *jobbágys*. Within the general context of the laws promulgated in 1351, giving greater homogeneity to the upper classes, the foundations of a dual structure of society were being laid down. It is in 1351 that begins a development culminating in Werböczi's legislation in 1514, which up to 1848 stood as an impassable barrier between those who have and those who have not.

It would be unreasonable to reproach Louis for developments which took place after his death, and which no one could have foreseen. At an epoch of grievous social disturbances—one only has to bear in mind the Jacqueries, the rising in Western Flanders or the insurrection of 1381 in England—Hungary under Anjou rule was an island of peaceful development, which not even the Black Death, which held Hungary in its grip between 1347 and 1350, could seriously impede.

The prosperity of the country provided the means to satisfy a craving for a more cultivated life. In the course of the Neapolitan campaigns many Hungarians learnt to know and to appreciate the refinements of Italian civilization, and it is but natural that, after their return, they should have tried to improve on local conditions. The kings themselves firmly rooted in the Western European cultured tradition, were, as was only to be expected, the chief promoters of a spiritual and cultural development unprecedented in Hungarian history. Louis himself was better known and more popular in Western Europe than had been any Hungarian king before him. Again and again he appears in contemporary Italian literature, it is as if he would justify with his life Wolfram von Eschenbach's claim that the Anjous were the last servants of the Holy Grail. A contemporary of the Black Prince and of Du Guesclin, Louis was a real knight, and it is interesting to see that we owe to Matteo Villani, historian of the battle of Poitiers, the greater part of our information on the Neapolitan campaign. Warrior at heart, and deeply religious, in his latter years he developed a leaning to a more secluded contemplative life. His inclinations were more scientific than artistic: he was greatly interested in astrology, and the horoscope of the Neapolitan campaign, established by Conversino di Ravenna, has come down to us. Conversino's son Giovanni, who was born in Hungary and was well known to Boccaccio, who calls him by the Hungarian word *chis*, i.e. *kis*, 'little', praises Louis for his great kindness and humanity. Though he was reproached by no lesser man than Petrarch for not paying enough attention to poetry, Louis was a great patron of historians. His desire to assimilate the Hungarian past must have played some part in this interest. We are fortunate to possess a beautifully illustrated chronicle by Marc Kálti, written in Latin at Louis's court.

Hungarian literature was virtually non-existent at the time of Chaucer, though oral literature was certainly flourishing. The adventures in Italy of the noble Nicholas Toldi, who accompanied the King there, must have been celebrated in many oral works before, almost two centuries later, Peter Ilosvai Selymes gave these a written form. In the nineteenth century they were to become the subject of a splendid popular epic by Arany.

In 1367 Louis founded in Pécs the first Hungarian University. The impulse for this was given by the foundation in 1347 of the German

University of Prague—the first institution of its kind in Transalpine territory.

We know very little of the architecture of the Anjou period, successive wars have almost entirely destroyed the not inconsiderable buildings erected at that time. The splendid statue of St George in Prague is the only extant example of the Kolozsvári brothers' fine work. Louis's endowments in Aachen and Mariazell are good examples of the King's generosity. There can be no doubt that the elegance and richness of his court were not unworthy of the power and authority of this great monarch.

CHAPTER II

SIGISMUND OF LUXEMBURG

LOUIS died without leaving a son, and his daughters Maria and Hedwig, respectively eleven and nine years old, were obviously too young to rule an empire of the size to which Hungary had grown under the Anjou kings. Maria was engaged to Sigismund of Luxemburg, son of the Emperor Charles IV. The young child was crowned without any opposition on the day following Louis's burial, but the Poles, in spite of the promise to the contrary they had given to Louis, refused to continue the union of Hungary and Poland under one ruler. They declared themselves ready to recognize Maria as their Queen only on condition that she renounced the Hungarian throne. As this was no longer possible, a compromise was eventually worked out, and Hedwig was crowned Queen of Poland (1384). She married the Lithuanian Prince Jagiello, creating thus a personal union between Poland and Lithuania.

In Hungary, the Queen Mother, Elisabeth, widow of Louis, ruled in the name of her daughter. Hungary was not lucky under a Queen Mother regent. Elisabeth displayed the same shortcomings as her namesake, mother of Ladislas IV. Jealous and capricious, she was completely under the influence of her favourite, Nicholas Gara. The magnates, quite rightly dissatisfied with the rule of this unreliable woman, sought and found an alternative in the person of Charles III, King of Naples, adoptive son of the late King Louis. Charles accepted the offer made by the Hungarian lords and, under the pretext of lending a helping hand, came to Hungary, where he was well received by the Queen. However, he soon put down his cards, forced the abdication of Maria, and in the presence of the humiliated mother and daughter, seething with rancour, had himself crowned King of Hungary on the last day of 1386. He had little opportunity to enjoy his success. On the instigation of Elisabeth, a murderous attack was made on Charles who, on February 24, 1387, died from the wounds he had received. The petticoat government was to continue.

The news of Charles's assassination caused great consternation, and the lords responsible for Charles's *coup d'état* joined forces with the Bosnian prince Tvartko who, with the help of Venice, had been trying to create unrest in the southern parts of the country for some time. Elisabeth, accompanied by her daughter, the Queen, tried to quell the rebellion by her personal intervention. However, she and her retinue were attacked, Gara and Forgách (who was directly responsible for Charles's death) were beheaded on the spot, and the queens were taken prisoner. Soon after Elisabeth was strangled—the second woman to pay in this way for her enmity towards Charles.

Sigismund, Maria's betrothed, who had never enjoyed the sympathy of the late Elisabeth, and who had been kept at a distance from Hungarian politics, now decided to intervene and to liberate Maria. He succeeded and, soon afterwards, was crowned King of Hungary, to rule jointly with his wife, the rightful heir to the throne.

Sigismund (1387–1437) ruled over Hungary for half a century; the length of his reign is second in Hungarian history only to that of the Habsburg Emperor and King Francis Joseph. It is inevitable that a reign of such length should leave a deep imprint on the history of the country; it is also inevitable that over a period of half a century, success and reverse, good and bad should alternate, making a simple assessment of Sigismund's activities impossible. There is a further difficulty: his reign belongs as much to European as to Hungarian history. To deal with it adequately would mean writing the history of Europe in the first half of the fifteenth century. We cannot attempt this, and in consequence our presentation must remain lopsided, dealing, as it does, only with the Hungarian aspects of his activities.

The coronation of Sigismund, though it seemed a reasonable compromise, did not meet with as much approval as might have been expected. The general uneasiness was already reflected in the wording of the coronation oath, in which promises of amnesty for those who had conspired against Maria and guarantees of reliance on Hungarian, not foreign, councillors, were incorporated. Having been crowned King, Sigismund sought to liberate Maria, but she had in the meantime been set free by the Venetians. Venice, eager to prevent any collusion between

Naples and Hungary which might endanger her Adriatic possessions, wished to see Sigismund firmly established in Hungary. It took Sigismund years and years to quell the rebellions which were constantly flaring up against his so-called foreign rule, and it was only in the second half of his reign that he enjoyed the sympathy and the confidence of the Hungarian people. He acted with considerable severity against rebels, and the execution of Kont of Hédervár, and of the thirty-two noblemen associated with him, has been reckoned amongst the great misdeeds of Hungarian history. Acts such as these were not calculated to create confidence in the King's government, and after Maria's death, in June 1395, many ceased to regard him as the rightful ruler of Hungary.

Sigismund's attention soon had to be focused on an external danger, the gravity of which had become obvious by that time to all concerned. The Turkish Sultan Beyazit I, following up the earlier successes of his father, Murad I, was making headway in the Balkans, and had attacked the Wallachian prince, subject of the Hungarian King. Though Sigismund's retaliation was successful, local successes were no longer enough to keep the Turks at bay. Sigismund decided to meet them on their own ground and to strike a decisive blow at Turkish expansionism.

Sigismund, realizing that Hungary's forces would be inadequate to the task and that preventive war would probably not be popular in the country, decided to lend to the campaign the characteristics of a crusade. In alliance with the Byzantine Emperor, Manuel II, and with the help of Pope Boniface VIII and of Venice, a western army, composed of French, Burgundian, Spanish and German elements, gathered around Sigismund and advanced through Serbia as far as Nicopolis. Here, on September 25, 1396, his heterogeneous army suffered a terrible defeat. Sigismund himself escaped, but it took him over half a year to return to Hungary via the Black Sea, Constantinople and Raguza.

The news of the defeat, and Sigismund's prolonged absence from the country, did little to enhance his popularity. On his return he had to face strong opposition, which manifested itself at the Diets, now frequently convened, at which the nobles tried to check Sigismund's indiscriminate favouritism. At one moment, April 1401, he was even taken prisoner by the rebellious lords. As they were unable to devise any alternative to his rule, Sigismund was set free seven weeks later; the action had achieved nothing but a deepening of the aversion between the King and his subjects, and the strengthening of the influence and power of those families, such as the Gara and the Cillei, who remained faithful to the King. Sigismund even took the somewhat unusual step of marrying, instead of some foreign princess, Barbara Cillei. He had no son and he decided, without proper consultation, that Albert, Duke of Austria, who was to marry his daughter Elisabeth, should succeed him on the throne. This high-handed fashion of disposing of the country as of some private property brought about some sharp reactions, and Ladislas of Anjou was called in as anti-King.

Ladislas, who enjoyed the moral support of the Pope, entered Hungary in 1403 at the head of a not very impressive army of Italians, Croatians and Hungarians who had joined him from the southern and eastern parts of the country. Sigismund was away in Bohemia, but his supporters met and defeated the army of the pretender, who then hastily withdrew and henceforth left Sigismund undisturbed. On his return the King had a number of the conspirators beheaded, and to commemorate his success founded the Order of the Dragon, a somewhat belated product of the spirit of chivalry to which the Hungarian King was much devoted.

Though Ladislas of Anjou had not achieved his aim, he remained in control of Dalmatia. In 1409 he sold his claims to these towns (with the exception of Raguza and Spoleto) to Venice, which thus acquired a strip of land which had long been a bone of contention between herself and Hungary. As usual, Sigismund was away from the country when this happened. Though between 1411 and 1413, and again between 1418 and 1419, Sigismund made repeated attempts to recover the lost territory, he failed and Dalmatia was to remain under Venetian rule.

Oddly enough, the general engaged in the wars with Venice was himself an Italian, Filippo Scolari, under his Hungarian name: Pipo of Ozora. His had been an interesting career. A Florentine apprentice-trader, he had come to Hungary in the company of an Italian agent, and about 1388 entered the service of the King. He was put in charge of the military organization of Southern Hungary and it was in this capacity that he had to contend with Venice and with the Turks, whose ever-growing activity on the southern borders of Hungary had become a constant menace. Following Italian practice, Pipo greatly improved the fortifications of the southern border, and in the town of Lippa caused a hospital to be built, probably to cater for those wounded in the border fighting. This hospital, of which, alas! nothing remains, was, on the evidence of contemporaries, a building of exceptional beauty.

Unfortunately Sigismund had little time to spare for Turkish affairs, for he had become Holy Roman Emperor (1410), and King of Bohemia (1420). Rushing to and fro between his distant countries, he was reproached everywhere for his constant absenteeism, and if he lost his causes it was mostly by default. The General Council of Constance (1414–18), of which Sigismund was the protagonist, diverted most of his energies, and the burning at the stake of John Hus—who had come to Constance with a safe conduct from the Emperor—had calamitous consequences for Hungary. First, the country had to put troops at the disposal of Sigismund, engaged in the murderous Hussite wars, then these wars spread to the north-western provinces of Hungary itself and decades were to pass before the last stubborn Hussite pockets could be absorbed.

The most important changes during Sigismund's long reign were in the constitutional, social and cultural fields. The eclipse of papal authority, and the general disorganization of the Church, gave Sigismund a good opportunity to settle the age-old and always latent problem of investiture to his own advantage. With the consent of the Diet held in 1404, he issued a decree, *Placetum regium*, in which he asserted his rights to exercise investiture and to grant benefices, and forbade the promulgation, without royal consent, of papal bulls and encyclical letters. Sigismund's policy considerably weakened the Church in Hungary, and resulted—a normal corollary of lay investiture—in a general lowering of the already not very elevated standards of the episcopate. He removed bishops who had been hostile to him and filled the vacancies according to his own interests. It is significant that Andrea Scolari, the brother of Pipo of Ozora, became Bishop of Zagreb and later of Nagyvárad, and that Pipo's cousin, Giovanni Buondelmonte, ended his life as Archbishop of Kalocsa. A clergy with very little spiritual strength could not meet the formidable challenge of Hussite teaching, nor could it give guidance amid the growing profusion of sects.

Sigismund's European policies put a heavy burden on his treasury; his constant travelling, the luxury of the royal household, the costly war against the Turks, had to be financed somehow, and to do so new ways of increasing the royal incomes had to be devised. The income from the royal domains had become manifestly insufficient and Sigismund had to rely in an increasing measure on taxation. Aware of the fact that the towns were likely to yield more than purely agricultural settlements, the King did much for their development and invited their representatives to attend the Diets. Commerce was also regulated, the export of gold and silver forbidden, and a uniform system of weights and measures introduced. Sigismund's efforts could not however produce proportionate results as long as he himself was dependent on the oligarchs; and no Hungarian king before him had been so at their mercy as he was.

The difficulties of having himself recognized as King of Hungary, the constant revolts against his rule, the war with the pretender Ladislas, all contributed to the creation of an immensely powerful privileged class, recruited from among the staunchest supporters of the King and drawn together within the newly founded Order of the Dragon. Some twenty to thirty families, many of them of foreign origin, shared among themselves estates which, at a rough estimate, were more than five times as great as those belonging to the King. More than half the country belonged to some sixty families which had obtained their immense possessions at the expense of the King and of other barons who had sided against Sigismund, and whose estates had been in consequence confiscated. Not only was the land shared out, but so were the high offices, ecclesiastical and secular; in fact the country was being exploited by a trust over which the King, though the principal shareholder, had no absolute control. It must be said that this group of nobles constituted, on the whole, a competent and devoted managerial class, whose members did their best to serve their country as long as this did not interfere with their own interests. They were instrumental in the success of Sigismund's western policy, which depended largely on the important sums which they advanced. Some of them, such as the *nádor* Nicholas Garai, accompanied the King in his travels across Europe, and enhanced his prestige by the pomp which they lent to his retinue.

It is understandable that in such circumstances the absentee King, on whose shoulders rested almost all the unsolved problems of contemporary Europe, should have lost contact with his lesser subjects. Though, theoretically, he wished to strengthen the burghers, he could not in fact increase their wealth and influence beyond a point considered harmless by the oligarchs. Even less could he prevent the growing exploitation of the lower classes. Though he repeatedly asserted the rights of the *jobbágy* to move if he were dissatisfied with his lord, in practice such movements became increasingly difficult. An unfortunate judicial reform brought the *jobbágys* under the primary jurisdiction of their lords, and a new military organization, the so-called *militia portalis*, introduced by Sigismund, shifted on to the lower classes the burden of military service which had hitherto been the duty and the privilege of the nobles. Over and above the 'ninth' introduced by Louis the Great, the barons continued to exact money as well as services and, under various pretexts, direct taxation was becoming more and more oppressive. Discontent was widespread, and well justified, and the admixture of Hussite ferment brought it to explosion.

Though Hussite teaching, and perhaps even more, the example of the Hussite wars, played a not unimportant part in preparing the ground for the *jobbágy* rebellion, the principal causes of the revolt lay elsewhere. The growing production of manufactured goods, and the improvement of the living standard of the middle classes, created a thirst for money which local resources could not satisfy. The lower strata of society, compelled to pay their taxes in cash instead of in products, hampered in their freedom of movement, suffering from overbearing lords, became more and more exasperated, until, in 1437, they took to arms. The spark which set the country ablaze came from George Lépes, Bishop of Transylvania. After 1433, when for three years Sigismund's coinage was much debased, Lépes omitted the collection of the tithe. In 1437, when the quality of the coinage had improved, he claimed, in good money, the arrears, as well as the tithe of the current year. When his exorbitant demands were not met, he placed his diocese, i.e. Transylvania, under interdict. The exasperated peasants revolted and, with some support from the towns and the lesser nobility, achieved notable military successes. The rebellion, unorganized at the outset, soon produced its own leaders, among whom Anthony Budai Nagy, himself a noble, seems to have been the most powerful personality. The first successes of the rebellion compelled the nobles to negotiate, and an agreement was signed which satisfied most of the demands formulated by the *jobbágys*. This agreement remained, however, a dead letter, and the signing of it by the nobility was only a device to save time. The *jobbágy* forces, sensing danger, did not disperse, and in a new clash reasserted their military superiority. Time played, however, in favour of the nobles, who by some concessions accorded to the burghers and to such nobles as had joined the rebels, succeeded in detaching the more well-to-do elements from the masses of the poor who formed the core of the revolt. Finally, the three privileged classes of Transylvania, the Hungarian nobles, the Székely (a Hungarian-speaking clan of unknown origin) and the Saxons, concluded an alliance, the *unio trium nationum Transylvaniae*, which was in fact a supra-national coalition aimed at maintaining the privileges of its members. The alliance was still unable to master the rebellion, and on October 6, 1437, the two parties decided, somewhat belatedly one would say, to submit their quarrel to the arbitration of the King. Sigismund, however, died on December 9th without having settled the dispute. His successor, Albert, by temporizing played into the hands of the privileged classes, who at last, not without the help of non-Transylvanian Hungarian nobles, succeeded in crushing the rebellion. Budai Nagy died in battle, nine other leaders were impaled and the cruelty of the repression, as is usual in such cases, was in proportion to the injustice of the victorious cause.

Thus the end of Sigismund's long reign saw the most grievous social unrest the country had ever known. This unrest revealed more than an undue lengthening of the social ladder, and its causes were not only economic. It was a symptom of the deep spiritual transformation which had affected more or less the whole country. Sigismund, though he had grown deeply attached to Hungary, was a cosmopolite, a man imbued with the spirit of early Renaissance humanism; he held a mundane view of life. Without any deep religious feeling, he sent more men to the stake for their religious beliefs than any other Hungarian king before or after him. There was in Sigismund a streak of cruelty which, with its premeditated 'civilized' character, is a strange by-product of a philosophy that claims to give more dignity to man. On several occasions he ordered retaliatory mass executions for political acts which an Árpád king would probably have put right without any bloodshed. The Hussite wars, the ruthless persecution of the heretics by men like the Italian Franciscan Jacob Marchia, led to a general degeneration of morals; the cruelties of Western Europe slowly started to permeate Hungarian life. The old order was destroyed, and an era of cut-throat competition inaugurated. Inhumanity in Hungary began with the dawn of humanism.

Undisturbed by starving peasants and tortured heretics, Sigismund's court was a centre of learning and of the arts. It was perhaps the last entrenchment of chivalry, a chivalry devoid of any content, purely formal, with little religion and no heroism. Sigismund enjoyed this pageantry immensely, he liked to think himself the head of the Christian world, a second Charlemagne, whom he tried to copy in many ways.

Sigismund's court was open to poets. The last great representative of the Minnesänger, Oswald von Wolkenstein, found in him a generous protector. Much of the *Livre de cent ballades* was written in Hungary, and Alain Chartier also visited that country. The dominating influence in Hungarian cultural life was undoubtedly Italian. We have already mentioned Pipo of Ozora who, with the help of the Florentine architect Manetto Ammanati, did much to improve the rather low standards of Hungarian architecture. The Italian humanist Pier Paolo Vergerio who, during the Council of Constance, had become one of Sigismund's advisers, followed the Emperor to Hungary and for many years remained his chief adviser on literary and historical matters. Vergerio also wrote a *De gestis Sigismundi Regis Pannoniae*, unfortunately lost. The moral atmosphere of the court fell very much below the standards of the courts of the Árpáds or Anjous. The Queen Barbara, who openly declared her disbelief in the existence of the human soul, was taken in adultery and escaped with a purely formal penance; and Sigismund himself was far from being strict in matters of marital fidelity. These were but symptoms of a general moral laxity, corollary of a disintegrating religious framework.

The superficial, epicurean atmosphere of the court, cultured but not very sure in its taste, stood in strange contrast with the grim fanaticism of the religious sects. It is worth noting that the only extant pieces of literature from this epoch are the products of these sects, fragments of the first possibly complete Hungarian translation of the Bible. The work of two Hussite preachers, this translation is a distant echo of Wyclif's activity.

The various facets of Sigismund's long reign can only be touched on in a history as short as this. To try to assess his character, while omitting the materials on which the assessment is based, would be meaningless. It would, however, be a serious omission not to mention the deep transformation which his relations with Hungary underwent over the years. The servant of the executed Kont could call Sigismund a 'Czech pig'—at the end of his reign he was abhorred by the Czechs and considered by the Hungarians as one of themselves. How could it be otherwise? The Emperor of the Holy Roman Empire swore in Hungarian . . . wherever he went he was accompanied by Hungarian knights, and when his death came he was buried, according to his own wishes, at Nagyvárad, beside the great king St Ladislas, whom he had so much revered as a knight, and of whom he had, in the spiritual field, fallen so far short.

CHAPTER 12

JOHN HUNYADI

WHEN Sigismund's son-in-law, Albert of Habsburg (1437–9), took over the conduct of Hungarian affairs they were in a state of considerable confusion. Soon after his coronation Albert became involved in a struggle with Czech Hussites, while an effective Turkish force was making a deep incursion into Hungarian territory, achieving notable successes, such as the taking of the important fortress of Szendrö after a siege lasting three months. Albert's short reign adds but a few lines to the long chapter of Hungarian history made by the wars with the Turks. It marks, however, an important stage in constitutional development. Albert had not been an heir to the throne; he was elected King of Hungary, and those responsible for his election, i.e. the nobles constituting the Diet, meant to have a king whom they could control. Some of the conditions Albert had to subscribe to were dictated by the desire to check growing foreign influence; others had more lasting effects. The highest dignity in the country, that of the *nádor*, hitherto held by a member of the royal household, chosen by the King, was henceforth to be conferred jointly by the King and the Diet. The King was not to marry his daughters without the consent of the Diet, and civil actions brought by the King or the Queen were to be judged by ordinary courts. Such restrictions of royal rights were not accompanied by a comparable alleviation of the King's duties. The defence of the realm remained his personal duty, to be undertaken by his own mercenary force; the help of the nobles could be invoked only in cases of great emergency, and in no circumstances were the nobles obliged to follow the King beyond the borders of the country.

Albert died of dysentery when, leading a weak army already decimated by the same disease, he was about to clash with the forces of Sultan Murad II.

When Albert died his wife, Elisabeth, was pregnant, and a few months later she gave birth to a boy, Ladislas. The Estates, now accustomed to electing a king of their choice, were unwilling to entrust the country to a newly-born baby and offered the throne to the Polish King, Vladislas III, who reigned over Hungary as Vladislas I (1440–4). The new King was the son, by another marriage, of Vladislas Jagiello, who had married Hedwig, the younger daughter of Louis I. He was expected to marry the widow of Albert and to recognize her son Ladislas as heir to the throne. He consented to do this, but Elisabeth, suddenly changing her mind, refused to accept this solution to which she previously had consented and, in May 1440, had her son crowned. The Estates retorted that it was their privilege to elect a king, and refused to recognize as valid the surreptitious coronation. Thereupon Elisabeth, together with her son, taking with her the crown, sought refuge with the Emperor, Frederick III. With the financial help of the Emperor she made use of Czech mercenary forces, under the command of Giskra, to gain by force what she had failed to obtain by consent. The warfare continued for about two years before Elisabeth finally renounced her claims, a few days before her death. It is significant that Giskra continued to occupy considerable portions of the Hungarian Highlands and there exercised almost sovereign rights. On September 1, 1443, in his own name, he concluded an armistice with Ladislas for one year.

While the Queen Dowager, with the help of foreign troops, was attacking her own country in the north, Murad continued his attacks from the south. The situation could easily have become catastrophic had the appearance of a great military leader, John Hunyadi, not changed the balance of power.

John Hunyadi is probably the greatest statesman and general Hungary has ever produced; he belonged to the rare category of men who put exceptional abilities at the service of excellent causes. His intervention stopped the Turkish advance and granted Hungary a lease of freedom for some eighty years.

Hunyadi was not born of particularly distinguished stock. His father, who had come to Hungary from Wallachia, had been a protégé of Pipo of Ozora, at whose instance, for services unknown to us, he was granted an estate in Transylvania, Vajdahunyad, from which the family then took its name. Though the Hunyadis had in this way become rich, they could not be reckoned, in rank or wealth, among the leading families of the country, who were to wage against them a lifelong and embittered feud. John Hunyadi, probably born in 1407, was a soldier by character and upbringing; he had great physical strength and his endurance saved his life many times. As a child he witnessed time and again the destruction and the massacres caused by Turkish irruptions, and his deep religious feelings, which remained an essential part of his character throughout his life, contributed to his growing opposition to the Moslem Turks. Serving as a page in various noble families, he tried to build up for himself a small mercenary army. His beginnings were modest; he commanded successively a group of six, and then of twelve mounted soldiers. In 1431 we find him for a while in the entourage of Sigismund, who lent him for two years to Philip Visconti, Duke of Milan. The young knight must have fared well, for on his return he was able to lend 1200 florins to the King and Emperor, always in need of the sinews of war. Clearly, John Hunyadi belonged to those children of light who are in their generation as wise as any of the children of this world. In Italy he had learned not only the art of war but also the clever management of fortunes, and he intended to put his knowledge to use. Sigismund, who was fond of him, was right in saying that 'the whole world could not satisfy' Hunyadi's ambition. Probably in 1428, Hunyadi married Elisabeth Szilágyi, who belonged to a family similar in status and fortune to that of the Hunyadis. The joint fortunes and influences of the two families were far from negligible, but also far from satisfying Hunyadi's hunger for land and its corollary, power. Under Albert, his influence grew steadily and he obtained command of one section of the southern border lands of the realm. On his accession Vladislas I made him captain of the important fortress of Belgrade, and put him in command of the whole southern border region. In 1441 he became Voivode of Transylvania. His career was thus not that of a courtier but that of a soldier, to whom more and more important commands were given in the most threatened parts of the kingdom. Hunyadi's initial successes were defensive. In the spring of 1442, however, the opportunity arose to deal a heavy blow to the Turks, who had penetrated in force into Transylvania and there defeated Bishop Lépes (prominent in the peasant revolt). The Bishop lost his life and Hunyadi barely escaped from an ill-conceived battle. But he did not accept defeat and his qualities as a true leader were given a splendid opportunity to show themselves. Within a few days he raised a popular army, badly trained but enthusiastic, with which he destroyed the Turkish forces. Retaliation was soon to follow, and a new Turkish army, estimated at 80,000 men, was sent against Hungary. Hunyadi met the challenge, and in a battle of annihilation fought beyond the Hungarian borders he destroyed the Turkish expeditionary force. The victory not only induced Murad II to make an offer of peace to the King; it prompted Elisabeth to abandon her claim to the throne (as mentioned already) and also strengthened Vladislas's position considerably.

The time now seemed ripe for an offensive. In the summer of 1443 Hunyadi set out on what is usually called the 'long campaign'. This campaign, in which the King also took part, was the first Hungarian attack against the Turks for many years. The army pushed towards the south, liberated Serbia (the Serbian despot Brankovitch had joined the Hungarians) and, having defeated the Turkish armies on a number of occasions, was compelled by the cold winter to return to Hungary. Though the offensive was an unqualified success and raised Hungarian morale considerably, it did not strike any decisive blow against the Turks. The Sultan thought it advisable, however, to make a peace offer, which the King and Hunyadi accepted. In July 1444 a treaty for ten years was concluded on terms very favourable for Hungary.

The success of the 'long campaign' roused considerable enthusiasm in Europe and, with the Pope as principal instigator, the idea of a European coalition against the Turks gained ground steadily. However, as there is a world of difference between sympathy and action, the actual help reaching Hungary was not more than a thousand warriors! It must be remembered that considerable financial interests, particularly those of Genoa, were involved in trade with the Turks, and these could have come to harm in the case of serious Turkish setbacks. The shower of empty promises fell on Hungary during the peace talks with the Turks, and Hungarian opinion was divided on the choice between peace or war. Hunyadi himself was in favour of continuing the war. It is difficult to know what made him sign the treaty of peace with the Sultan; it is even more difficult to understand what made him break his oath a few months later; perjury seems to be so little in keeping with his character. The fact remains that Vladislas and Hunyadi, at the head of a small but efficient army, penetrated into the Balkans. Murad, who had sensed the danger, crossed the Bosphorus in Genoese boats and rushed to the help of his northern armies. The surprised Hungarians found themselves facing a considerable army headed by the Sultan himself. The decisive engagement took place on November 10, 1444, near Varna, and for a time neither party could force a decision. Then Vladislas fell and victory went to the Turks. Losses on both sides were heavy, but the real catastrophe was the King's death. Had Murad decided to follow up his victory with an offensive he would perhaps have achieved what, in fact, only the battle of Mohács was to effect. As things stood, Murad himself was too weakened by the battle of Varna to risk a major operation against Hungary with Hunyadi still alive.

Hunyadi escaped from the battle only to be taken prisoner by Vlad, Voivode of Wallachia. He was, however, soon released and could take part in the Diet of 1445. The problem to be solved was a difficult one, for some doubt remained concerning the death of King Vladislas. There was general agreement that, in the case of the King's death being established, and subject to certain conditions, the crown should be offered to Albert's son Ladislas. Meanwhile, seven captains-general were elected to act as the executive of the royal council, which continued its function. The royal prerogatives were not exercised by anyone. It goes without saying that Hunyadi, who had been a member of the council, was one of the captains-general. These represented much more the individual interests of the great baronial families to which they belonged than those of the country as a whole. The institution of these captains-general was less an effort to unite the country's forces than a quasi-recognition of the fact that the country was divided between seven groups of interest. Fortunately for Hungary, Hunyadi proved to be the most powerful among them.

Ambitious, Hunyadi was clever enough not to try to become King of Hungary, an idea that must have crossed his mind. At the Diet of 1446 he succeeded in having Ladislas elected King of Hungary, but as the King was still detained by Frederick he had himself nominated Regent (*gubernator*), a dignity that had no precedent in Hungarian history. Hunyadi thus obtained prerogatives similar to those of the King. He was to be assisted in his office by a council of twelve, composed of six nobles, two prelates and four barons.

Hunyadi was thus given powers which no one before him had obtained, and which few statesmen were to acquire in Hungarian history. History tells of many men reaching the summits of power by violence or unscrupulous methods. Few, if any, have achieved them by economic means. Hunyadi was one of them. True, he was an excellent soldier, and personally a brave man. But his military successes barely outweighed the reverses he had suffered and were due more to the excellent armaments and efficient organization of his forces than to the tactical brilliancy of their general. Hunyadi had set his mind on one great goal: the liberation of Hungary from the Turkish danger. In order to achieve this he needed a powerful army, and to organize and maintain one he needed money. It was idle to expect that in a country torn by internal feuds, divided by barons each pursuing his individual interests and paralysing any effort to create a strong centralized government, such an army could be built up by collective effort. Power, wealth, was in the hands of the barons—so Hunyadi had decided to become one of them and to beat them on their own ground. With a remarkable unity of purpose he had set himself to acquire as much land as possible and time and again we find him lending money to the King and obtaining a mortgage on some estate. By the time of his election as Regent, he had become by far the richest magnate of the country his estates covered, at a rough estimate, 5,900,000 acres! But Hunyadi was not content with possessing these huge estates, and did not exploit them with the short-sighted and inhuman methods of the barons. As far as was possible he maintained order and the rule of law, and instead of ruthlessly exploiting the peasants he secured their co-operation. It would be anachronistic to speak of industry, but such artisan resources as were available, Hunyadi put to good use in equipping his armies. The barons despised and hated him, but to the nobles he was the champion of their own cause, and it was their intervention which swept Hunyadi to power in 1446.

Hunyadi's endeavours to forge an army with effective striking force could not lead to success as long as the *banderia*, devised by Charles Robert, remained the basis of the country's military organization. To face the splendid infantry of the janissaries, a well-trained and well-armed force was needed of permanent mercenaries, and for many years the nucleus of such an army had been kept up at Hunyadi's own expense. He also contributed enormous sums to the preparation of his offensive campaigns. Now, having become the head of the country, he secured a measure that a uniform and not inconsiderable tax be voted, payable by the barons or nobles in proportion to their estates, for the purpose of creating a permanent mercenary army.

The skirmishes on the southern borders continued unabated during the first years of Hunyadi's rule, but not until 1448 did Hunyadi feel strong enough to launch a new offensive. Once again he penetrated deep into the Balkans and met the main Turkish force at Kossovo Polje (in Hungarian: *Rigómezö*), a plain situated near the town of Pristina. The Hungarian army suffered a crushing defeat, more serious even than that of Varna, but Hunyadi once again escaped and after a memorable and lonely journey, during which he was more than once taken prisoner, reached safety in Hungary.

The defeat weakened Hunyadi's authority considerably within the country and on some points he had to make concessions to the barons, whom he only could keep at bay by coming to some sort of terms with some of them and playing these off against the others. In 1450 an uneasy alliance was concluded between the Cillei and Garai families on one side, and Hunyadi on the other.

The situation with Austria was also far from satisfactory. Frederick, who was still holding the young king Ladislas as a quasi-hostage, was a permanent nuisance on the western borders, and the connivance of some Hungarian barons, such as the Cillei (who were of Austrian origin and still held huge Austrian estates) made things even more awkward. In the north-west the troops of Giskra owed allegiance, at least formally, to Frederick. Further to the south the Emperor's own troops were holding Hungarian towns such as Györ. In 1446 Hunyadi decided that the time had come for action. He attacked Styria and Carinthia, devastated Wienerneustadt, Frederick's usual residence, but to secure the sympathy of that great city, avoided Vienna. On June 1, 1447, an armistice was concluded and Frederick undertook to evacuate Györ. The armistice, though it did not settle the outstanding problems, had at least the advantage of opening the roads for trade, a benefit Hunyadi seems to have appreciated. Not many generals engaged in conflicts on three borders would have paid so much attention to the commercial interests of citizens; we have here a striking example of Hunyadi's all-embracing genius. On July 21, 1447, Hunyadi concluded with the other great war-lord, Giskra, an agreement which recognized Giskra's *de facto* rule over the territories then under his control, assured him considerable income and an important sum in cash, but also—and this was Hunyadi's principal aim—contained guarantees to the effect that the Czech general would use his considerable forces for the maintenance of internal peace. It was with the knowledge that his hinterland was fairly secure that Hunyadi had embarked on the campaign which ended at Kossovo Polje.

On his return as a defeated general all his previous achievements with Giskra and Frederick were brought to nothing. In September 1447, the former defeated an army sent by Hunyadi to put a check on his renewed raids. Not being able to bring about a favourable decision in the endemic conflict which opposed him to Frederick, Hunyadi in 1450, accepted a compromise: Ladislas was to stay with Frederick until he reached the age of eighteen; in the meanwhile Hunyadi was to continue as Regent. Though, for the first time, a clear date had been set on the return of Ladislas, thus ensuring that by 1458 Hungary would again have a king, it seems likely that the idea of remaining Regent for another eight years was not one to displease Hunyadi. Things, however, turned out differently. In 1452 the Austrian and Czech Estates, impatient to secure the freedom of Ladislas, who, as the son of Albert of Habsburg, was heir to their respective thrones, forced his release, and Hunyadi, whatever his deepest thoughts may have been, had to accept the fact that in the person of the young boy Hungary had again a king.

Ladislas V (1452–8) was twelve years old when he assumed, theoretically at least, the leadership of the country. It is not surprising that he exerted barely any influence on state affairs and was little else than a pawn in the hands of such formidable statesmen as Hunyadi, Giskra and Ulrich Cillei. The last of these, his maternal uncle, who acted as his guardian, tried to keep him away from Hungary. Thus the young King, who had taken the by then customary oath to reside in the country, spent most of his time in Vienna or Prague and relied, as far as politics were concerned, on the advice of his uncle.

Hunyadi, who—owing to the force of circumstances—had relinquished his regentship, maintained his grip on the control levers of the state. The young King made him Captain-General of the Realm and Administrator of the Royal Revenue (*Capitaneus regie maiestatis in regno Hungarie constitutus administratorque proventuum regalium*). It is difficult to follow the ups and downs of Hunyadi's power and impossible to see with clarity the fluctuations in his relations with Cillei. In Hungarian history these two play traditionally the respective rôles of hero and villain. Such a distribution of rôles is probably fair in so far as Hunyadi's political conceptions stood far above those of Cillei, but to blame the latter for everything that went wrong with them is to simplify history. It is often assumed that Cillei used his influence with the King against Hunyadi, but, in fact, had he done so the King would certainly have yielded to his suasions and Hunyadi would have been dismissed from favour. Nothing of the sort happened, and the two antagonists seem to have found a *modus vivendi*. Ladislas's accession as King of Hungary, Austria and Bohemia meant that the pie to be shared out had grown so big that even appetites like those of Cillei and Hunyadi could be satisfied simultaneously. Cillei who, we remember, was himself Austrian, held supreme power in his homeland, Hunyadi ruled over Hungary, and power in Bohemia was in the hands of Podiebrad. Cillei was obviously a man of lesser calibre than the two other proconsuls; the Austrians, dissatisfied with his nefarious influence, forced him to retire. The helpless King, now crowned also King of Bohemia, came under Podiebrad's influence, and it is probably in this that we have to seek the cause of some attempts to concentrate in the King's hand powers held by Hunyadi. Podiebrad had the appetite of a newcomer to the feasting-table, and had as yet little opportunity of learning the 'live and let live' principle. Early in 1455 Ladislas returned to Vienna, and his uncle Ulrich Cillei was able to stage a spectacular comeback to the political scene. The precarious balance of power between the factions had more or less been re-established.

In 1453 a tremendous event, the fall of Constantinople, had shaken Europe, and it seemed for a moment that Western Europe was awakening to the danger of Turkish imperialism. The moment soon passed, and a year after Mahomet II was able to launch a well-prepared attack against Serbia. Once more, only Hunyadi offered him resistance. He achieved local successes but could not, at this stage, engage on a decisive battle. Simultaneously with his military preparations, considerable efforts were made to raise a European army strong enough to eject the Turks not only from Serbia but from Europe as a whole. These efforts faltered because of the general lack of enthusiasm of the western powers, particularly of Frederick III. Such moral help as came, came from the Pope Calixtus III, who did his best to break through the general apathy.

The spirited Franciscan, John Capistrano, put his powerful oratory at the service of the great cause and did much to secure for Hunyadi the support, not only of nobles, but also of the broad masses. In the spring of 1456 Mahomet started a new offensive, and at the beginning of July the siege of Belgrade began. The move had been foreseen for some time, and to remind people of the imminence of the Turkish menace the Pope had ordered that a special prayer be said daily at noon. The Catholic custom of ringing the church bells at midday dates from this epoch. Hunyadi did his best to prepare Belgrade—defended by his brother-in-law, Michael Szilágyi—for the attack, and he himself gathered such armies as he could to meet the enemy at the walls of the city. Only a few of the barons put their forces at his disposal; but many from the lower classes answered Capistrano's call for a crusade and flocked in untrained, ill-armed but enthusiastic crowds to join Hunyadi's army. The first Turkish onslaught on the fortress failed, and the few days' respite gave Hunyadi an opportunity to give some training to his popular troops and organize the relief of the hard-pressed town. He succeeded in joining the garrison and the final assault, which began on July 21st and continued throughout the night, was victoriously resisted. The following day a Hungarian counter-attack was launched. In spite of the great numerical superiority of the Turks, the Hungarians gained a complete victory. The greater part of Mahomet's army was annihilated, and the rest, including the Sultan himself, was put to flight. Hunyadi's excellent military organization, aided by Capistrano's fanaticism, and the courage of both leaders, won a victory for which the great hero, then in his sixties, had been labouring all his life. It was the finest, and very nearly the last, day of his life, a life spent in the service of his country and his people. He died on August 11th of a fever contracted on the field of battle.

It is not diminishing Hunyadi's outstanding achievements to recognize his shortcomings; they were typical of his time and of his country. His unbridled ambition was certainly the dominant feature of his character. But to satisfy it he relied on virtues, on heroism, devotion, justice. He was not a champion of the common people, but his aim was not to exploit them; he himself became the most powerful baron of Hungarian history, but he never lived in the fool's paradise of his like. His memory has been cherished in Hungary, and has inspired many poets. He was a great man by any standards.

Hunyadi's elder son, Ladislas, had been, in his father's lifetime, entrusted with important offices in which, without excelling, he showed himself capable enough to command some support. Sons of powerful and rich fathers seldom have to show outstanding abilities in order to obtain public recognition; the immense family fortune inherited by Ladislas Hunyadi predestined him for what is called, with mild euphemism, public service. It is likely that the King and his advisers, chiefly Cillei, thought the moment opportune to clip the wings of the Hunyadi family; it is certain that Ladislas intended to maintain and possibly to augment its influence. Things were probably not all too secure for him, for he only consented to attend the Diet convened by the King at Futak with a safe-conduct in his possession, guaranteeing that neither of John Hunyadi's sons would be called upon to render account of their father's management of the royal revenue. Ladislas Hunyadi must have left this Diet in considerable anger for, contrary to his expectations, not he but the old foe, Cillei, had been nominated successor of John Hunyadi as Captain-General of the Realm. Soon after, the King visited Belgrade, which Szilágyi was most reluctant to hand over to him. During the visit a quarrel broke out—with or without premeditation it is now impossible to say—in which Cillei lost his life. With Cillei murdered before his very eyes and himself within the fortress —Hunyadi and Szilágyi had been careful not to let the royal escort enter the walls—the young King showed a cunning worthy of his late uncle and tutor. He appointed Ladislas Captain-General of the Realm, in succession to the murdered Cillei, and issued a series of letters exonerating him from what had happened. On his return to Buda, passing through the house of John Hunyadi's widow, he guaranteed the immunity of her sons—though it is difficult to imagine in what measure he was then free to choose another course of conduct. But the King's entourage, all the old enemies of the Hunyadis, were now determined to put an end to their rule. The pack was closing in; even Giskra was mobilized. On March 14th Ladislas and his younger brother Matthias, invited to the royal palace, were arrested and two days later Ladislas was put to death.

As the name Hunyadi had a magic ring for many Hungarians, the execution of his son caused considerable stir, and the choleric Szilágyi engaged in a military campaign against the supporters of the King, who, taking with him the young Matthias Hunyadi, withdrew to Vienna and thence to Prague. A Hungarian delegation of extraordinary splendour was sent to France to arrange the marriage of Ladislas with Magdalene, daughter of Charles VII. It was during these negotiations that a sudden illness put an end to the young King's stormy life, providing yet another example for Villon's *Ballade des seigneurs du temps jadis*.

CHAPTER 13

MATTHIAS HUNYADI CORVINUS

FOR some eighteen years Hungary had been virtually without a king and now, when at last it seemed that the King was going to rule effectively, he died, leaving no heir and a country on the brink of serious civil war. There was no lack of candidates for the vacant throne, but none of them could put forward claims as strong as Matthias Hunyadi. Michael Szilágyi took the lead in the election campaign, which achieved its purpose: the Diet assembled on New Year's day, 1458, elected Matthias King of Hungary (1458–90).

The young King was still in Prague, a quasi-prisoner of Podiebrad. The latter thought the moment opportune to betroth his daughter Catherine to Matthias, but not before he had obtained a considerable ransom did Podiebrad consent to hand Matthias over to a Hungarian delegation headed by Szilágyi and John Vitéz, Bishop of Várad, a staunch supporter of the Hunyadi family.

Matthias was a spirited young man, who found it fairly natural to rule Hungary and was determined to rule it alone. This had not been the intention of those electing him, and particularly not that of his uncle, Michael Szilágyi, whom the Diet had appointed Regent and tutor of the King, and who probably envisaged a relationship with Matthias similar to that which had existed between Ladislas V and Cillei. Matthias's ideas were different. Very soon Szilágyi had to resign, and shortly afterwards he was imprisoned by his young nephew, who was little inclined to leave at liberty someone potentially so dangerous, when he still had to assert himself in the face of enemies as powerful as the Emperor Frederick III and Giskra.

Ever since the young Ladislas V had taken refuge with the Emperor, the crown of the Realm had remained in his possession, and this fact already gave him some semblance of right to the throne. On Ladislas's death he had rather half-heartedly put forward his claim to the succession, but his chances became real only when some barons, dissatisfied with Matthias's determination to rule himself, in February 1459 'elected' Frederick King of Hungary. The act had little practical meaning, for the Emperor showed no more enthusiasm for securing the throne of Hungary than for any of his previous undertakings. So, after some minor clashes, an agreement was worked out in 1462, partly through the good offices of Pope Pius II, according to which Frederick, against a payment of 60,000 pieces of gold, handed the crown to Matthias, but reserved for himself the title King of Hungary and the right to the succession. The terms of the treaty were so unfavourable for Hungary that the only reason one can give for its acceptance by Matthias was his desire to have a free hand in his various other enterprises. These were numerous and compelled the King to remain permanently on a war footing. Almost simultaneously he had to face renewed unrest caused by Czech brigandage in the Highlands, and wars in Wallachia, Serbia and Bosnia. The first of his undertakings was a complete success; the Czech brigands were wiped out and Giskra, who had ceased to make common cause with them, was finally won over to Matthias. Wallachia and Serbia were made to recognize Hungarian rule without undue difficulties, and the Serbian campaign brought the King the perhaps not entirely unhoped-for benefit of Szilágyi's death. The King had set his uncle free on condition that he should reconquer Serbia, of which he was to become Prince; but the Turks succeeded in taking him prisoner and he was beheaded in Constantinople. Bosnia, nominally, had always remained attached to Hungary, but now the Turks attempted to annex it. Their plans were effectively resisted by Matthias, who launched a counter-offensive. It seemed for a while that the King was willing to continue John Hunyadi's aggressive Turkish policy. But, though more support was forthcoming from abroad, particularly from Pius II, than there had been in Hunyadi's time, Matthias showed little interest in Balkan affairs. Pope Paul II, continuing his predecessor's policy, sent further sums for the purpose of prosecuting the Turkish wars, but the King put the responsibility for his own slackness on the Western Powers who did not help him sufficiently, and refrained from attacking the Turks. Though Matthias was undoubtedly right in his estimate of the help received from abroad, his father, with even less help, had been willing and able to continue the struggle. When, after his solemn coronation in 1464, Matthias ceased to pursue an active Turkish policy, it was not because he felt unable to do so, but because he thought it more rewarding to focus his attention on Czech and Austrian affairs.

In order to achieve his aims in foreign policy—aims which, at least at this stage, were not very clearly formulated—Matthias had to create an army, and to sustain an important striking force he had to dispose of the necessary financial means. He was thus faced with roughly the same problems as his father had been. He too realized that the *banderia* were neither strong nor reliable enough to form the core of his army, and therefore he further increased the military duties of the lower classes by ordering, in 1458, that every twenty, and from 1465, every ten *jobbágy* households should contribute one armed mounted soldier to the *militia portalis* introduced under Sigismund. The forces thus levied could be used beyond the borders of the kingdom, for a period not exceeding three months. The forces of the nobles and the *militia portalis* could only be mobilized in case of war. Matthias therefore established an impressive hired army of highly-trained professional soldiers which—an unusual feature in the Europe of his day—had a permanent character and could thus be used at very short notice. Composed of about 20,000 cavalry and 10,000 foot, both heavily armed, the so-called 'Black Army' constituted a military force of outstanding value. The soldiers serving in it were largely foreigners, Germans, veterans of Giskra's; and it is interesting to note that shortly before his death Matthias was engaged in negotiations for the employment of a Swiss contingent.

To maintain such an army, new, and very heavy taxes were needed, and in fact Matthias had to reorganize the taxation system. By giving new names to old taxes the King invalidated old exemptions and he also secured for himself the tolls. Though the burden of the new taxes had to be borne by the *jobbágys* the nobles also found cause for dissatisfaction in the new system, for the King, as a rule, favoured the tax-paying layers of the population. His social and judicial measures brought in in their favour counter-balanced, in the eyes of the peasants, the unpopularity of his financial and military exactions. The nobles also resented the fact that those of them who had no *jobbágys*, i.e. those who were the poorest of their class, were compelled to pay the new royal taxes. This meant that a financial consideration overrode the judicial distinction between nobles and non-nobles, the former losing their principal and characterizing privilege of exemption from the payment of taxes. The bitterness caused by these dispositions led to two conspiracies (1467 and 1471) which, however, failed to obtain their abrogation.

An army similar to that of Matthias is usually not forged without the desire to make use of it. During the whole of his reign the extraordinary military gifts of the King were used to obtain the Czech and the Imperial crowns. It is difficult for us to see the reasons that made Matthias abandon his father's policies and embark upon what could only be considered an adventure. It has been argued, and the argument was put forward already in Matthias's time, that to obtain a decisive victory over the Turks the King felt it necessary to have at his disposal forces superior to those Hungary could muster. Probably this was only a pretext serving to justify a policy that could not be justified by more direct arguments, and it would be unfair to Matthias's splendid intelligence to suppose that he actually believed it. The years spent by him as a prisoner in Vienna and Prague certainly contributed to giving these towns, in the eyes of Matthias, an outstanding importance. If we may hazard a guess, it is probable that, together with the discovery of the higher degree of civilization these places represented compared to that of the family estate where he had spent his early childhood, the desire to return as ruler where he had been a prisoner must also have influenced the King's mind. We usually prefer the esteem of our childhood's world to that of any other society and, perhaps, Matthias—quite wrongly—attached more importance to Bohemia than to Turkey and therefore considered its conquest of more moment.

When Matthias had returned from Prague to occupy the throne of Hungary he was affianced to Podiebrad's daughter, and he resisted the pressure of his nobles to break the engagement. One could, therefore, have expected a cordial collaboration between him and his father-in-law, Podiebrad. The Czech King had been on good terms with John Hunyadi and tried to maintain good relations with Matthias. His aim was to call a new General Council at which Hussite teaching might obtain some sort of recognition, and to form a European coalition against the Turks. On the death of his daughter Catherine, Podiebrad offered the hand of another daughter to Matthias, who refused it; by

that time his ambitions had grown and he was ready to jeopardize
Czech friendship in order to obtain the support of the Emperor and the
Pope in his great scheme: his election as King of the Romans. His
dream was to become Holy Roman Emperor, but he realized that this
was beyond his grasp as long as Frederick III was alive. As the Emperor
was a middle-aged man—in fact he outlived Matthias—the King could
not wait for death to bring a solution to his problem; he therefore
purposed to become elected King of the Romans, hoping that, invested
with this dignity, he would be able to exert considerable influence on
the affairs of the Empire. It was building on shifting ground to rely on
Frederick, who used Matthias merely to counter-balance Podiebrad.
Pope Paul II, annoyed by the Czech King's reluctance to take measures
against the Hussites, encouraged the Hungarian King to act. Thus
prompted, Matthias in 1469 made a totally unwarranted attack on
Moravia, occupied Brno and Olomouc, and with the help of some
Catholic lords was crowned King of Bohemia in May of the same year.
Understandably Podiebrad took this act in bad part, and to ensure
foreign help, by-passing his own son, offered the heirship to his throne
to Vladislas, son of Casimir IV, King of Poland. He died soon afterwards
and Matthias had to face the joint Czech and Polish forces. The
Emperor himself recognized Vladislas, and Matthias, though militarily
undefeated, found himself in a quandary.

The Czech wars had strained the country's finances to the utmost,
and even friends as reliable as the old Bishop John Vitéz and his cousin,
the famous humanist Janus Pannonius, felt impelled to take steps
against the King. These took the form of a conspiracy aimed at replacing
Matthias by Casimir, son of the King of Poland of the same name. This
desperate step was taken after the King, through a fit of rage, had
jeopardized plans to marry him to the Emperor's daughter, then aged
five. By then it was clear that good counsel could not prevail on Matthias,
entirely taken up with his chimeric ambitions. At the Diet of 1470, when
the Estates were reluctant to vote further taxes, Matthias, losing his
temper, struck Bishop Vitéz, imprisoned others, and had the taxes
collected without the consent of the Diet.

Casimir IV, accepting the invitation addressed to him by the conspirators, prepared to attack Matthias. Faced with this imminent
danger, the King displayed his great human qualities. When he learned
about the conspiracy he showed remarkable self-control and took great

care to appear as if he were unaware of the preparations. Through his great personal charm and through favours judiciously accorded, he secured one by one the sympathy of a great number of lords, and at the Diet held in September 1471 he proposed remedies, apparently on his own initiative, for most of the complaints voiced by the conspirators. By the time Casimir crossed the Hungarian border with 17,000 soldiers, Matthias had secured the loyalty of many of the Hungarian lords. Though preparing his army, Matthias did not hasten to combat Casimir; the latter, realizing the change that had taken place in favour of Matthias, found it wiser to withdraw. The crisis was over and, for once, it had not been solved by arms. It left a deep impression on Matthias's mind, and as far as it was compatible with his general policies, he tried thereafter to show more consideration for the wishes of his subjects. A certain lassitude manifested itself also among the Estates; the two men with the most cultivated brains, John Vitéz, at that time Archbishop of Esztergom, and Janus Pannonius, disappeared from the political scene and soon afterwards died, and the nobles seem to have abdicated their responsibility in conducting the affairs of State. The Diet on its own request, adjourned itself for two years.

With his continuous wars Matthias had made himself a nuisance to all concerned in Eastern Europe, where he could no longer reckon to find real help or sympathy. A coalition composed of all the neighbouring states was being formed, and Matthias had no choice but to strike. Once more he was brilliantly successful, and he soon entered Breslau, which a vast Czech and Polish force gathered to besiege. Though the enemy was about seven times superior in numbers, and had the advantages an assailant always possesses, Matthias defeated them. The extraordinary thing happened, that the besieging army surrendered to the beleagured garrison. An armistice was signed for four years on the expiry of which, on December 7, 1478, a peace treaty was concluded at Olomouc, according to which Matthias and Vladislas were both to use the title 'King of Bohemia' and each of them kept the territories in their possession. This meant that Moravia, Silesia and Lausitz remained under Matthias's rule, though it was stipulated that at his death they could be bought back at a price of 400,000 pieces of gold.

The victorious conclusion of the Czech wars meant no respite for Hungary. The Turks made good use of the lull, and whilst Matthias was involved in the north, they made several successful raids into

Hungary and built on Hungarian territory, on the banks of the River Sava, a powerful fortress: Sabach. The victorious garrison of Breslau, reinforced by *banderia*, laid siege to this powerful stronghold which surrendered after a resistance of six weeks, on February 15, 1476.

Relations between Matthias and Frederick had never been really cordial, and since Matthias had broken his engagement to the Emperor's daughter they had become frankly bad. Matthias quite rightly felt that he had nothing to expect of the Emperor's friendship, and that, therefore, the conquest of Austria would bring him nearer to the imperial crown than any negotiations. In the thirteen years between 1477 and 1490, Matthias led three campaigns against Frederick III. The first two Austrian wars ended in the Emperor's seeking peace on Matthias's terms, which included the handing over of Bohemia by Vladislas. As Frederick did nothing to respect the obligations he had undertaken, hostilities again flared up, and in 1485 led to the occupation of Vienna. Here Matthias died on December 6, 1490, worn out by the strain of an exceptionally arduous life.

Matthias's foreign policy was unrealistic, but he should not be judged on this alone. He was also a soldier of exceptional ability and was, in fact, more successful than his father had been. But his conquests brought no permanent gains to the country, and he neglected the most serious problem, the Turkish one, with which Hungary was presented. Matthias's victories, fought and obtained by mercenaries, had comparatively little popular appeal, though the fall of Vienna captured the imagination of the people. Public opinion was focused on the Turks, and it is no mere accident that the siege of Sabach should have inspired the only epic poem written in Hungarian that has come down to us from that period.

How is it then that Matthias ranks not only among the most powerful, but also among the most popular, kings of Hungary? His organizing abilities, and particularly his love of justice, together with his generous support of arts and letters, achieved for him what his policies and victories had failed to do.

Matthias established a strong centralized government and considered the Diet as a necessary nuisance, hampering rather than advancing state business. This was transacted by his own chancellery and the royal council, both manned by men, often rather young, who had been chosen on the strength of their own capabilities rather than for their birth or fortune. In fact, Matthias methodically kept the barons removed from any real source of political power, and relied on a nucleus of men, very similar in their function to modern Civil Servants. A curious feature of Matthias's centralizing policy was the strengthening of the power retained by the departments (*megye*), the two being in apparent contradiction. But he augmented the powers of the *megye* notably in judiciary matters, at the expense of the barons. These, though they kept their fortunes, were being deprived of their political and administrative functions.

Matthias's legal reform was of the greatest benefit for the country, and it is not without reason that the Hungarian people surnamed him 'the Just'. The tribunals of the first instance were organized on a departmental basis, and meeting at regular intervals were composed of the *föispán* (the King's permanent administrative representative in the *megye*), four *szolgabirós* (elected judges of the *megye*) and ten *homini regius*. In the case of an appeal being lodged, this went first to the *tabula regia judicaria*, presided over by a *protonotarius*, representing the King, who was a professional judge. The supreme court was composed of the King in person, assisted by some members of the royal council. The reforms introduced by Matthias all served the same purposes, the defence of the rights of the common man, the speeding up of procedure, the prevention of bribery. Earlier than in many countries of Europe, the administration of justice in Hungary was made independent of political administration.

Matthias's conquests were soon lost, and his social policy, with its achievements in justice and humanity, was not to survive the troublesome times which followed his reign. The most lasting influence he has exerted on Hungarian life was in the cultural field; he made his court a centre of humanist culture, a source of light for the subsequent dark centuries. To this source Hungarians have often returned to find moral comfort and faith in their destinies.

Matthias was certainly not the first Hungarian king to show an interest in the humanist culture; in this respect, as in some others, Sigismund can be considered as his principal forerunner, and had Ladislas V lived he too would probably have become a patron of learning. John Hunyadi himself, though he had little time for study, was an enlightened patron of the humanists and it was under him that the leading figure of John Vitéz gradually emerged. Approximately of the same age as his great patron, John Vitéz too had started his career in Sigismund's entourage. Bishop of Nagyvárad since 1445, he was nominated Archbishop of Esztergom in 1465. For more than thirty years he served the two Hunyadis, helping them with deeds and counsel in the shaping of their policy. He was instrumental in securing Matthias's election, fulfilling thus the wish of his old friend, John Hunyadi, who on his death had committed his sons to the care of the Bishop. He took part in many diplomatic negotiations, including those which led to the recovery of the Holy Crown from the hands of Frederick III.

His bishopric, where his immediate predecessors were Italians, the already mentioned Andrea Scolari, and Giovanni Milanesi da Prato, had for some years been a centre of humanist culture. Vitéz laid there the foundations of a library which was soon to become famous. He employed good copyists, and works belonging to the library were sent to men as distinguished as the Cardinal of Cracow and Aeneas Sylvius, the future Pius II. The latter great humanist, since 1443 in the service of Frederick III, was at first a great opponent of the policies advocated by Vitéz, but above political controversies their common interest gradually drew them together; Vitéz recommended Aeneas for the cardinalate, the latter intervened in favour of Vitéz when he was held prisoner by Ladislas V. Though he himself never attempted to write works other than letters, speeches, memoranda, Vitéz's style was excellent. In Nagyvárad, and even to a greater extent in Esztergom, he succeeded in gathering around him scholars of merit; his house was a *confugium bonorum omnium ac literarum asylum* and his support extended to scholars living outside Hungary. He showed great interest in astrology. Commissioned by Vitéz, George Peuerbach produced his *Tabulae Varadienses* for the calculation of lunar and solar eclipses, and the famous Regiomontanus from Königsberg wrote in Esztergom his *Tabulae Directionum* (1457), which he dedicated to Vitéz. Among the more important achievements of Vitéz we must count the foundation of a University at Pozsony, which, however, outlived its founder by a few years only, and the splendid architectural improvements brought to Esztergom. Unfortunately, these did not fare better than most of the other buildings previous to the Turkish occupation. Only a spade can bring to light the remains of ancient splendours.

Another outstanding figure of Hungarian humanism is Vitéz's

nephew, John Csezmicei, better known under his Latin name: Janus Pannonius. In many respects the careers of both resemble each other; uncle and nephew were both bishops, both were imbued with the spirit of humanism, both became involved in politics and fell together after the unsuccessful conspiracy of 1471. But though their outlook was similar, their approach to life was different: Vitéz was above all a statesman, Pannonius a poet. In their minds the balance between the humanist and national ideals was tilted in opposing directions. The younger man was educated in Italy, whence he returned to his native country at the age of twenty-four as a poet of repute. Vitéz promoted humanistic studies, his nephew excelled in them. The greater part of Pannonius's poetical output dates from his stay in Italy: panegyrics, epigrams, epithalamia, having practically no connection with Hungarian civilization. Most of his earlier poems are in a light vein, some of them even obscene. With his return to Hungary his tone changed; his new dignity (he had been nominated Bishop of Pécs), his part as a statesman and also his own circumstances, his illness and his longing for more civilized surroundings, gave his later poetry an intensity of feeling and an individuality which ensures for him a very honourable place among the Latin poets of his age. He was also an excellent Greek scholar, a translator of Plutarch and Demosthenes.

We have already mentioned that the abortive conspiracy which aimed at replacing Matthias by Casimir had left a lasting mark on Matthias's mind. The death of Vitéz and of Janus Pannonius disturbed the evolution of Hungarian humanism and the King, disappointed, felt no inclination to protect a school of thought which, to his mind, formed traitors. But a suite of literati was, at this epoch, an indispensable requisite of a prince of Matthias's standing, and the King could not dispense with it for long. In fact, it is from this second period that date most of the achievements which have ensured a lasting fame for Matthias's court.

The beginning of this new era was marred by Matthias's marriage in 1476 to his second wife, Beatrix, daughter of Ferdinand of Aragon, King of Naples. With her arrival direct Italian influence became the principal feature of the royal court. Among the many Italians living there, special mention is due to the historians: Galeotto Marzio, Antonio Bonfini and Pietro Ransano.

Galeotto, a student-friend of Janus Pannonius (a joint portrait of them by Mantegna has, unfortunately, not come down to us), spent some eight years of his life full of vicissitudes in Hungary. In Buda he wrote his book *De homine libri duo*, which was to cause him endless troubles. His work *De dictis ac factis*, written for John Corvinus, contains much useful, though not always reliable material on contemporary Hungary.

Galeotto, second-rate both as a scholar and as a man, cannot compete for our esteem with his compatriot Bonfini. His *Hungaricum Rerum Decades IV et dimidia*, presented in forty-five books the .history of Hungary until 1496. Of no particular value for the older epochs, his work becomes increasingly important from the second part of Sigismund's reign onwards, and is our main, and very valuable, source for the reigns of Matthias and his successor Vladislas II.

It is interesting to watch Bonfini's efforts to cloak Hungarian history with Roman garments. The protagonists act and speak like Romans and deliver speeches in the best humanist style. One should note also the revival in Matthias's court of the cult of Attila. Bonfini's book is largely responsible for the survival and popularity of the historically unwarranted Hun-Hungarian identification. His Attila behaves in Roman fashion and resembles Matthias; in fact, Hun history as presented by Bonfini brings justification for Matthias's policies. It is an odd, probably unparalleled, attempt to merge admiration for Roman and Barbaric ideals, and to find a compromise between the chauvinism of national traditions and the supra-national worship of all things Roman.

Under these conditions it is not surprising that the Hunyadis should have bestowed upon them a Roman origin. Bonfini traces the family back to a Roman Consul, Marcus Valerius, himself a descendant of Lacedaemon, son of Zeus and Taygeta. It was Marcus Valerius who, having once been helped by a raven, adopted the name Corvinus. Thus the origin of the name under which Matthias is known in European history is to be found in Bonfini's fanciful genealogy.

A short *Epitome rerum hungaricarum* has Pietro Ransano, Bishop of Lucera, as its author. His stay in Hungary was comparatively short, from 1487 to 1490.

The writing of history was not, however, limited to Italians. The *Chronica Hungarorum* of John Thuróczy is much less affected by humanist mannerisms and presents, as it were, a Hungarian version of national history. He was the first to launch the new cult of Attila, and his material was largely put to use by Bonfini. The great interest in history which characterizes the reign of Matthias is further exemplified by the fact that the first book ever printed in Hungary was a work of history, the so-called Chronicle of Buda (1473).

It will be noted that the first Hungarian printing-press was senior by three years to that established in England by William Caxton. The first printer was a German, Andrew Hess, and among his earliest productions figure a *De legendis poeticis* by St Basil and an *Apologia Socratis* based on Plato.

This last work is but one sign of the strong Neoplatonist trend which pervaded Matthias's court. Janus Pannonius, Galeotto and many other men belonging to his entourage were great admirers of the Greek philosopher and kept close contact with the Florentine Marsilio Ficino, perhaps the most eminent Platonist scholar of his time. Several of Ficino's works are dedicated to Hungarians, two of them to Matthias himself. It is interesting to note that Filippo Buonaccorsi, alias Callimachus, a former companion of Pomponius Laetus, and later Polish (!) ambassador to Matthias, made his first contacts with Neoplatonic thought in Hungary, whence he transplanted them to Cracow. A small example to show that the humanist circle around Matthias was not only receptive, but acted also as a point of radiation.

It is not surprising that the interest of humanists, particularly that of the historians, should have turned towards the Roman remains then still very numerous in Hungary. Bonfini quotes several inscriptions found in Hungary, but the real founder of Hungarian, more precisely Dacian, epigraphy was John Megyericsei (1470–1517).

The greatest single cultural achievement of Matthias was probably the creation of his library, the famous Corvina. Started in the early 1460's, the library grew rapidly once the King had put in charge of the acquisitions Taddeo Ugoleto. Matthias's buyers, copyists, illustrators, were busily working in many Italian towns, and also in Vienna. The workshop in Buda employed some thirty men on copying and illustrating. Some early prints also found admittance to the library, though only one, a five-volume Venetian edition (1483–4) of Aristotle's works has come down to us. After Matthias's death the splendid library was promptly dispersed, and many distinguished scholars borrowed its volumes—never to return them. Their pilfering proved beneficial; had the library remained intact, the Turkish occupation would have destroyed more of it. As it is, some 170 volumes have been preserved and we know the titles of more than three hundred. The diaspora of the library served European humanism; early editions of Pliny, Ptolemy, Heliodorus, and Latin translations of Greek historians are often based on manuscripts which had belonged to the Corvina.

The settings of Matthias's court were worthy of all its intellectual activity. His castles and summer palaces forced the admiration of the numerous foreign visitors; sculpture, painting, the minor arts, were all represented, and even music reached a very high standard.

No Hungarian King lived in greater luxury than did Matthias—a way of life rarely appreciated by the common people. And yet it was not viewed with envy. His fame abroad rests on his army and his library, at home on his justice: 'Matthias died, justice has disappeared' goes the Hungarian saying. His humanist court, the flourishing of Latin literature within its precincts, marks the zenith of a Hungarian, almost nationalistic, civilization. Matthias was proud of being called, in Latin, *secundus Attila*! His foreign policy was unrealistic and mistaken; like many great statesmen before and after him, Matthias identified the country's good with his own glory. Had he lived longer his social reforms would have struck deeper roots and—why should we put a brake on our own imagination?—he would, perhaps, have realized that the great task had remained the containing of Turkish expansion. Time did not allow him to tackle this task. The colonnade of the Corvina, ornate with Verocchio's fountain and overlooking the Danube, no longer defended by the Black Army, was to tumble in the approaching cataclysm. Matthias, the last Hungarian King of Hungary, was the greatest, the most civilized of them all. Of common stock, he lifted the people with himself; Hungarian, he knew how to merge the national with the general human element. His achievement shows what the country could have become had it not been abandoned by Europe in its struggle against the Turkish foe.

SOCIAL UPHEAVAL—NATIONAL
DISASTER

MATTHIAS died, leaving no legitimate son. He had, however, a natural son, born of a self-effacing German mother, whom in his latter years Matthias considered as his heir. John Corvinus would have had some chance to obtain recognition had he been able to secure the collaboration of Beatrix, the widowed queen, and had he shown more energy. He enjoyed part of Matthias's immense prestige, possessed the huge family fortune, detained the Holy Crown; but John Corvinus realized too late that all this was not enough to put him on the throne without any action on his part. He took up arms only when it was already too late, when the Estates had already decided to elect Vladislas, of Jagello stock, King of Bohemia. Matthias's former lieutenant, the splendid Paul Kinizsi, was sent against John, who suffered defeat, and who, up to his early death, played only a tiny part on the Hungarian scene.

Vladislas was certainly not the only foreign pretender to the throne. Maximilian, Frederick III's vigorous son and John Albert, a Polish prince, had also put in their claims, and there was also a Hungarian pretender, Stephen Zápolyai, Governor of Vienna, one of the late king's most trusted men. The election of Vladislas II (1490–1516) was due to two principal factors. The first was the determination of the Estates to enthrone a king as weak as possible; the second, Beatrix's desire to remain Queen. She had supported Vladislas's candidature on the strength of his promise to marry her. Vladislas, who already had a wife, promised to do so, and on Beatrix's insistence even had a mock ceremony arranged. The Queen was dupe of his weak cunning. Once King of Hungary he never went near her and, owing to his previous marriage, had no difficulty in obtaining a decree of nullity from the Pope.

This little incident may serve to show what traits of character the Estates had sought in their future king. In this respect their choice could not have been better, for Vladislas II, surnamed *dobzhe* (from the Czech word *dobrý* 'good', in the sense of 'all right') pushed to the extreme that virtue rare among kings: submissiveness. From the first moment he touched Hungarian soil, the weak King was nothing but a powerless and, on the whole, not unwilling executor of others' decisions. Without private means, he could not compete with the barons, who, having regained the political importance they lost under Matthias, became once again the actual rulers of Hungary, thanks to their huge wealth. Two among them were particularly influential: John Zápolyai, son of Stephen, *nádor* by that time, and Thomas Bakócz 'Matthias's slave, Vladislas's Lord', who, from an obscure secretaryship in Matthias's court, had become successively Bishop of Eger and Archbishop of Esztergom.

Vladislas II's reign opened with a series of external disasters. Maximilian not only reconquered Matthias's Austrian possessions but—without encountering any serious opposition—penetrated deeply into Hungary. Though the situation was far from hopeless, as Matthias's army still represented a considerable force, a hasty peace-treaty was concluded at Pozsony (1491). This fantastic document, negotiated by Bakócz, was a wholesale barter of the country to a foreign prince on the sole condition that he would respect the privileges of the nobles. Matthias's conquests in Austria were abandoned, a few Hungarian towns on the western border given up to Maximilian, who was entitled to call himself King of Hungary (!), and who was to receive a compensation of 100,000 pieces of gold. Another major part of the treaty stipulated that, after Vladislas's death and in the absence of direct male heirs, Maximilian or one of his descendants was to become King of Hungary. The treaty was ratified by the King and a group of nobles, but the Diet refused, in 1492, to recognize its validity.

In the meanwhile the Black Army had been called back to Hungary. Silesia, Moravia, Lausitz, were lost without war and with no compensation forthcoming. The splendid mercenary force, under the command of the German Haugwitz, regained Hungary in perfect order, awaiting instructions. On two occasions it drove out the Polish pretender John Albert and had it been given an opportunity, it would probably have coped with Maximilian. As the abolition of the special military tax

introduced by Matthias had been one of the conditions on which the
barons agreed to elect Vladislas, there were no funds available to pay
the army which, however, moved southwards to join the forces of
Kinizsi, who had fought victoriously against renewed Turkish attacks.
Unpaid, the mercenaries had to wring their livelihood from the local
population, until Kinizsi annihilated the bulk of their force, while the
remnants, withdrawing towards Austria, were dispersed by Maximilian.

The disappearance of this superb army was not resented by a government which had no policy to pursue. National interest was completely
lost to sight, and the ambition of individuals was the only driving force
in political action.

The first years of Vladislas's reign saw the sudden and vicious
deterioration of the relations between barons and the King on one side,
and the nobles on the other; a gulf appeared which proved unbridgeable.
The barons and prelates sided with the Habsburg Maximilian, whose
growing power offered more temptation to their appetites than the
prospect of a national state, on the pattern set by Matthias, which if
powerful and prosperous, could only cause their own eclipse. The nobles
displayed a stronger national feeling which, however, was not moved by
motives exclusively idealistic. They had learned that what was good for
the barons was bad for them, and so they came quite naturally to oppose
the pro-Habsburg policy.

The leader of the nobles was John Zápolyai whom, in 1511, Vladislas
nominated Voivode of Transylvania. Through this act, devised by the
King in order to remove Zápolyai from the capital, the centre of gravity
of the nationalist policy moved eastwards; a further wedge, geographical
this time, had been driven between the contending groups.

Slowly the group of nobles secured various concessions. They
secured that, of the twenty-four members of the royal council, sixteen
should be selected from their ranks, and they established the responsibility of the royal councillors. It was also decided that decrees issued
by the King without consultation with his councillors were to be
considered invalid. The Diet held in 1504 decided that in the future
taxes would not be levied without the consent of the Estates. Though
they had earlier claimed the right to vote taxes, it was only now that this
was formally recognized. Hungary reached this important step in
constitutional development almost a century after England. The
following year, becoming gradually more and more the instrument of

growing opposition, the Diet passed a resolution for ever debarring foreign rulers from election as kings of Hungary. The resolution, though hardly complimentary to Vladislas, was in reality aimed at Maximilian, and it must be set against the background of Vladislas's matrimonial policy.

Among the few virtues of the Czech King must be counted the fact that he was what we would call today a family man, and his heart's desire was set on the normally laudable object of making his children happy. He was therefore prepared to jeopardize the realm—to which he had, understandably, little sentimental attachment—as long as this would secure to his children a 'decent future'. Not unnaturally he thought that the future lay with the Habsburgs and, though the Diet in 1505 had shown unmistakably its displeasure at foreign rule, in 1515 he concluded with Maximilian a double betrothal. His first-born child, Anne, was affianced to Maximilian's grandson Ferdinand, and his son Louis, born on July 2, 1506, was to marry Maria, Ferdinand's sister. This matrimonial agreement, concluded with complete disregard of the already-expressed intentions of the Estates, meant in reality a deal between the hitherto hostile families of the Habsburgs and Jagiellos—a deal over Hungary.

By this time Hungary had gone through the most terrible peasant revolt of its history, and this was followed by a repression just as terrible, but more stupid and inhuman, which sealed the fate of the *jobbágys* for more than three hundred years and made Hungary for the same period the scene of a social exploitation which in duration and ruthlessness is probably matched in Europe only in the Baltic States.

The national irresponsibility of the barons went hand-in-hand with a reactionary social policy, aimed at curtailing all the small concessions Matthias had made to the lower classes, in fact aimed at a degree of exploitation which had never hitherto been attained in the course of Hungarian history. We have seen how, from Louis, through Sigismund and Matthias, the great kings had resisted the barons, how they had tried to bolster up the burghers, lesser nobles and peasants in face of the voracious greed of the great oligarchs.

The short-sighted exploitation of the peasants, who according to a contemporary French traveller 'were treated like beasts' by their lords, was all the more unpardonable as it was not justified by the country's economic situation. The terrible predicament of some of the peasants was not due to an economic crisis; on the contrary, an economic crisis—affecting only the lower classes—was brought about by the over-greediness of the lords. It was man's inhumanity to man that caused the hardship which, in its turn, led to revolt. As the basic conditions of production and marketing had not changed for the country as a whole since Matthias's death, the seething discontent cannot be attributed to any other cause.

Successive Diets had heaped increasing burdens on the shoulders of the *jobbágy*, and as soon as the barons seized the reins of government, at the Diet of 1492, it was decreed that the *jobbágy* was allowed to move only with the consent of his lord. This Diet thus marked the triumph of a trend to reduce the peasants to virtual slavery, a trend which had hitherto always been effectively resisted by the kings. Once the *jobbágy* had been deprived of his only effective weapon, that of leaving a place where conditions had become untenable, it was possible to bleed him even more. The lords, unable to create means of production different from primitive agriculture, the income of which was no longer enough to satisfy their growing needs and those of the peasant tilling the soil, thought that, by tying the peasant to the soil and by enforcing atrocious labour dues, they would be able to stop evolution and remain prosperous. Evolution they did stop—for a while; but they also destroyed the economic basis of their own prosperity. However, the consequences of their actions were not at once visible, and the barons went on merrily to kill the goose laying the golden eggs.

In 1504 a law was enacted forbidding hunting and fowling to the lower classes. We know from English history the bitterness that cruel forest laws could cause; this was among the grievances of Wat Tyler's rebels, at an epoch when conditions in Hungary had been much better. The tragedy of Hungarian history is that of a decline from heights once reached, and at this time the decline was very rapid indeed.

Nevertheless, the peasants' rebellion might never have occurred had the unbridled ambition of one man found an outlet elsewhere. This man is not, as one might expect, Dózsa, the leader of the revolt, but Cardinal Thomas Bakócz, Primate of Esztergom.

We have already met the cardinal's name, but a few more words on his career may help to a better understanding of his extraordinary character. Bakócz was born of peasant stock about 1442. He studied for the priesthood and visited successively the universities of Cracow,

Ferrara and Padova. On his return to Hungary he was employed in Matthias's chancellery, became secretary to the King and in 1486 was nominated Bishop of Györ. On Matthias's death he sided with Vladislas (it was Bakócz who staged the mock ceremony of the King's wedding with Beatrix), became chancellor, and in 1497 was invested with the bishopric of Eger—the richest in the country. Almost at once he moved again to become Archbishop of Esztergom. The manner of this move is really extraordinary, even by the standards of that epoch: Hippolytus d'Este, the then Archbishop, simply exchanged his office with that of Bakócz. Hippolytus, a cousin of Beatrix, had been nominated to the archbishopric of Esztergom at the age of six, against the opposition of the Pope. At the age of fourteen he was made a cardinal. Not un-naturally his popularity was not great with the Hungarians, and Bakócz's clever manœuvring secured the help of the Pope and of the Estates, only too glad to see an Italian boy removed from the leading position in the Church of Hungary and replaced by an adult Hungarian. In 1500 Bakócz became a cardinal, thanks to Venetian support. Bakócz's relations with the Republic had been excellent and he hoped by her help to achieve the great aim of his life: to obtain the tiara. To accomplish this he spent two years in Rome, where the splendour of his suite and his munificence caused a considerable furore. Perhaps he even overshot the mark (there were rumours of bribery), for Leo X was elected Pope in 1513. As compensation Bakócz had to satisfy himself with a papal bull authorizing him to preach a crusade against the Turks, the surprising outcome of a failure to reach the highest degree of the ecclesiastical hierarchy. This Hungarian, a Julien Sorel of the sixteenth century, suddenly chose *Le Rouge*, for *Le Noir* was no longer able to satisfy his ambition. If he failed to become Pope, he would at least try to find the glory of a Hunyadi or a Capistrano in combating the heathen.

On April 16, 1514, Bakócz published the bull calling for a crusade. He did so in spite of counsel given him by men not viewing with pleasure the fact that arms would be handed to any who asked for them, and that valuable labour would be diverted from farmwork. The very same reasons, however, prompted great crowds to take up the Cross. It was an unexpected opportunity to escape from the claws of the exploiting lords, a chance to be seized. The peasants and mercenary soldiers out of work gathered in great numbers, and as they gathered they grew conscious of the force they represented, and also of how widespread was the discontent in the country. Few were the nobles joining the forces assembled by Bakócz, and the barons felt no inclination whatsoever to fight the Turks. For reasons difficult to understand Bakócz entrusted the leadership of the crusaders' army to a little-known noble soldier, George Dózsa, who organized it fairly well. Having this force at his disposal, Dózsa, quite rightly, felt that it was a power which could be used for many purposes, and he was little inclined to obey orders enjoining him to move southwards—towards the Turks. It is impossible to say whether Dózsa ever had any intention of coming to grips with the Turks, but it seems reasonable to suppose that he was unwilling, with the nobles sabotaging the whole campaign, to have his men massacred either by the Turks or, as happened with the Black Army, by the forces of the nobles. It gradually became clear that Bakócz would have to take sides and show whether the idea of a crusade was nearer to his heart than the interests of the oligarchy. It is not surprising that he should have favoured the second: on May 23rd, just over a month after its proclamation, the crusade was suspended. But this was no longer enough to put back into the bottle the genie which had been let loose: the army refused to disband. In a famous speech delivered at Czegléd, some forty miles from Buda, Dózsa definitively fixed its aims: the overthrow of the nobility and an end to the exploitation of the lower classes. The ideological foundation of Dózsa's revolution—because that is what the crusade had turned into—was remarkably sound and coherent, and it is regrettable that the whole movement is so little known to western historians. We cannot attempt here to try to place it within the framework of other European peasant revolts. As far as action goes it followed the usual pattern of burning, plundering, murdering. In spite of considerable initial successes, Dózsa could not obtain a decisive victory, and with the passing of time he saw the chances of ever achieving one slip away. Barons and nobles, setting aside their mutual grievances, joined forces against the foe who was imperilling their common privileges, and even the usually apathetic King exerted himself to call in Czech troops. The middle classes of the epoch, burghers, artisans, after some sitting on the fence, decided to abstain from action. The forces of the nobles slowly became organized, particularly in Transylvania, where John Zápolyai, to whom the rebellion brought a welcome opportunity to show his capacities as a leader, successfully revived the *unio trium nationum*, which under Sigismund had proved the right instrument of repression against the rebels of Budai Nagy. The rebels of Dózsa, under his own command, were laying siege to Temesvár, defended by Stephen Báthory, when a relief force led by his personal enemy Zápolyai attacked them. It was victorious, and Dózsa, together with some of his lieutenants, was made prisoner. Though isolated groups of peasants held out, particularly under the leadership of Mészáros, a priest, their fate was sealed, and by October 1514 the attempt to secure freedom for the great majority of the people had failed. For more than three centuries to come the broad masses were to know an oppression which their like in Western Europe have fortunately been spared.

We have mentioned how, since the reign of Sigismund, with the weakening of real religious feeling, brutality was slowly increasing in Hungarian life. Dózsa's peasants were no angels, but they never came near the atrocious brutality with which the 'civilized' and 'humanist' nobles wreaked vengeance. Distasteful as it may be, it must stand here that Dózsa—not in the first black rage following the battle, but later—was set on a red-hot iron throne and crowned with a glowing iron crown (still preserved), and that some of his own men, who had previously been starved, were compelled to bite pieces out of his roasting flesh.

Dózsa's end has haunted the conscience of Hungary's leading classes ever since. Zápolyai himself remained for the rest of his life a man badly tormented by conscience, and the name of Dózsa has reached a symbolical significance, outstripping even his real achievement and echoing down the centuries through Hungarian literature.

But the death of Dózsa, however cruel, was but a crime against an individual. More cruel and more wicked were the decisions taken at the Diet held at the end of this fatal year for Hungary. History probably knows of no legislation more shameful: for none of the discreditable acts of history, such as the withdrawal of the Edict of Nantes, or the racial laws of Hitler, affected such a great proportion of the population, nor have they been upheld for so long a time. The Hungarian nobility can claim the doubtful privilege of having, by legislation, reduced most of their own countrymen to abject servitude for 'eternity' (as they claimed), in fact for centuries.

The Diet held at the outcome of the rebellion suppressed definitely the right of the *jobbágy* to move, fixed considerable taxes, compelled the peasant to make good the damage done by the rebellion, and in case of

their failure to do so, subjected them to further fines, 'if they still have
something left' with which to meet them. 'Innocents' of the crime of
rebellion should not be punished, at least 'not more than four or five to a
village'. All those peasants guilty of actual crimes committed during the
rebellion should pay with their lives. Such were some of the sanctions
taken against the lower classes of the society, quite irrespective of
whether or not the individual had taken part in the rebellion. All
peasants were potential enemies to their lords 'by nature', the nobles.
Such being the punishments meted out by the Diet, one shivers at the
thought of what torments private vengeance must have devised to
punish rebels or simply to satisfy lust for cruelty. One lord we know of
had all his *jobbágys* branded like cattle. . . .

Perhaps the decisions of the Diet would have defeated themselves by
their own inhumanity, perhaps individual charity would have softened
their hardship, had, as a crowning misfortune, a brilliant lawyer,
Stephen Werböczi, not had at this very moment, codified Hungarian
customary law, and had he not, under the influence of events, exposed
with admirable clarity a legal and social doctrine which solidified into a
permanent form the hitherto fairly fluid division between noble and
not-noble.

Werböczi's *Tripartitum*, as his work was called, summed up in the
following four points the privileges enjoyed by the nobles: (1) No noble
can be arrested without judgment; (2) The noble has only one superior,
the King, but not even he can do anything detrimental to the noble's
person and property without legal proceedings; (3) The noble can
dispose of his income as he pleases, he does not have to pay taxes, duties
or tolls, and only in case of a defensive war has he the obligation of
military service; (4) If the King disregards the foregoing principles, the
noble acquires the right to resist him.

These points gave the nobles more rights than any citizen in any
democratic country has ever had, without putting any obligations on
him. The ill-defined duty to assist the King in a defensive war could
hardly be considered as such. All the nobles were held to be equal, no
legal distinction was drawn between barons and lesser nobles. Though
this principle had been upheld since Louis's reign, in practice it had been
little respected. The immense authority of the *Tripartitum* succeeded,
however, in obtaining its universal and uncontested recognition.

'There is no King unless elected by the nobles, and there are no nobles save those who were granted nobility by the King.' The Holy Crown is the symbol of the community of the nobles, all land belongs to it, it is the supreme liege lord. It is the real seat of power even if there is no King to wear it. It ensures that only the nobles have rights, but they have all the rights, as their community forms the body politic, the nation itself. Other men have no rights whatsoever and, particularly, have no right to possess or acquire land which *per definitionem* is in the possession of the Holy Crown, i.e. of the nobles.

The *Tripartitum*, though theoretically a codification of customary law, was, in fact, the product of wishful thinking, a projection into reality of a political theory extolling the exclusive virtue of one class, a Marxism turned upside-down. The fantastic thing about it is that, by asserting that land, of necessity, had always belonged to the nobles, it deprived *jobbágys* of holdings they had had for generations, and by asserting—without any proof but by an obvious falsification of historical facts—that all rights had always belonged to the nobility, it reduced the hitherto free masses of the country to slavery. The influence of the *Tripartitum* is a staggering example of the harm political theorists can do when let loose. No king, dictator or tyrant could have achieved what a single volume had; Hungary has not yet outlived the evil done by this book.

The adoption of the *Tripartitum* constituted a great victory for the lesser nobles. Their position was further strengthened by the fact that one of their ranks, John Zápolyai, had secured the defeat of the rebellion. The barons, and Bakócz in particular, had emerged rather badly from the great trial of strength, and the Cardinal, himself the son of a *jobbágy*, found it wiser to keep quiet when the Diet decided that henceforward no priest of *jobbágy* origin would be eligible for a bishopric. The runners-amok of the Diet were trying to fill in the last gap, however narrow, left in the prison wall which they were building so busily around the majority of their countrymen.

These, the *jobbágy*, were henceforth excluded from national life. Individual skill, honest work, perseverance, were of no use to them, they could not acquire land, they could not amass a fortune, they could not even leave their abodes. Their only hope—and it is easy to imagine how slender it was—consisted of obtaining nobility through some extraordinary chance. But it was not only among the *jobbágy* that individual effort had been stifled. The *Tripartitum* had a disastrous effect also on the nobles, tied to their land, which theoretically belonged to the Holy Crown, and enjoying undeserved privileges in conditions of unnatural security and lack of competition. Narrow-mindedness, backwardness, lethargy, were the natural results of the new order. It has been argued that the sense of enjoying common privileges, by forging the various noble factions into an indissoluble unity, created a class consciousness which helped the country to tide over the hardships of coming centuries. But this is a fallacy, for most of the incredible difficulties the country was to face were precisely due to the fatal cleavage in Hungarian society. A nation undivided, commanding the solidarity of all its children, could have weathered infinitely better the storms which were to break loose upon it.

Vladislas II died in 1516 and was followed on the throne by his ten-year-old son, Louis II (1516-26). It appeared that Vladislas had appointed the Emperor Maximilian and the Polish King Sigismund as guardians. The Diet, reluctant to submit to such a degree of foreign influence, decided that a royal council be appointed to assist the King, officially emancipated, in the performance of his duties. The King, a talented youth, not devoid of charm but depraved, had little to say in the running of the country, which once again became a battlefield of conflicting interests among the nobles. The death of Maximilian on January 12, 1519, meant only a temporary lull in Habsburg expansionism towards Hungary. The double marriages arranged by Vladislas II and Maximilian were soon brought to pass. In May 1521 Ferdinand wedded Vladislas's daughter Anna, and on January 13th the marriage of Louis II with Maria was celebrated.

Herberstein, the Emperor's ambassador in Hungary, gives a depressing, though probably accurate, picture of the conditions then prevailing in the land. 'If the Hungarians were united—we are told—the richness of their country would enable them to defend it in face of any enemy. But they are of the worst type in the world, everyone is seeking his own profit and, if he can, lives on the fat of public property. They have no esteem for other countries. Though they feast together as if they were all brothers, surreptitiously they fight each other. There is no case so evil that it should not be won by the bribing of two or three men. They are haughty and proud, unable to command and to obey but unwilling to accept advice. They work little as they spend their time with feasting and intrigues.'

Indeed the country was in a pitiful state. The Diets, held in quick succession, achieved nothing, for decisions taken there were not implemented. That unreliable blockhead, Stephen Báthori, became *nádor*, and his old antagonist, Zápolyai, made it a point of honour to defeat all his decisions, setting an example of irresponsibility and violence that was followed by all.

It is not surprising that with such leaders the financial and economic situation of the country swiftly worsened. One-third of the rapidly dwindling national income was spent on the royal household! Even so, the King's chest was so empty that he was compelled to borrow often ridiculously small sums in order to meet day-to-day expenses. The King's personal conduct was scandalous by any standards, and his inconsiderate prodigality would have squandered the largest fortune. The main sources of royal income, the mines, were let out to private enterprise. The copper mines of the Highlands were exploited by the family Thurzó and also by the famous German bankers, the Fuggers. The commercial interests of the latter covered the greater part of Northern Europe and they disposed of immense capital. As a security on the money lent to the King, the Fuggers obtained the monopoly of the copper mines, the products of which they exported. The large-scale silver smuggling, organized jointly with this export, led to their temporary eclipse in 1525, but the bankrupt King could not dispense with their services and the Fuggers were soon reinstated in their functions, on terms even more favourable than they had previously enjoyed. The exploitation of the Transylvanian salt mines was hardly more profitable for the country. Some of these were leased out on terms very unfavourable for the King, others were used to pay in kind the salaries of certain officials. These, in their turn, had to sell the salt, so becoming rivals of the King. Considerable quantities of salt were simply stolen from the mines, and sold below the official price, diminishing thereby the already scanty royal income. Not only was the product of the mines misappropriated, the miners themselves were also badly treated and in April 1526 serious unrest occurred in Besztercebánya, the centre of the mining district. The only thing capable of stirring the nobles to 'constructive' action was social unrest. Werböczi—totally unable to cope with all the other emergencies in the country—had soon suppressed the revolt, and the ring-leaders were executed in spite of the fact that the local tribunal had found most of the grievances justified.

It was in a state of complete anarchy that Hungary was to face the renewal of Turkish attacks. Since the accession in 1520 of Soliman II, the Turks had once again turned their attention towards Hungary. For everyone concerned it was perfectly clear that the Turkish menace loomed undiminished on the country's southern border. Sultan Selim, actively engaged in Asia, had been rather eager to renew the peace-treaties with Hungary, but the King and his government, hesitant and undecided, had lost the opportunity of coming to terms with the Turks. They were also unable to raise foreign aid and the military preparedness of the country was next to nothing. Only the Pope showed any real interest in the defence of Hungary, and Burgio, Nuntius of Clement VII, did what he could to make the Hungarians realize the gravity of the situation. But, as he wrote in one of his dispatches: 'If it were possible to save Hungary from the turmoil at the price of three florins, I do not think that one could find three men ready to make this sacrifice.' Indeed, when early in 1521 it was obvious that Soliman was to attack Belgrade, there was no one to put up the fifty florins necessary for gunpowder. . . . Belgrade and Sabach fell after a heroic resistance by the undermanned, unpaid, half-forgotten garrisons. No Hungarian army had come to their rescue.

The warning, though stern, went unheeded. The appeals sent out for foreign help were vain, as they always had been and always were to be. By the end of 1525 it was well known that Soliman was preparing a major campaign against Hungary. 'This country', wrote Burgio on January 18, 1526, 'is unable to defend itself. . . . I am not experienced in military matters but even the little experience I have is enough to make me realize that if the Sultan attacks with a strong army there is no hope to save the country.' His estimate proved to be accurate; on August 29, 1526, at Mohács, a smallish, ill-equipped, and badly-led Hungarian army was cut to pieces by Soliman. Hungarian losses were terrible, only a few hundred men survived; the King himself lost his life during the flight.

The battle of Mohács has always been considered as perhaps the greatest national catastrophe in Hungarian history. In the words of the poet Kisfaludy (nineteenth century), Mohács was 'the great graveyard of our national grandeur', but the road leading to it could have been avoided. The military defeat itself was not more disastrous than others had been before; and the havoc wrought by the Mongol invasion had been infinitely more ruinous. Internal strife had weakened Hungarian resistance then, even as it paralysed every effort before Mohács. But now there was no Béla IV to take upon himself the task of reconstruction, and the great majority of the population, disowned by their fellow-countrymen, reduced to poverty and servitude, was basically indifferent to the destiny of a country which, they had been told, belonged only to their masters. The real catastrophe happened, not in 1526, but in 1514.

The main reason why the battle of Mohács must be considered as a major landmark in Hungarian history is that it marks the begining of the Habsburg reign over Hungary, a reign that lasted for almost 400 years. Not until the end of that period could Hungary regain full independence, and that only at the price of a dismemberment in many respects worse than that caused by the Turkish occupation. Liberty and territorial integrity were never again to be simultaneously attained by Hungary.

PART FOUR

THE DIVIDED KINGDOM

CHAPTER 15

THE COUNTRY TORN ASUNDER

LOUIS II lost his life after the battle of Mohács, and there was little cause to shed tears on this account. His disappearance, however, caused an administrative vacuum, which had to be filled, and the struggle for the throne, whilst further poisoning the political atmosphere, resulted in the simultaneous election of two kings. The two pretenders were Ferdinand, Archduke of Austria, brother of the Emperor Charles V, and John Zápolyai.

Ferdinand had really excellent claims to the throne; he was the brother of the widowed Queen Maria, and husband of the late King's sister. The treaty concluded in 1491 between Maximilian and Vladislas, and the engagements contracted in 1515, in his own eyes, made his case so strong that he thought he could dispense with a formal election by the Estates. The case was not as simple as that, because not only had it become a tradition that the King must be elected, but the Diet had passed a resolution in 1505, against the election of foreign rulers to the throne of Hungary. But Ferdinand was not stubborn and followed closely the advice given by Maria who, shedding her former frivolity, had become her brother's staunch and clever agent. Following precedent, she set up the Queen's council in Pozsony, refused Zápolyai, who presented himself as suitor, and started to win over the barons one by one. She did not always succeed, as the price she could offer, in the name of Ferdinand, was often lower than that which was asked; but she gathered a fair number of supporters, particularly those barons who did not rank among the most powerful.

Those barons who felt that they would fare better under Zápolyai as King, joined his party, which also included the majority of the lesser nobles, anxious to avoid the rule of a foreigner. This group could legally refer to the already-mentioned decision, taken at the Diet of 1505, and, generally speaking, was thought of as representing the 'national' interest as opposed to the policies of the 'German' party. Zápolyai had, by this time, become the richest man in Hungary; he was the master of about one-twelfth of the country's *jobbágy* population and as Voivode of Transylvania he also commanded the support of the Székely. As he had taken no part in the battle of Mohács he had at his disposal a fairly strong and intact army, and, though he could boast of no success against foreign foes he had been the vanquisher of Dózsa; a reason strong enough to make Werböczi join him. On November 10, 1526, Zápolyai was elected by the Diet King of Hungary, and subsequently crowned. Though there could be no doubt as to the validity of his election, Ferdinand refused to stand down and Zápolyai hesitated to make use of force. As a consequence, in his turn Ferdinand too was elected King, at Pozsony, on December 17th, by a comparatively small gathering of nobles. From the end of that fatal year, Hungary had two rulers: John Zápolyai (1526–40) and Ferdinand I (1526–64).

At the beginning of their contest Zápolyai was in a much more favourable situation than his Habsburg opponent. He was the rightfully crowned King of the country, he was a Hungarian, and he commanded immense local resources. Ferdinand had none of these advantages and Charles V was much too occupied elsewhere to be able to help his brother to secure the throne of Hungary. As Ferdinand was, however, a much better politician than his opponent, and also had the energy and determination conspicuously lacking in Zápolyai, he steadily gained ground. At the time of his election Ferdinand had only a token force, and had Zápolyai seized the opportunity he could easily have driven Ferdinand from the country. As he failed to do so, Ferdinand gained time to raise troops, and in the summer of 1527 undertook a campaign to conquer his own land—Hungary. He was to be successful; in August, without encountering serious resistance, he entered Buda, and whilst his troops were pressing Zápolyai he had himself crowned on November 3rd of the same year. The Holy Crown had been handed over to him by Peter Perényi, a former supporter of Zápolyai turned traitor, and the ceremony was performed by the same bishop who, barely a year earlier, had crowned Zápolyai. These are but instances to show the complete lack of principles, characteristic of the Hungarian nobles, who by then were flocking around Ferdinand. Zápolyai himself fled to Poland.

In his struggle against Zápolyai, Ferdinand had a somewhat unusual ally, the 'prophet' Ivan the Black, a fanatic Serb, who took the title of 'Tsar' and who succeeded in gathering around him a considerable peasant force. First an ally of Zápolyai, he went over to Ferdinand, who promised to recognize him as despot of the Serbs. Finally, Czibak, a lieutenant of Zápolyai, dispersed his army and a short while later Ivan the Black lost his life. His rôle had not been a significant one and, even had he lived, he would not have reached the stature of a Dózsa. But Ivan the Black is important as a symptom and exemplifies the military value of untapped popular forces. It is interesting to note that neither of the anti-Kings had thought of assembling a popular army, probably the only one which would have held its ground against the Turks.

Zápolyai put all his confidence in foreign help and combed the European courts in vain for aid. He even went so far as England, where Henry VIII showed sufficient realism to refuse politely to become involved in eastern European affairs. He received more attention, though, as it turned out, no more help, from Francis I. Quite understandably the French king was eager to encourage anyone likely to cause annoyance to the Habsburgs, and the creation of what we would call today a second front seemed the best way to do so. On October 28, 1528 a treaty against the Habsburgs was concluded at Fontainebleau between Francis I and Zápolyai. Thus in the first half of the sixteenth century we encounter already a political pattern which until modern times was to determine some important aspects of relations between Western and Eastern Europe. France, and later the western powers in general, tried to create disturbances at the back of the Habsburg Empire; the smaller countries of Eastern Europe, anxious to defend their very existence against German expansion, sought allies for themselves in Western Europe. In spite of the real community of interests, these alliances never worked effectively—at least not so far as Hungary was concerned—because France was not able, for purely geographical reasons, if not also for others, to give the necessary help. So Hungarians (and very often Poles too, but this is not now our concern) had to sacrifice themselves so as to alleviate the burden of the French, or of the western powers in general. To complete the tragedy, from the Hungarian point of view, whenever a power sufficiently strong to attack the German world emerged to the east of Hungary, this country was unhesitatingly handed over to it as a sop. No one can blame western European statesmen for trying to ease the pressure brought on their own people by creating, or encouraging, a diversion. What is less pardonable is the inability or unwillingness of Hungarian statesmen to recognize the vanity of any hopes attached to western aid.

Zápolyai, though most incompetent, had no experience to draw upon, and is not therefore to be blamed for seeking a French alliance. The French, quite naturally, put their trust rather in the Turks, who were much more powerful. The Franco-Turkish alliance seemed shocking to contemporaries, because some of the official ideals of the crusades could not yet be publicly denied. For Hungary the problem lay at a more practical level; either they sided with the Habsburgs and bled to death in defending the prosperity of Austria, or they allied themselves with the Turks, in which case their country would again become a battle-field. It is not surprising that both solutions found advocates.

It is difficult to know in what circumstances Zápolyai had made up his mind to seek Turkish alliance. It is probable that Rincon, Ambassador of Francis I, did his best to remove the obstacles on the road that should lead Soliman to Vienna. The negotiations between the Sultan and Zápolyai were conducted by a Polish adventurer, Jerome Laszki. Soliman promised to help Zápolyai, whom he treated as a vassal. Turks and French had nothing to lose and much to gain by supporting Zápolyai against Ferdinand. Had he not existed they would have had to contend with the whole strength of a united Hungary.

On November 3, 1528, Zápolyai returned to Hungary and in seven or eight months he conquered Transylvania almost completely and also a reasonably large part of Eastern Hungary. The word 'conquered' should not here be given an exclusively military meaning, for, though clashes did occur, the conquest consisted mainly in securing recognition by the barons. In the autumn of 1529 Soliman led in person a strong Turkish army whose aim was to re-instal Zápolyai as King of Hungary and then to attack Austria. Zápolyai met his master at the blood-sodden plain of Mohács, offering him as a present one of Matthias's diamond rings. Times had changed indeed. In Buda, Thomas Nádasdy resisted, but he was betrayed by his own soldiers, and Zápolyai was able to enter the capital once more, whilst Soliman proceeded further towards Vienna. It is not our task to describe the heroic defence of this city, which finally compelled the Turks to retrace their steps without achieving anything. On his return Soliman handed the Holy Crown over to Zápolyai and left the country which, thanks to him, he could consider himself to have conquered.

This was an opinion not shared by Ferdinand and by many Hungarians. It must be said that many of Zápolyai's supporters viewed his pro-Turkish policy with considerable misgivings and did not hesitate to declare their opinions. So, for instance, few Hungarians were willing to accompany Zápolyai to his humiliating meeting with Soliman at Mohács, and their absence, as well as its motives, did not go unnoticed by the Turks. As soon as Soliman left Hungary, Ferdinand returned and, reinforced in the spring of 1530 by troops sent by Charles V, achieved the conquest of some important towns. Buda was not among them, because Thomas Nádasdy, who a year earlier had defended it against Zápolyai, put up a very effective resistance. In his task he was aided by an Italian adventurer, Gritti, who—a curious fact—commanded the Turkish troops left in the fortress by Soliman, and who shortly after was to become a most important personage.

The deadlock at Buda prompted both kings to scrutinize the possibilities of a compromise. The two adventurers, Laszki and Gritti, found here a golden opportunity to render themselves indispensable, and very soon the cunning Italian scored an unprecedented success: Zápolyai appointed him regent (*gubernator*) of the realm. It will be remembered that this had been the office of Hunyadi at a time when there was no king to rule over the country. With Zápolyai there was no possible cause to justify the presence of a regent, and the appointment was tantamount to a public admission that the King, Zápolyai, was in his own eyes no longer capable of coping with the tasks of government. Aided by his accomplice Laszki, who, in order to give time to Gritti, dissuaded the Sultan from interfering at this stage, Gritti started conversations with Ferdinand. In fact his aim was to replace Zápolyai and it was to achieve this that his first act after his appointment as regent was to pay a visit to the Sultan. His connections in Turkish circles were very good, since, at an earlier stage of his picturesque career, he had been a purveyor of jewels to the Sultan. It was his own unscrupulousness and greed that caused his early death. In a short period he had amassed considerable riches and had murdered a number of men of Zápolyai's entourage in whom he suspected potential opponents. Bishop Czibak was one among them, but his nephew sought vengeance and at the end of a private war, on September 28, 1534,

Gritti was beheaded, without the impotent Zápolyai intervening to save his favourite.

The four years of Gritti's 'reign' had not been uneventful. In 1532 Soliman made another attempt to conquer Vienna. Though by that time he could use without hindrance the road leading along the Danube, the Sultan chose another route, going, roughly speaking, eastward along the River Drava, turning north towards Nagykanizsa, Szombathely, Köszeg. This latter place was defended by Nicholas Jurisics, who put up a defence which can be reckoned among the most glorious feats of Hungarian history. The fortress of Köszeg was rather insignificant and, as it was not on the usual route of Turkish invasions, it was practically unmanned; the regular garrison consisted of some twenty-eight hussars and a few German soldiers. Jurisics not only reinforced his garrison with *jobbágys* drafted from the neighbourhood, but also organized peasant resistance in the rear of the Turkish troops. The Turkish attack started on August 10th, and in the following fortnight nineteen assaults were repelled; as time was pressing Soliman had to make a peace-offer. The compromise eventually reached was a fairly complicated one: Turkish troops were not to enter the fortress which, however, had to fly the standard of the Sultan. Jurisics also had to hand over all the silver he possessed. The delay caused by Jurisics's resistance jeopardized the original Turkish plans; by the time the Turks reached Austria snow was falling and as the Sultan was reluctant to face with a tired army the imposing forces gathered around Vienna, he returned through Croatia to the Balkans.

The fact is that for once Ferdinand had succeeded in gathering an army sufficiently strong to be set against Soliman's. Charles V, most reluctantly, shared in the general effort, and Spanish, Italian and German troops, Catholics and Protestants, a whole impressive array of picked forces, was standing by and watching Köszeg's heroic resistance, presumably with great interest. During the siege, Jurisics succeeded in sending a messenger asking for help—none was forthcoming. It would be wrong to suppose that the inaction of the Imperial and Austrian troops was due to some strategic consideration; it must rather be ascribed to their reluctance to fight. Ferdinand, it must be said, was bitterly disappointed to have missed the splendid opportunity and to watch disband, unused, the army he had taken so much pains to raise. There was only one course open to him, that which he had been advised to take by his brother the Emperor: to try to reach some form of agreement with the Turks. Charles V, who was ready to make great efforts against the Turks in the Mediterranean, somehow did not seem to connect his enemies with the enemies of Ferdinand; his half-hearted support in 1532, coming after many years of complete abstention, must have convinced Ferdinand of the necessity of toeing the line of imperial policy.

The time was favourable for a peace-offer. The Sultan realized that the conquest of Austria and Germany was beyond his power; his lines of communication were too extended to be safe in the case of a campaign beyond Hungary, nor were the Hungarians themselves entirely reliable from his point of view. Though ambassadors from both their kings were imploring peace, individual diehards of Jurisics's type could cause him, as in the past, serious inconvenience. Soliman was, moreover, contemplating a campaign against Persia and things in the Mediterranean had also been somewhat complicated by the activity of Charles V's admiral, Andrea Doria. For all these reasons it was not difficult for Ferdinand to conclude with the Sultan a treaty, which *mutatis mutandis*, was the exact counterpart of the agreement concluded in 1529 with Zápolyai. Soliman found himself in the curious position of having as vassals two Hungarian kings who, moreover, were fighting each other. He could indeed be satisfied with such results, achieved with comparatively little sacrifice, thanks to the fratricidal struggle of the two Hungarian factions. This was well exemplified during Ferdinand's peace negotiations in Constantinople by the anxiety with which the ambassadors of Zápolyai watched that the 'other' Hungary should not obtain terms of peace more favourable than their own.

It slowly dawned on the two anti-kings that they too would have to work out some sort of compromise. The nobles themselves grew tired of the situation they had helped to create, and realized that there was a point beyond which the weakness of the ruler was no longer beneficial for their own schemes and ambitions. The supporters of Ferdinand were deeply disappointed by his incapacity to put up an effective reistance against the Turks, whereas the opinion of the followers of the irresolute Zápolyai is probably best exemplified by the saying of one of them: 'I am bored with His Majesty.' The murder of Gritti, and the fact that Francis I transferred Rincon from the court of Zápolyai to Constantinople, helped Zápolyai to realize that he could no longer hope for foreign help. Ferdinand could also see that his military resources were insufficient to oust his rival from power. The pressure brought upon both kings by the nobles resulted in the Treaty of Várad, signed on February 4, 1538. The main clause of this was to the effect that on Zápolyai's death, whether or not he had children (he was at that time still unmarried) the country should elect either Ferdinand or his son to the throne; it was this operative paragraph that Zápolyai was determined to dodge. Hardly a year after the conclusion of the Treaty of Várad he married Izabel, daughter of the King of Poland, who expeditiously bore him a son, John Sigismund. The good news reached Zápolyai a few days before his death and perhaps his last political act, fitting to a life of continuous blunders, was to repudiate the Treaty of Várad and to designate the new-born child heir to the throne. On July 22, 1540, Zápolyai, the last national King of Hungary, died.

Quite understandably Soliman had viewed with serious misgivings the Treaty of Várad, and a punitive expedition by the Turks could only with difficulty be averted. The Sultan therefore readily recognized the rights to the succession of John Sigismund, as his very existence promised to perpetuate the division of the country. Of course he was to be a vassal of the Sultan, and the conditions of his vassalage were to be heavier than those granted to his father. Henceforward, the King of the eastern parts of Hungary would have to pay taxes to the Sultan.

Ferdinand's military weakness prevented him from giving substance to his claim, fully justified by the Treaty of Várad, to rule the whole country. Though the majority of the nobles sided with him, a handful of men, the immediate entourage of Izabel and her son, could prevent the unification of the country. Almost immediately after the death of Zápolyai, an attempt by Ferdinand to occupy Buda failed, and in 1541 a considerable German force, led by Roggendorf, attacked in vain the fortress defended by only some 2,500 Hungarians. The fortress was finally relieved by Soliman, who put to flight the besieging army and by a ruse took possession of Buda.

The fall of the country's capital into Turkish hands would in itself have been of the greatest significance. Soliman, however, was not content with this, and extended Turkish occupation as far east as the River Tisza. The territories thus occupied were simply incorporated in the Turkish Empire. 1541 thus brought to fulfilment the processes which began at Mohács. The country was divided into three parts: the western in Habsburg hands, the central, comprising great parts of Transdanubia and the plain between Danube and Tisza, under Turkish occupation, and finally Hungary east of the Tisza and Transylvania. The Turkish wedge could never be driven as far to the north as to cut the country into two: in the Northern Highlands the eastern and western parts had a common frontier. The development of these three parts proceeded on different lines and for centuries to come determined the peculiar aspect of Hungarian history. The final evacuation of the Turks from the occupied territories took place in 1699, and only in 1848 was Transylvania again fully united with the motherland.

Before we come to trace the great lines of the particular development of the different parts of the divided country, mention must be made of a joint attempt by the two Hungarian kings to drive out the Turks.

Since Zápolyai's death, a certain monk, commonly called Frater George, or by his mother's name, Martinuzzi, had become the most influential person in the Eastern Kingdom. Of Croatian origin, he fully identified himself with Hungarian interests, and Zápolyai made him Treasurer of the Royal Household. In this task he excelled, displaying as he did a quality uncommon among his contemporaries: thrift and financial adroitness. An extraordinary intelligence, commanded by an uncompromising conscience, made Martinuzzi the most remarkable Hungarian statesman of the sixteenth century. The dying Zápolyai appointed him one of John Sigismund's three guardians and made him swear that he would never abandon the infant. To this oath Martinuzzi remained faithful though, more than once, it proved to be difficult to bring the interests of John Sigismund into harmony with those of the country.

Martinuzzi's career as a senior statesman began with a gigantic blunder, the consequences of which he endeavoured to mitigate for the rest of his life. He is to blame for the successful defence of Buda against Ferdinand, a defence which resulted, as we have seen, in the loss of the capital to the Turks.

In December 1541, Ferdinand and Martinuzzi signed an agreement at Gyalu which, in its essence, was a renewal of the Treaty of Várad. John Sigismund, in return for a generous material compensation, was to hand over the Eastern Kingdom to Ferdinand. Martinuzzi succeeded in convincing the Estates of the necessity of raising troops and joining Ferdinand in a great effort to rid the country of the Turks. Exceptionally, the German Estates had showed some understanding, and in the summer of 1542 a considerable mixed German and Hungarian force, under the command of Joachim Brandenburg, gathered under the walls of Buda. It never came to a siege because the army—a textbook example of that military inefficiency which so curiously characterizes Habsburg rule—disbanded without having even tackled the task for which it had been raised. This military failure prompted Martinuzzi to abandon any hope of uniting the two parts of the country in the immediate future.

The Turkish reaction was almost immediate. The next year (1543) Soliman led his sixth campaign against Hungary; he occupied a number of important towns such as Pécs, Székesfehérvár, Esztergom. Though Ferdinand succeeded in raising an army some 30,000 strong, once again this army watched with folded hands the Turkish advance. Ferdinand considered it a success that in 1547 the Sultan condescended to conclude a peace-treaty, for five years, which included for Ferdinand the obligation to pay a tribute of 30,000 pieces of gold a year. The Diet, meeting at Nagyszombat, had no choice but to accept the fact that the question, which to the hearts of all Hungarians was a matter of life and death, had been shelved. Simultaneously, plans to unite the kingdom had lost all their purpose: there was no point in handing over the Eastern Kingdom to a foreign ruler unable to defend the country against the Turks.

CHAPTER 16

INTERNAL CONDITIONS

THOSE parts of Hungary which were under Ferdinand's rule were too small and impoverished to be able to influence decisively the shaping of Habsburg policy. Ferdinand, though much more accessible, much more humane and kindly than his brother, was very much under the influence of Charles V and had little sympathy with parliamentary rule. He was a man of goodwill, having at heart the prosperity of his subjects; but these belonged to many countries and their interests were not always in common. He could not be expected to put Hungarian interests above those of, for instance, Austria, and circumstances were most unfavourable for establishing a close link between country and dynasty. In 1531 Ferdinand was elected King of the Romans and from 1558 he was Emperor; he had already shed most vestiges of his Spanish education to adopt German customs. There was no room left for Hungarian influence. Ferdinand could not speak Hungarian, and since the fall of Buda—which he vainly attempted to conquer—there was no town in Hungary where he could have taken up permanent residence. Thus there was little opportunity for king and country to make close acquaintance and the Habsburg incomprehension of things Hungarian dates back to these first years of their four-centuries rule of Hungary.

The *raison d'être* of a foreign king was—from the Hungarian point of view—the hope that with the might of his other possessions he could liberate Hungary from the Turks. It was therefore normal that there should be an attempt at co-ordination and that Hungarian affairs should be dealt with in the same way as those of Ferdinand's other countries. Only a strongly centralized government was capable of coping with the problems of a multinational empire, and the governmental system of Hungary had to adapt itself to the new contingencies.

The major administrative and political changes which took place in Habsburg-Hungary, can be summarized as follows:

The country's new capital was Pozsony, conveniently near to Vienna, conveniently far from the Turks. A smallish town, suitable perhaps as the seat of administration, but not as the residence of the King. There was no longer to be a Hungarian royal court and household. The old Royal Council was rapidly losing its former decisive influence, and was replaced by the so-called *helytartótanács* (*Consilium Regium Locum-tenentiale Hungaricum*), of permanent character, presided over by the *nádor* who, according to old Hungarian usage, was *per officio* the *locum tenens* of the King absent from the country. As the *nádor*, however, precisely by the tradition attached to his office, was likely to represent the country versus the King, his office was viewed with misgivings, and was not always filled. From 1562, for forty-six years, the kings did not fill the post but simply appointed a *helytartó*, i.e. a *locum tenens* of the King. The new administrative organ was much more efficient than had been the old Royal Council, but it was, by its very nature, more pliable to the King's will. Even more distant from the heart of Hungarian matters were the Royal Chancellery, where Hungary was represented by secretaries, and the Austrian Royal Council, the *Hofrat*. As early as 1527 Ferdinand had offered two seats in the *Hofrat* to Hungarians. These were not accepted, as it was felt derogatory to discuss the affairs of the country in a non-Hungarian council. As is so often the case with procedural inexperience, a small mistake had disastrous consequences. The *Hofrat*, as the King's principal advisory and executive body, continued to decide matters concerning Hungary without that country having a say in the discussions. The Hungarians, by asserting their independence and refusing to partake in the deliberations of a body where the other countries of Ferdinand were also represented, cut themselves off from the possibility of having direct influence on the nerve-centre of the Habsburg Empire, on which they nevertheless depended.

It is obvious that financial matters had to be settled centrally. A special Hungarian Treasury (*Kamara*), set up in 1528, worked entirely on Austrian and Czech patterns and after 1548 was no longer dependent on the *Helytartótanács*, but, on any matter of importance, had to refer to the King who then, presumably, in most cases followed the advice of his own treasury (*Hofkammer*).

The military situation was even more disastrous for Hungary. One of the reasons telling against the maintenance of the office of the *nádor* was that he was, *ex officio*, Commander-in-Chief. It was felt that, as Hungary was no longer capable of defending herself alone, this post should be filled by a national representing the power making the greatest contribution to the war effort. Such propositions are seldom popular, because they invariably mean that the immediate interests of the local population are subordinated to the exigencies of some principles of general strategy, often rather ill defined. These, as a rule, happen to coincide with the interests of the major power in question, in our case with those of the Habsburgs. Hungary was unusually unfortunate in that its army became incorporated in the worst military organization a great power has ever produced, and in that for centuries it had to provide the best fighters in an exceptionally inefficient army. We shall see later how adversely foreign command affected the country's defence against the Turks.

Clearly there could in the circumstances be no independent Hungarian foreign policy, and not until after the First World War did things change. Ferdinand's ambassadors to Constantinople were rarely Hungarian, the King being afraid that they would represent the special interests of their own country, often opposed to those of his other lands.

It must be emphasized that in many respects Ferdinand improved considerably on former administration and that it was not his aim purely and simply to incorporate Hungary into the Empire. Head of a multinational and multilingual state, he simply endeavoured to reconcile conflicting interests. Though he favoured a strongly centralized government, Ferdinand showed no inclination to do away with the Diets. These were called together at frequent intervals—one session usually lasted five to six weeks—and the privilege of the Estates (from 1530 they are officially referred to as *Status et ordines*) to vote taxes and soldiers was not seriously challenged. It is, however, obvious that the nobles who, under the Jagiellos, were almighty, and with their dishonesty and incompetence brought ruin to their country, were pushed into purely defensive positions. There they were to remain until their final disappearance in the nineteenth century.

Internal developments of the Eastern Kingdom proceeded on different lines. Since the 'Union' of the three nations, concluded in 1437, Transylvania had gradually come to be regarded as a political

entity referred to as *Regnum Transylvaniae*. Under the reign of Zápolyai
the separatist trend became more marked and Martinuzzi gave a
definite shape to what must be called a new state. It cannot, however, be
sufficiently emphasized that what we have called a separatist tendency
was always considered even by its staunchest champions, as a *pis aller*, a
provisional arrangement devised to preserve national independence for
at least one part of St Stephen's kingdom. Martinuzzi himself considered
it the aim of his life to unite the country torn asunder, and the future
princes of Transylvania were satisfied with their title and did not seek
to become kings.

The task of organizing the Eastern Kingdom of Zápolyai into a state
was not an easy one; geographically, historically, ethnically, the area
was heterogeneous, for it was not the result of any historical development
but comprised simply the territories which happened to remain under
Zápolyai's sway. These were Transylvania proper, and a number of
megye, the so-called 'Parts' (*Partium*), lying east of the Tisza and the
region of the River Temes, which used to stand under a separate royal
commander, the *Bán*. In fact the new principality included all those
territories in the south of Hungary which, not occupied by the Turks,
were separated by the Turkish zone from Habsburg-Hungary. In 1542,
at Torda, the three nations of Transylvania, i.e. the Hungarians, Székelys
and Saxons, renewed their former alliance. The Prince (*fejedelem*)
elected by them was to rule jointly with the Transylvanian Estates,
according to their constitution. The Prince resided at Gyulafehérvár,
and was assisted by a council composed of twenty-two members, seven
for each of the three nations and one representing the Prince himself.

The social consequences of the creation of the new state were
considerable but not always happy. Compared with the more progressive
political ideas of the Habsburg dynasty, Transylvania perpetuated a
system basically medieval, and the trend towards equalization, so
marked in Western Europe—and which in Hungary proper led to the
merging of all the lower social classes into one large group, that of the
jobbágy, opposed to that of the nobles—did not affect its social structure.
Transylvania became to some extent an historical anachronism and the
fact that its population did not fare worse than that of the more advanced
region gives food for thought. It is interesting that the new state had in
many respects a federative character, and theoretically each of the three
nations kept a certain autonomy, though any of the nations had to abide

by decisions brought by the other two. Conflicting interests often set the nations at odds and helped to augment the power of the Prince or (as in the case of Martinuzzi) of his minister. The Prince, as in a medieval monarchy, had a decisive influence in almost every sphere of the country's life: in his hands were centralized the affairs of the army, the finances and foreign policy; he was the chief judge who appointed the others, just as he was responsible for all the other public appointments. The Transylvanian Diets did hardly more than rubber-stamp the decisions already taken. When one considers the notable achievements of Transylvanian history and recalls the splendid accomplishment of the Árpáds, the Anjous and Matthias, one cannot escape the conclusion that absolute government—as long as it remains national—seems to produce the best results in Hungary. The capacity for endless talk, the reluctance to take decisions, unless spectacular, has made democratic rule in Hungary singularly ineffective. Foreign attempts to rule the country usually broke down on the same pigheadedness which has generally prevented one Hungarian from seeing the point of view of another. But respect for authority, for legal fiction (as with the doctrine of the Holy Crown), have had a strong appeal in Hungary and absolute monarchy, mitigated by a semblance of popular consultation, would seem to bring out the best in the Hungarian character.

Western and Eastern Kingdom, Habsburg-Hungary or Transylvania, they both continued Hungarian traditions. Lopsided, they were nevertheless direct heirs to the independent kingdoms of Hungary; but wedged between them, covering for a century and a half about one-third of the country's territory, was the Turkish zone of occupation, which had no other justification than sheer force. An alien body embedded in the living flesh of the country, not assimilable, it had no ties with Hungary's past and had nothing to offer to and nothing to receive from Hungarian civilization.

For the country's population the Turk was the enemy *par excellence;* none of the Hungarian statesmen of the sixteenth or seventeenth centuries could, even temporarily, forget this basic axiom of Hungarian political life. If political necessity, the hope of sparing lives and of limiting destruction, compelled statesmen, particularly in Transylvania, to effect a compromise, to flatter the Sultan or his entourage, they did so in the conviction that this was only another way of fighting the archenemy.

The occupied territories were organized according to the methods of Turkish administration, with a total disregard of local circumstances. At its greatest expansion the Turkish zone was divided into four *vilayets*, with Buda, Eger, Kanizsa and Nagyvárad as their respective centres. Turkish administration was in many respects admirable, but its aims were different from those of its contemporary European counterparts. It served only one purpose, to secure Turkish supremacy over the conquered territories. The interests of the local populations were only taken into consideration in so far as they were directly relevant to the well-being of the Turkish occupiers. This attitude was, in more than one respect, beneficial to the Hungarians because, in practice, it was often a rudimentary liberalism. The Turks by ignoring Hungarian institutions often preserved them. As long as duties towards the occupiers were fulfilled, the latter were unconcerned with the internal affairs of the subjected population. Communal autonomy not only remained but developed, and often the permission of former landlords or of officials from Habsburg-Hungary was sought for undertaking projects which did not officially affect the Turks. In fact people seeking Turkish help, or taking their grievances to Turkish authorities were frowned upon.

In the eyes of the Turks there was no difference between noble and *jobbágy*—and—this was perhaps the only beneficial effect of this terrible plague—many *jobbágys* succeeded in liberating themselves and their descendants by asking for and obtaining the much-coveted parchment making them freemen. This freedom was, at that time anyhow, an empty word—probably a reason why such charters of emancipation were easier to get.

As the nobles could no longer enjoy their privileges they fled in great numbers; as so often in history, the rich had the possibility of escape, leaving the poor, the peasants tied to the soil, to face alone the rigours of the occupation. This, in historical perspective, was rather fortunate; it was the peasant's faithfulness to the land, of which he was not the owner, which ensured the continuity of Hungarian presence. We will discuss later the causes and results of the depopulation of the occupied areas; at this stage we simply record that, at a time when administration and landlords abandoned their posts and homes, only the peasants and the clergy remained at what had become the outpost of Hungarian and Christian civilization.

The Turkish attitude towards religion conformed to the pattern already mentioned with regard to political institutions. The absolute contempt of the Muslim for the 'useless ceremonies and empty rules' of Christian worship never degenerated in straightforward persecution. As long as Christians respected the rules set by the Turkish authorities, rules which, it must be said, limited their activities considerably, they could lead their miserable existence basically undisturbed. For miserable it was through lack of funds, absence of facilities for training priests, and partial disintegration of the hierarchy. In Turkish eyes Catholics and Protestants were equally despicable, and if at some time they seemed to be harder on Catholics, their attitude had nothing to do with religious considerations. Catholics have always been the *bêtes noires* of every strongly-centralized totalitarian régime—unless it was Catholic itself.

All proprietary rights previous to the Turkish occupation were considered void, the whole land became owned by the Turkish state, just as all men became serfs. One-fifth of the occupied land remained State property, the rest was distributed among Turkish soldiers and civil servants. The right to these properties was not hereditary, in fact the beneficiaries of this system were not the owners but only the usufructuaries of the land for the duration of their stay in Hungary. It was a policy of Turkish administration to make frequent changes, and the higher the official was, the shorter his stay in Hungary. In the 145 years during which Buda was in Turkish hands, the highest administrative post in the occupied country, that of the Pasha of Buda, had ninety-nine holders. It is understandable that in such circumstances the Turkish lessee had no other aim than to squeeze out the maximum immediate profit, during his short tenure, quite regardless of the effects this might have in the long run. Most of the tenures were in the hands of the *spahis*, Turkish mounted soldiers, whose duties were dependent on the income of his tenure, a system not conducive to augmenting real productivity but which encouraged illegal extortions—not controllable by the tax-collectors.

Taxes, as a rule, were extremely heavy and manifold. Direct and indirect taxation, taxes collected on behalf of the State or the lord, all together put an unbearable burden on the population. Even the worst Hungarian lord had usually taken care not to push exploitation so far as to cause the ruin of his *jobbágy*. Such consideration did not hamper the

Turkish landlord, never certain whether the coming year would not find him at another border of the Turkish Empire. On the lands belonging to the state, the exploitation of the population was much less ruthless.

In several regions taxes were payable both to Turkish and Hungarian authorities. This was the case particularly in the border regions which, though nominally on Hungarian territory, were regularly raided by Turks. The *de facto* situation was taken into consideration both by Turkish and Hungarian authorities, who abstained from claiming all the taxes theoretically due. It is most remarkable that villages well within the boundaries of the Turkish area continued voluntarily to pay taxes to the Hungarian state and to their former Hungarian lord. This is an outstanding example of the sense of solidarity which the subjected populations felt for the motherland. Often, in their extreme poverty, their payments took little more than a symbolic value, intended to show that in spite of their inescapable duties towards the Turkish occupants they never disowned their Hungarian allegiances. For a century and a half, in every aspect of their life, there was a stubborn, methodical rejection of everything Turkish. It must be said that the by no means unfranchisable border-line between Turkish and Hungarian territories contributed considerably to maintaining the national spirit. There was a constant coming and going across the frontier; merchants, priests, preachers, moved across it quite unhindered. The terrible plight during the Turkish occupation was not, primarily, due to Turkish administration. It was partially the suffering inherent in continuous warfare, partially the inevitable outcome of a more backward civilization conquering a more developed country. We shall examine later the tragic balance-sheet of this period.

CHAPTER 17

THREE-CORNERED FIGHT

AFTER the treaty between Ferdinand and the Turks had been concluded, in 1547, Martinuzzi found it necessary to find a *modus vivendi* for Transylvania. For an annual payment of 10,000 florins, and by recognizing Soliman II as his liege lord, Martinuzzi ensured a precarious existence for Transylvania and made use of the respite to create conditions in which Ferdinand could unite the two parts of the realm. It was a double game if ever there was one, and the monk played it with supreme skill and not without finding in it his own enjoyment. He was considerably hampered by the Queen Izabel, jealous of his power and unable to grasp the principles of his policy. The victory at Mühlberg over the League of Schmalkalden in 1547 strengthened Ferdinand's position considerably, and it seemed likely that he could resist a retaliatory Turkish campaign, bound to be launched in the case of Transylvania recognizing him as king. Martinuzzi felt that the time had come to hand over Transylvania to Ferdinand. His aim was to find an agreement, after the pattern of that of Várad, which, whilst securing the personal welfare of Izabel and John Sigismund, would unify the country. After long preliminaries lasting for about two years, Martinuzzi achieved his aim in July 1551. A treaty was concluded in which the Queen, in the name of her son, renounced his claims to the throne of Hungary, handed the Holy Crown over to Ferdinand, and recognized Ferdinand's descendants as future heirs to the throne. As compensation John Sigismund was to receive the dukedom of Oppeln in Silesia and the hand of one of Ferdinand's daughters. The Queen Dowager was to receive 140,000 florins, the value of the lands presented to her as a betrothal gift by her late husband, Zápolyai. When the time came to implement the treaty, Izabel, with her usual inconsistency, changed her mind. But it was already too late. Called in by Martinuzzi, Ferdinand's troops, under the Italian Castaldo, were entering Transylvania, and the reluctant Queen was forced to leave the country. Martinuzzi accepted the charge of Voivode of Transylvania, and did his best to avert the fury of the Sultan. The task was not an easy one, as Ferdinand's army reoccupied a number of fortresses in the south of the country, and connivance between him and Martinuzzi seemed obvious. With a consummate diplomatic skill the monk provided acceptable explanations for everything and made Turkish reaction less forceful and less immediate than was to have been expected.

Unfortunately he was less successful with Ferdinand's officers. Italians, Spaniards and Austrians, feeling very much isolated in these foreign parts, they watched with growing suspicion the turns of Martinuzzi's diplomatic game. Unable to follow the meandering of his path they sensed treason, and the powerful, impressive, but somewhat uncanny personality of the monk, by then a cardinal, seemed to them invested with almost demoniac powers. Ferdinand himself found it difficult to believe in Martinuzzi's integrity and had left a considerable freedom of action to Castaldo, an honest, simple-minded soldier, most uneasy in his task, feeling uprooted in these strange surroundings. On December 17, 1551, a group of Italian and Spanish officers, with Ferdinand's tacit consent, stabbed Martinuzzi to death. To him alone was it due that, after twenty-five years, all the Hungarian territories not subjected to the Turks were united under one head of state. Only he would have been able to keep for Ferdinand what he had obtained. Martinuzzi's devotion to his political aims was as great as his skill in achieving them. Without personal ambitions, honest, courageous, supremely intelligent, he ranks among the greatest statesmen of Hungary.

There was no man to fill the breach caused by Martinuzzi's death. The attempt to unite Transylvania and Habsburg-Hungary prompted the Sultan to take action both vindictive and preventive, and early in 1552 he launched a campaign the ultimate aim of which was the cutting of Hungary into two. Three separate Turkish armies were operating simultaneously, two coming from the south, and one, under the command of Ali, Pasha of Buda, having as its base the capital of the country. The first major stronghold conquered by the advancing Turkish armies, Temesvár, could perhaps have been saved, had the heroic commander Losonczi received relief, or, before the siege had begun, sufficient material help prepared for the attack. This was to be the pattern of the whole campaign, in which the heroic resistance of Szondi, commander of the tiny fort of Drégely, some twenty-five miles north of the bend of the Danube, stands out as a remarkable feat of military prowess. With a very small garrison he resisted the far superior forces of Ali and lost his life, with all the last defenders of the place, in the final assault against the fortress.

Ali then defeated an imperial army, and, joining the Turkish forces coming northwards from Temesvár, joined in the attack on Szolnok. The town proved an easy nut to crack, for the foreign mercenaries simply abandoned it. The united Turkish armies, advancing further north, laid siege to Eger, the last fortress capable of offering serious resistance on the road towards the Polish border. The commander, Steven Dobó, lacked none of the qualities required by his difficult task, he was as good as an organizer as he was brave as a soldier, and he knew how to gain the enthusiastic support of the local population. For five and a half weeks Eger resisted the furious assaults of the Turks; professional soldiers, peasants, women, all did their best and their ingenuity and courage together defeated the Turkish efforts. The Turkish plans had to be abandoned and a peace-treaty, this time for eight years, was once again concluded between Ferdinand and Soliman. The defence of Eger inspired one of the best historical novels in Hungarian literature, the *Stars of Eger* by Gárdonyi (1901), and the desperate heroism of Szondi is celebrated in an exceptionally fine poem by Arany (1856).

The senseless murder of Martinuzzi had not only brought about the retaliatory campaign against Hungary; Ferdinand had also to pay for it by the loss of Transylvania, and on October 22, 1556, Izabel and John Sigismund (1556–71) were finally reinstated. Their return was generally welcomed, for the vexatious conduct of Castaldo's mercenaries had made Ferdinand's rule thoroughly unpopular. Ferdinand had no means to prevent the restoration. Dobó, the defender of Eger, at that time Voivode of Transylvania, was equally helpless. Thus Martinuzzi's great work, the unification of Hungary, barely survived his own lifetime. His efforts to give a solid structure to the Transylvanian state proved more durable and their effects were felt down the centuries.

Ferdinand died in the same year, and his son, Maximilian I (1564–76),

the second of this name on the Austrian throne, succeeded him unopposed. He inherited the basic goodwill characteristic of his father,
but had little energy and in religious matters was at variance with his
entourage. He led a life withdrawn, and disliked the adjuncts of
constitutional government. He, however, saw clearly that the Turkish
danger must have priority in the conduct of affairs, and it was not his
will but his power that was in default when opportunity came to
challenge the Turks.

In 1564 a war flared up between Maximilian and John Sigismund
who, since his mother's death in 1559, had ruled alone in Transylvania.
The Imperial forces were successful and the Turks, in order to prevent
the renewal of Habsburg rule in Transylvania, launched a major attack
against Hungary. The aged Soliman came in person to lead his seventh
campaign against Hungary, which proved to be the last. His original
plan had been to proceed northwards across Hungary towards Eger. A
raid on his armies by Nicholas Zrinyi made him change his mind; he
turned westwards and laid siege to Szigetvár, Zrinyi's fortress. Of
Croatian origin, but proudly Hungarian, Nicholas Zrinyi, a man of
passionate temper, was one of the richest lords in Southern Hungary.
He also enjoyed Maximilian's confidence, in uncommon measure for a
Hungarian lord, and the Emperor made serious efforts to bring help to
Szigetvár. But his council could not prevail over the narrow-minded
cowardice of his generals, and an Imperial army, some 100,000 men
strong, stood in readiness near Györ, awaiting an attack which was not
to come, whilst Zrinyi and his companions, in a resistance of epic
grandeur, lost their lives in the defence of their country. From August
6th till September 8th they performed miracles of heroism, and the
siege cost the life of some 20,000 Turks. Soliman himself, too old to
take part in the battle in person, died, angered, so it seems, by the loss
of so many of his best soldiers. His death was kept secret and his armies
won an important victory. But Zrinyi's defence had not been in vain.
He stopped the Turkish advance, and the siege of Szigetvár marks the
zenith of Turkish might in Hungary. With Soliman's death a new
period began, characterized by the slow decadence of Ottoman power.
Soon Turkish occupation would be due less to the strength of the
occupier than to the division of the Hungarian forces.

Soliman's successor, Sultan Selim II, was of a different temperament
from his great predecessor, and a peace-treaty signed between him and

Maximilian in 1560 was less unfavourable to the Emperor than could have been feared. This treaty, valid for eight years, weakened John Sigismund's situation considerably. Since, in the case of a conflict with Maximilian, he could no longer reckon with Turkish help, but would have to rely on his own forces, he found it more prudent to reconsider his relations with the Habsburgs. The agreement ratified in Speyer in 1570 was once more a patching up of the Treaty of Várad. An important innovation was that John Sigismund and his successors, if any, were to renounce their title of Kings of Hungary and, though continuing their rule over Transylvania, were to do so as vassals of the King. Transylvania was thus recognized as forming an integral part of the Habsburg realm; and if the Zápolyais became extinct it was agreed that it should be administered, as before, by a Voivode. Soon after, John Sigismund died, leaving no child, and this agreement thus became operative. The Transylvanian Estates, unaware of the existence of such an agreement, and prompted by the Turks, still anxious to maintain a satellite Transylvania, elected Stephen Báthori (1571–6) in succession to the defunct John Sigismund. Báthori, the first elected Prince of Transylvania, having defeated Maximilian's candidate, Békés, hastened to assure Maximilian that he felt himself bound by the Treaty of Speyer. The compromise seemed admirable and, as Báthori continued to pay what was due to the Turks, could have lasted had it not been for Békés, whose intrigues brought about an armed conflict. On July 10, 1575, Báthori defeated Békés, supported by Maximilian's soldiers, and thus his co-operation with the Emperor came to an end. Maximilian and Báthori were both competing for the throne of Poland. Báthori achieved success and, leaving his younger brother Christopher (1576–81) in charge of Transylvania, left his country to become one of the most glorious kings of Poland. His original idea, to use the joint forces of Poland and Transylvania against the Turks, could not, however, come to fruit. The first two Báthoris, the younger mainly as executor of his brother's will, did much to consolidate the young Transylvanian state. Their efficient government left to Christopher's son, Sigismund Báthori (1581–97), a country capable of pursuing a constructive foreign policy. No one could then foresee what catastrophes this capacity would bring about.

In 1576 Maximilian died and was followed by Rudolf, the second of this name on the imperial throne (1576–1608). This is not the place to recount the personal story of this odd, tragic ruler. His madness developed only gradually, and in his early years he showed himself a capable and well-meaning monarch; but from 1579 his illness gained ascendancy and made him more and more suspicious, more and more withdrawn. Though one of the most learned men in Europe, he paid less and less attention to the affairs of state, until anarchy assumed tragic proportions in his many lands. During the reign of Rudolf, secluded and almost inaccessible in distant Prague, the gap between Hungary and its foreign ruler widened to the extent of becoming unbridgeable. Ferdinand had known the Hungary of his day, important and independent in spite of all its internal dissensions; Maximilian was already both more distant from and less interested in Hungarian affairs, and these, for Rudolf, were but a particularly irksome burden: the governing of an alien, impoverished, rebellious and disgruntled people, who were always complaining, always asking for help, and who were yet fiercely independent and more exigent than the other peoples of the Empire. Hungarians had to be distrusted, their country had to be governed to an ever greater extent by reliable Germans. It seems, therefore, rather surprising that Rudolf's reign should have witnessed the longest sustained effort so far undertaken to oust the Turks from Hungary. Though he did not initiate the outbreak of new hostilities, it was Rudolf's stubbornness, together with the impotence of his generals, which made the oncoming war a long drawn out and sorry undertaking.

Sigismund Báthori and Rudolf had one thing in common: their mental illness. But in his seclusion the syphilitic Rudolf was harmful only through his lack of interest in public affairs; Báthori's depressions found relief in bloodthirsty outbursts of bestial cruelty, changing into feelings of bitter regret and despair. As a child Sigismund had come very much under the influence of the Spanish Jesuit, Alphonso Carillo, who implanted in his mind the conviction that the struggle against the infidel must be his principal task, and that in order to achieve this he must seek an agreement with the Habsburgs. It is undeniable that the obvious weakening of Turkish power opened possibilities of pushing the Turks back into the Balkans. It will be remembered that since 1658, officially at least, there was peace between the Turks and the Habsburgs. Although this meant very little or no relief to the populations living on the borders, at least no major campaigns were launched and the Turkish zone of influence remained fairly constant. But as in every epoch vested interests in war were at work, and these found a leader in the octogenarian Great-Vezir, Sinan, who saw in a new Hungarian campaign the only possibility of strengthening his own influence and of grabbing even more money than he already possessed. Murad III (1574–95), who by that time lived as secluded as Rudolf, undermined by the excesses of a dissolute life, had even less influence in the actual governing of his lands than his Habsburg opponent; Sinan, with the help of court intrigues, was able to begin hostilities in 1591, which led to what is known in Hungarian history as the Fifteen Years War (1591–1606).

The first campaign began with a series of Turkish successes which prompted Sinan to call on Sigismund Báthori for help against the imperial troops. Sinan's idea was that, because of his victories, Sigismund would lack courage to refuse him aid and that, with Transylvanian forces joined to his own he could perhaps drive the Habsburgs out of Hungary. He was not far off the mark in his calculations, for an important group of the Transylvanian lords were ready to make concessions to the Turks, whom they feared to antagonize at a moment when they were apparently regaining their former strength. Transylvania's obvious hesitation made the Turks order their vassals, the Tartars of Crimea, to attack that country. Sigismund abdicated in favour of his cousin Balthasar Báthori and withdrew. Two weeks later, helped by his powerful lieutenant Stephen Bocskai, he returned in strength and in a horrible blood-bath wiped out the supporters of the Turkish alliance. The action was so unexpected and so horrible that all opposition was silenced and Sigismund was able to act according to his own wishes. He sent Bocskai to Prague and on January 28, 1595, a treaty was concluded by which Sigismund, whilst recognizing the Emperor as King of Hungary, obtained that he and his descendants should be recognized as hereditary Princes of Transylvania. The alliance was sealed by the match between Sigismund and the Habsburg princess Maria-Christina. This was an exceptional honour, and showed that, this time, the agreement between the Habsburgs and Transylvania was really meant to be lasting. The marriage was celebrated on August 6th but was to remain unconsummated. The handsome, stalwart Sigismund, a splendid weight-lifter and swordsman, proved impotent. Those who like to deny the rôle of the individual in the shaping of history may profitably ponder on the consequences of Sigismund's infirmity. His mind, never particularly well-balanced, grew more and more distressed and he became dominated by the mania of avoiding his wife. First he threw himself into military campaigns and conquered Moldova and Walachia, which had been lost for a long time to Hungary. He drove Sinan out of Transylvania, and his army, which included soldiers from Habsburg, Hungary and Poland, under the capable command of Bocskai, pursued the Turks and won a great victory over them at Giurgiu on the Lower Danube. At long last the Hungarian forces were on the offensive, and the Imperial troops, essentially Hungarian, achieved promising successes further west. It seemed that the Turks would be driven out, and even Europe's imagination was stirred by the prospect. Once again it was the Pope, this time Clement VIII, who made the greatest sacrifices to help Rudolf and Báthori defeat the Turks. Up to 1597 he spent one and a half million florins to support their efforts. By the end of 1596 a considerable army gathered, and Hungarian and foreign Imperial troops, commanded by the worthless Archduke Maximilian, joined forces with Transylvanian troops to inflict a decisive defeat on the harassed Turks. These, commanded in person by the Sultan Mahomet III, lived up to their former reputation perhaps for the last time. The battle of Mezökeresztes, fought on October 26, 1595, ended in their victory, which secured their domination over Hungary for another eighty years. The Fifteen Years War went on, fluctuating, without either party achieving major successes, without even decisive battles. The great strategic principle of the epoch, that of avoiding battles in which the armies could be destroyed, was scrupulously observed; the generals prospered, and the tormented and despoiled populations—decimated by war, the brutality of mercenaries, famine and illness—went slowly under in a maelstrom of blood, dirt and decay.

The war ended in 1606 with the peace-treaty of Zsitvatorok, which opened a new era in Hungarian–Turkish relations. The ten years leading up to it had brought untold sufferings to Transylvania. The immediate cause of this was Sigismund's instability. Had he remained firmly at his post, the energetic Bocskai would have been able to maintain the liaison between the two parts of Hungary; had he abdicated, Rudolf would have been entitled to incorporate Transylvania into his realm; but Sigismund Báthori abdicated four times within eight years, and returned thrice, thereby utterly marring Transylvanian politics.

His first abdication, in 1597, was in favour of Rudolf, who offered him (by then a customary arrangement) the principalities of Oppeln and Ratibor, together with a fixed annuity. Sigismund's main motive in renouncing Transylvania was his hope that Rudolf might obtain for him a divorce from his wife. Rudolf had neither the money to face his obligations nor the strength to take possession of Transylvania. The Imperial agents sent there to prepare for the arrival of the governor-designate, the Archduke Maximilian, committed the major blunder of relieving Bocskai of his post of Commander-in-Chief, the most ardent supporter of Habsburg rule and the most capable soldier and politician of Transylvania. A Turkish invasion seemed imminent, and in face of the obvious inability of the Habsburgs to defend the country Bocskai staged a *coup-d'état*. After eight months in exile, in August 1598, Sigismund returned to Transylvania. Somewhat to his surprise he there met his wife, whom he had earlier sent back to Austria, and who, with uncommon magnanimity, stood by her nominal husband. New deliberations were begun with Rudolf, but even before they could be brought to fruition, on March 17, 1599, Sigismund once more abdicated, this time in favour of his cousin the Cardinal Andrew Báthori. The Cardinal was an honest, well-meaning man, who had spent most of his life abroad and was unable to understand, and even less to direct, Transylvanian politics. Incited by Rudolf, the cunning, courageous but uncouth Michael, Voivode of Walachia, attacked Transylvania, where, aided by the Székelys (who bore a grudge against the Báthoris for Sigismund's reign of terror) he defeated Andrew on October 28, 1599. Michael was clever enough to make a gesture of submission towards Prague, but he could not allay Rudolf's distrust. An Italian general, George Basta, was dispatched to take over the government. Understandably, Michael felt reluctant to abandon the fruits of his victory and demonstrated his offensive spirit and military power by occupying Moldova. His tone became more and more menacing, and he began to threaten to invade Imperial territories. The social element was to play an increasing part in the ensuing struggle. The Székelys, anxious to preserve their rights, sided with Michael, but the nobles who, in any case, found the rule of the primitive Roumanian repugnant, threw in their lot with Basta; Michael was defeated and had to flee. The Transylvanian lords, wearied with the contest of two foreigners for their country, appealed again to Sigismund Báthori. For the third time that unstable prince returned; but at the news of his arrival Basta and Michael joined forces, and on August 3, 1601, they defeated Sigismund, compelling him to seek refuge in Moldavia, where his stay was to be short. A few days after their common victory, Michael was assassinated on the orders of Basta, who found no use for his former ally, who by motiveless massacres was about to alienate such modest sympathy among the lower classes as remained after his constant pilfering. Basta, who on his arrival at this distant place of appointment was pleasantly open-minded towards Hungarians, gradually developed a hatred towards them which, fanned by Rudolf's entourage, reached extraordinary proportions. His mental attitude was similar to that of his compatriot Castaldo, who had exerted such a baleful influence on Transylvanian history. Unable to control his mercenaries, who pillaged everything within their reach, he reduced the country to a misery hitherto unknown. For a fourth time Sigismund returned to Transylvania and appealed for help to the Turks. The little help they could provide caused as much distress as if they had come as enemies. Sigismund tried to court favour with the Székelys, whom he confirmed in their former status as free men, whereas Basta appealed to the Saxon towns. The Habsburg policy, continued by Hitler, to play the German minorities against the people who had taken them in, dates from this epoch. Sigismund's prospects were good when, unaccountable as ever, he changed his mind, concluded an armistice with Basta in February 1602, and soon after made yet another agreement concerning the disposal of Transylvania. This time his indecision amounted to high treason towards all who had supported him against Basta. The Hungarian nobility of Transylvania, exasperated, took to arms; their leader, Moses Székely, attempted in vain to make a surprise attack on Basta, and he was defeated at Tövis on July 2, 1602. An era of ruthless terror began. Basta, and indeed the Imperial Court, now considered Transylvania as conquered enemy country, and refused even to recognize the rights of jurisdiction of the Estates. Imperial commissaries were sent to Transylvania, and with complete disregard of the country's internal structure a reorganization was undertaken. Their work was interrupted by the reappearance of Moses Székely who, reinforced by Turkish troops, undertook to liberate the country. He was enthusiastically received by everyone save the Saxons (already drugged by the mysticism of German unity), and was elected Prince of Transylvania. Basta had to quit Transylvania, but now the Roumanian Voivode, Radul, attacked the unfortunate country. Székely met him on July 17, 1603, near Brasso and there lost his life. Once again Transylvania was at the mercy of Basta.

'Mercy' is the right word in the circumstances; there was no question of rights, and this mercy (in the form of a safe conduct) had to be bought and had to be carried on one's person to ensure a modicum of personal security. Basta's own bestial cruelty was directed against the nobles and the burghers—excepting the Germans, who had become a privileged class. The common people were subjected to the inhuman vexations of his soldiers, whom he was unable to control. Indeed, man had become a wolf to man; and reduced by pestilence, famine and spoliation to the utmost misery, those who could afford it bought human flesh sold openly on the market. . . .

Though the physical terror and misery which characterizes Basta's régime in Transylvania was not equalled in Habsburg-Hungary, conditions there were only a shade better. The sufferings caused by the Fifteen Years War were augmented by the short-sighted rapacity of the Imperial Treasury. It was the Treasury which was directly responsible for a step which was to provoke rebellion and to lead to a complete reversal of the political situation. Political power rested more than ever in the hands of the owners of huge estates. Yet though traditionally these men could expect to play a political rôle commensurate with their wealth, they found themselves more and more by-passed in the affairs of state, and the government of Hungary came to be almost exclusively in the hands of Germans or Italians. Deprived of an outlet for their political ambitions, the great lords could find no compensation in enlarging their estates. The King had no more domains to give away, and in courting his favour the lords could not expect an extension of their lands. There was, therefore, a general sense of frustration which, though less spectacular than the other aspects of the terrible trial the population was undergoing, made the great landlords into another factor of instability. Their faculty of resistance was underestimated by Rudolf and his councillors. In permanent need of money, Rudolf devised a very simple method to increase his revenues. Lawsuits were instituted on trumped-up charges against the richest lords, and these, having been found guilty, were punished by the confiscation of their property. As legal proceedings, however fraudulent, were often slow, confiscations were often carried out before any judgment was passed, by methods which, by a modern euphemism, one could call administrative. As was to be expected, these expropriations benefited the many foreign lords in the Imperial service, and nationalist feelings ran high in their wake. When Stephen Illésházy, one of the richest and most influential nobles, was condemned to death and to the confiscation of his fortune (the original verdict of 'not guilty' having been falsified to 'guilty' by the president of the tribunal), it was clear to everyone that the only right remaining was that of might. Illésházy escaped to Poland, and the Treasury, with the active help of Barbiano-Belgiojoso (the Imperial Captain-General of the Highlands), soon turned its attention to its next victim, Bocskai.

We have already met Bocskai's name in connection with Sigismund Báthori's eventful life. Many of his actions deserve reproof, but he was the greatest Hungarian statesmen of the second half of the sixteenth century. Moderate and prudent, he was neither swept off his feet by success nor disheartened by reverses. His approach to problems was essentially practical; he was not a rebel by nature, and he showed uncommon patience during the negotiations between Sigismund Báthori and Rudolf. Since 1602 he had lived in retirement in the *megye* of Bihar, in Eastern Hungary (but not in Transylvania), in the middle of his immense estates, acquired by methods not always blameless. A familiar of Rudolf's court, he was well acquainted with the weaknesses of the mad Emperor. He probably considered it as the great failure of his own life that he had not succeeded in his initial project of uniting Transylvania peacefully with the rest of the country, and that the extension of Habsburg rule had brought Basta upon that once-flourishing land. A number of Transylvanian nobles, menaced by the terror of the Italian general, sought refuge with the Turks, and Bocskai maintained contact with some of them. One émigré, Gabriel Bethlen, tried to convince Bocskai of the advantages of an alliance with the Turks, and entreated him to accept the charge of Prince of Transylvania, and to take on himself the struggle against aggression. Bocskai, though with no illusions left concerning the Habsburgs, felt reluctant to ally himself with the Turks, particularly as the latter were too weak to be able to offer decisive help. A copy of a letter sent by Bethlen to Bocskai fell into the hands of Imperial troops, and Belgiojoso considered it as an excellent pretext for dispossessing Bocskai. With Illésházy's fate before his eyes, Bocskai could easily imagine what would be his own if he were to stand trial. Reluctant to flee, he decided to resist. He succeeded in organizing the redoubtable *hajdús*, fearless but terribly savage Hungarian soldiers who had done immense harm to populations whom they had despoiled, quite irrespective of their nationality. The alliance of these miserable, landless, lawless, godless creatures of an inhuman epoch with the great lord Bocskai was to achieve an improvement for the wretched country.

The attack came from the Imperial troops, whose surprise assault on one of Bocskai's small fortresses was successful. Belgiojoso's military operations started at the beginning of October 1604, and on the 15th of this same month Bocskai won an important victory. News of this had a considerable effect on public opinion, but so bad was the *hajdús'* reputation that the population was slow to give support to what was in fact a national insurrection against alien oppression. It took some time also before Rudolf realized the magnitude of the danger. Basta was put in charge of the repression and, though he was victorious in a few open battles, the guerilla warfare waged by the *hajdús* during the winter 1604–5 caused the attrition of his forces and left Bocskai master of the Hungarian Highlands; he even occupied Pozsony, where he seized the Holy Crown. Bocskai was elected Prince of Transylvania on February 21st, and two months later, at a Diet held at Szerencs, Prince of Hungary, a title hitherto unknown and representing a compromise between the *de facto* situation and Bocskai's reluctance to usurp the royal prerogatives. It must have cost him much to accept Turkish support (obtained for him by Gabriel Bethlen), but, after a lifetime spent advocating the unification of Hungary under Habsburg rule, it was clear to him that this was not the solution to his country's problems. According to his new conception, such a solution was to be found in an independent and prosperous Hungarian state, Transylvania, which, wedged between the two great powers, the Turks and the Habsburgs, could preserve Hungarian civilization and the idea of a Hungarian state until such time as, the Turkish flood having receded, a fresh political start could be made. The greatness of Bocskai lies not so much in his political and military successes as precisely in this conception of Hungary's future; for a century it determined the direction of Hungarian development.

Bocskai, though he held practically the whole territory of Habsburg-
Hungary and of Transylvania, tried hard to negotiate a compromise
with Rudolf. The seclusion of the Emperor made this task particularly
arduous, as negotiations had to be conducted with the Archduke
Matthias, who was bent on duplicity and whose status, as a negotiator,
was not clearly defined. With Illésházy, who now returned from exile,
as a mediator, the Treaty of Vienna in 1606 put an end to Bocskai's war.

The terms of the treaty showed Bocskai's remarkable moderation.
They included guarantees of religious freedom for the Protestants, and
of the legislative rights of the Diet. The Emperor promised to fill at the
next Diet the vacant post of the *nádor*, and to govern the country
exclusively through Hungarians. In fact the Treaty of Vienna reasserted
the constitutional rights of the Estates. The fact that the clauses of the
treaty were guaranteed by the Austrian and Czech Estates contributed
to their efficiency, but was a step towards equality between the three
countries, and helped the Habsburgs' centralizing efforts. The treaty
recognized the independent principality of Transylvania, with Bocskai
at its head. Bocskai also kept a number of *megyes* belonging to the
Highlands, though, after his death, these were to return to Hungary
proper. The estates confiscated in illegal lawsuits were returned to their
rightful owners.

A few months later Bocskai died, but even the short period of peace
which he was allowed to enjoy was marked by two important achievements, namely the settlement of the *hajdús* and the conclusion with the
Turks of the Peace-Treaty of Zsitvatorok. The *hajdús* ceased henceforth
to be the dangerous marauders they had been, and, enjoying the
privileges of nobles and having, at last, fixed abodes, they became a
useful class of Hungarian society. Bocskai's act, by which he helped the
most disinherited stratum of society, is far in advance of the general
practice of his own time, and the Diploma of Korpona, by which he
conferred nobility upon all the *hajdús*, has an uncommon humanitarian
interest.

The Peace-Treaty of Zsitvatorok, which, as we have seen, put an end
to the Fifteen Years War, could not have been concluded without
Bocskai's consummate diplomatic skill. Only his influence was strong
enough to induce Ahmad I to accept an agreement which, though it
accepted the territorial *status quo* was, in other respects, a marked
success for the Emperor. Against a single payment of 200,000 *Talers*, the

Emperor was exempted from any further obligations and the Sultan agreed to address him as 'Emperor', a title which hitherto had not been used by the Turks. The Sultan also agreed not to exact taxes from Hungarian nobles living on territories under Turkish occupation. Though this last measure affected only a few, this was the first time that the Turks had been willing to take cognisance of a Hungarian constitutional distinction.

The Treaty of Zsitvatorok marks the beginning of an era in which the Turks, though still redoubtable, had to recognize, in an increasing measure, that their enemies must be treated with a modicum of consideration.

CHAPTER 18

REFORMATION. LITERATURE

THE clause on religious freedom incorporated in the Treaty of Vienna, shows that, as was to be expected, the effects of the Reformation had extended also to Hungary. Religious considerations often played a part in the political events which took place after the battle of Mohács, and only the requirements of clarity have prevented us from giving them so far the space they deserve. Now the time has come for a very brief account of the impact which the Reformation had on the course of events in Hungary during the sixteenth century.

The history of the Reformation in Hungary does not follow closely that of Western Europe. It is one of the peculiarities of the Hungarian character that it has little bent for religious speculation, and so the first adepts of Lutheranism were recruited among the Germans and from the entourage of Queen Maria, wife of Louis II. In 1525 the Diet (on a proposal from Werböczi, always ready to oppress) enacted a severe law against the new heresy, but the aim of this law was more political than religious; it was to counteract German influence. After the battle of Mohács the increasing anarchy was favourable to the spread of the new faith. The decadence of the Catholic Church, direct cause of the Reformation, had, ever since the Anjous, been apparent also in Hungary. Political events, and in particular the Turkish occupation, annihilated even the material framework of the Church, and the new faith found, therefore, less resistance in Hungary than it had in other countries. Vacant bishoprics remained unfilled, and the estates belonging to them were occupied by laymen. These used all their influence in favour of the prolongation of their interregna and the kings, anxious not to alienate the magnates, abode by their desire. Bishops of the Turkish zone took refuge on royal territories and, deprived of their income and of their flock, led an existence as miserable as it was useless. The lower clergy, left to themselves, could do little, and in growing numbers accepted the new faith.

Hungary's first Habsburg rulers, Ferdinand and Maximilian, though they remained Catholics, had much sympathy with Luther's teaching, and the converts of the new religion were, as a rule, not persecuted. In fact, a very great number of the realm's high dignitaries were Lutherans. One of the greatest practical assets of the Protestant religions was the use they made of local languages. The practice of worshipping in Hungarian had its appeal, but the use of particular national languages (in the case of Lutheranism, the use of German), hampered the spread of the new religions. After Luther's death the teachings of the Swiss reformers, who wrote in Latin, found easier access to the Hungarians. Up to the present day Lutheranism is in Hungary limited to Germans and Slovaks, whereas the majority of Hungarian Protestants is Calvinist. The beginnings of religious persecution in Habsburg-Hungary date from Rudolf, and only Basta used force against Protestants. On January 7, 1604, Belgiojoso occupied the, by then, Protestant cathedral of Kassa and handed it over to the Catholic Bishop of Eger, who had been made homeless by the Turks. The principle of *cuius regio eius religio*, accepted in the Treaty of Augsburg, was in general use also in Hungary, and the towns were eager to assert their right to determine the form of religion to be practised within their walls. The flagrant violation of this right at Kassa prompted the nobles and burghers to join their protests at the Diet of 1604. Though they were successful in their undertaking, and a law on religious freedom was enacted, the Archduke Matthias, acting on behalf of Rudolf, outwitted them by simple fraud. To the decisions taken at the Diet Matthias added yet another, the ill-fated twenty-second paragraph, forbidding the discussion in the future of any religious question by the Diets. It was because of this unscrupulous procedure that in the Treaty of Vienna the principle of religious freedom (not for the individual but for a given region!) had to be reasserted.

In Transylvania Protestantism gained ground rapidly, and Martinuzzi had to accommodate himself to the changing circumstances. The Diet held at Torda in 1557 asserted the freedom of religious practices and the scale was slowly tipping in favour of Protestantism: first Lutheranism, then Calvinism. From 1571 onwards Unitarianism was also recognized, and the Transylvanian constitution was based on the axiomatic equality of the three nations (Hungarian, Székely, Saxon) and of the four religions (Roman Catholic, Lutheran, Calvinist, Unitarian). This was a remarkably liberal attitude for the epoch, and it seems to be unparalleled in other parts of Europe. Majority was with the Protestants, but areas with a Catholic population were left undisturbed. Clearly not even in Transylvania was it possible for any individual to worship differently from the majority of the region in which he lived. But he was free to move, and no hindrance stood in the way of regional worship, whatever the religion. Religious freedom became an idea accepted by all in Transylvania, and this caused that country to become its champion during the Counter-Reformation in Hungary.

The Reformation exerted a considerable influence on Hungarian literature. The greatest single achievement of the outgoing sixteenth century was certainly the complete translation of the Bible produced in 1591 by Gáspár Heltai. This was to play an important rôle in the development of a Hungarian literary language. Literature in the national language developed much later in Hungary than it did in the countries of Western Europe, and it was only under the impact of the Reformation that Latin irretrievably lost its predominance. The sixteenth century in Hungary was one of continuous struggle and confusion, most unfavourable for artistic creation. Literature, unable to free itself from the general current of events, was essentially of a polemic character, and its only objective merit lies in the fact that, written in Hungarian, and, for the purpose of gaining popular support, addressed to the broad masses, it brought within the circle of letters classes who had hitherto been illiterate.

If there is nothing very particular in all this, there was another development during the sixteenth century so original that anyone not acquainted with Hungarian literature may find it difficult to visualize. We can only hint at it here. The phenomenon known in Hungarian history as 'the life on the marches' was a way of life shaped by the incessant Turkish wars, and by the realization that whatever paths the policies of the absent King might follow, the supreme duty of the Hungarian lay in defending his country. In the fulfilment of this task were welded together all the defenders, whether powerful lords or *jobbágys*, whether Catholics or Protestants, of the blood-sodden soil of the marches. In an epoch when military discipline was at its lowest, when the population learned to dread the German or Walloon mercenaries supposed to defend it as much, if not more than, it did the Turks, a chivalrous code with a self-imposed discipline came into flower among these half-forgotten and despised warriors. Foreign generals, seldom successful, and almost always indifferent to the destinies of Hungary, met uncomprehendingly the ideals animating these men, ideals of chivalry long forgotten in the Europe they defended. Assuredly they were tough men, as all must be who have to face death ceaselessly, but they were also noble, splendid products of that 'school of heroism' that was Hungary. We are fortunate that among the many occasional poets they produced there was one of genius, Valentine Balassi (1554–94), whose evocation of his own life and of that of his companions inspired from him some admirable poems. It was from the great line of these 'warriors of the marches' that sprang the tradition of the chivalrous heroism of which the Hungarians are so proud. The vanity of their sacrifice made it yet more precious, their gallantry was an atonement for the criminal egoism of their fathers, and has shone through the following centuries of Hungarian tragedy.

CHAPTER 19

THE GOLDEN AGE OF
TRANSYLVANIA

THE year 1606, in which the Treaties of Vienna and of Zsitvatorok were concluded, and in which Bocskai died, is in more than one respect an important landmark in Hungarian history. Though the Turks maintained their grip on those parts of the country they had conquered, their aggressiveness seems to have ceased. Bocskai's rebellion changed the relation between Hungary and the Dynasty and the creation of an independent Transylvania, whose religious freedom was respected by all, was to exert a powerful influence on events to come.

Rudolf, by his reluctance to honour the above-mentioned peace-treaties, risked jeopardizing the very real achievements they represented, and could have brought about the fall of his dynasty. To forestall this danger, the Archduke Matthias, who for a number of years had borne the burden of actual government, with the full consent of the family-council of the Habsburgs, marched against Prague and compelled his brother to abdicate from all his countries save Bohemia. In November 1608, Matthias II (the first of this name among the Emperors) was elected and crowned King of Hungary (1608–19).

Matthias obtained his throne with the help of the Estates and even before his accession he had to give important guarantees that the clauses of the Vienna Treaty would be respected. The fact that Matthias was elected by the Estates was an important constitutional step as, since Ferdinand, the Habsburg Emperors had succeeded to the throne without the Estates having been consulted. A new system was devised for the filling of the controversial but very important part of the *nádor*. The Diet of 1608 agreed that from four magnates, two Catholic and two Protestant, designated by the King, the Diet should have the right to elect the *nádor* of the country. The first *nádor* thus elected was the Protestant Stephen Illésházy. Since 1528 it had been customary for the Diet to divide into two houses. In 1608 this custom was embodied in a law, and the system then adopted remained in use until 1848.

The Estates of the Realm (*Status et Ordines Regni Hungariae*) numbered four: the higher clergy (*praelati*), the lords (*magnates*), the nobles (*nobiles*) and the representatives of the free townships. The Upper House consisted, roughly speaking, of members of the first two Estates and holders of higher administrative posts. The two houses of the Diet communicated by exchanging messages. The division of the nobles was similar to that made by the English Parliament between *barones majores* and *barones minores*, and was in contradiction with Hungarian tradition as formulated by the law of 1351 and the *Tripartitum*.

The constitutional guarantees given by Matthias, and the existence of an independent Transylvania, theoretically capable of counterbalancing German influence, augured well for the country's gradual recovery. Things, however, were to develop differently.

Matthias II was an old, tired man when he took Rudolf's place, and his main preoccupation was to lead a happy and quiet life. Already before his accession much of the business of government had been transacted by the president of the *Geheimrat*, the Cardinal Khlesl, an adept of the then new political theory of absolutism, and so, both as a German and as an absolutist, the avowed enemy of the Hungarians. It was under the influence of Khlesl that the 'rebellious Hungarian' became a stock-concept of Austrian political thought. In Khlesl's opinion any attempt to circumscribe the ruler's power was equivalent to rebellion and, as such, could and should be resisted by arms. Khlesl's absolutism had none of the positive features of the enlightened despotism which in the eighteenth century was to produce such remarkable results. His was a primitive, administrative tyranny, based on sheer force. His policy could find no real justification in the attitude of the Hungarian Estates, basically loyal. The Spanish or German mercenaries who, on Khlesl's advice, accompanied Matthias to the Hungarian Diet achieved nothing else than to perpetuate and increase the Hungarians' distrust of their sovereign. Khlesl's administration represented a definite backward movement in political development, and as it was not redeemed by any improvement in efficiency and integrity, it would have been an unattractive example to follow even had it shed its anti-

Hungarian character. There was all the less inducement for Hungarians to accept the Habsburg system, as Transylvania, under the rule of Gabriel Bethlen, demonstrated for all to see the superiority of a purely Hungarian state.

Bocskai's early death was followed in Transylvania by a period of unrest during which Sigismund Rákóczi and Gabriel Báthori were successively princes. The latter, the last representative of a family marked by a tempestuous temperament, was in the end murdered at a time when Gabriel Bethlen had already been elected Prince of Transylvania (1613–29).

Owing to the rôle he played in the Thirty Years War in Western Europe, Gabriel Bethlen is one of the better known Hungarian statesmen. Judgments on him vary according to the political and religious bias of their enunciator; and it must be admitted that during his lifetime his shifting, cunning, secretive political conduct put to a hard test the patience of friend and foe alike. Most of his contemporaries felt at a loss before the circumvolutions of his apparently contradictory actions; and historians of later ages have found it no easy task to assess, or even to understand, his conduct. The perspicacious Sir Thomas Roe, often exasperated by Bethlen's behaviour, without however ceasing to admire him, openly admits to not understanding his character. Bethlen had inherited from Bocskai the conviction that as long as the Crown was in the possession of a foreigner belonging to a nation more powerful than Hungary, it was essential that a strong Transylvanian principality should act as guardian of the nation's permanent values. Just as Bocskai had done, Bethlen envisaged this rôle as a temporary one only, though, in the circumstances, of unlimited duration; and the future of Transylvania, for which he did so much, was always seen by him in the context of Hungarian interests as a whole. Where Bethlen differed from Bocskai, and indeed from all previous Hungarian statesmen, was in his attitude towards the Turks. For Hungarians who had not been openly hostile to the Ottoman Empire, alliance with it had been but a *pis aller*, intended to ensure the survival of Transylvania. The Turk remained, as we have already said, the enemy *par excellence*. Matters appeared differently to Bethlen, who had spent his youth in Turkey, driven there by Basta's terror. He had a sincere admiration for Turkish military power, and considered that the menace of the Habsburg Empire engulfing Hungary was the most acute the country had to face. In the long run Bethlen was probably not more Turcophile than the majority of Hungarians; he wanted a country ultimately free from Turkish as well as from German domination. But until such time as this aim could be achieved, he was prepared to make the greatest possible use of Turkish force to counterbalance the growing German danger. Without it, he held, Transylvania was bound to succumb. History proved him to be right.

Bethlen's foreign policy embraced the whole of Europe; his diplomatic activity, so difficult to follow, aimed principally at the weakening of the Habsburgs. Although a pious Calvinist, religious controversy and persecution was not to his liking, and during his reign the four recognized religions were left undisturbed in Transylvania. It was therefore for political reasons only that he took advantage of the Thirty Years War to join forces with the Protestants. Not for a moment did he forget his aims, and his fixity of purpose, which did not coincide with that of his allies, explains most of his double dealings.

The absolutist tendencies of the epoch were not alien to Bethlen, and his political theories were not unlike those of James I, whose *Basilikon Doron* was translated into Hungarian in 1612. Similar theories were expressed by John Pataki Füsüs in his *Mirror of Kings* (1628), perhaps the most outstanding work of its kind in the flourishing political literature of Transylvania. Bethlen considered Transylvania as a financial and economic entity. With almost unrestricted powers, he was able to carry out his economic plans, and under his rule Transylvania enjoyed prosperity enviable even by western standards. His measures to increase production in agriculture and mining were as successful as his efforts to encourage foreign trade. With its credit balance Bethlen's treasury stood in sharp contrast to its insolvent Habsburg counterpart.

It is not surprising that Bethlen took great care to forge an army adequate to the needs of a country pursuing an active foreign policy. A judicious assessment of his country's resources in manpower led him to develop a light cavalry, which was reluctant to engage in major battles, but which by its rapidity and elusiveness, was a constant menace to the enemy, who, during the Thirty Years War learned to fear its interventions. Bethlen's army was, for the epoch, well disciplined; looting and pilfering were limited to the enemy, which was great progress when we consider the indiscriminate savagery of the *hajdús*.

Bethlen's rule in Transylvania marks the apogee in that principality's

history. He showed that the Hungarian genius, which had animated St
Stephen, Béla IV, Charles Robert and Hunyadi, was still very much
alive and needed no Habsburg nursing to fulfil its historic function. In
fact, as in the past, it was spiritually vastly superior to the alien pattern
to which it was expected to adapt itself. Bethlen represented an ideal
much more advanced than that of Matthias II or of his immediate
successors; and the 'fairy-garden' Transylvania of his creation
represented the fulfilment of wishes which most Hungarians nursed in
their hearts.

Matthias's reign ended in the chaos caused by the Bohemian revolt.
Ferdinand II (1619–37), the narrow-minded grandson of Ferdinand I,
whose intransigence as King-Elect had done much to poison the
situation, ascended the throne firmly resolved to eradicate heresy. He
had no sympathy either for constitutional government and, a man of
mediocre intellect, he could not even grasp the moving force behind
Hungarian or Czech national aspirations. He belonged to a type of ruler
which was to become fairly common in the Habsburg dynasty. He was
basically honest, religious and conscientious; ruling the Empire
consisted for him in signing documents, attending meetings, and in
general transacting business with the mentality of a subordinate civil
servant. Opposed to constitutional government, he did not himself want
to rule: he left the task to his ministers, hardly better equipped than
himself to make decisions, but mildly dishonest, who (to cover their own
indiscretions) raised no objections to the King's costly pleasures. The
Habsburgs lacked probably some of the Bourbon vices; they also lacked
their imagination and their good taste. They were a pedestrian race and
it is this quality which explains why they succeeded in ruling for almost
four centuries, and why they were driven out, at the end, by foreign
intervention rather than by their own people.

At the outbreak of the revolt in Bohemia, the consolidation of
Transylvania was sufficiently advanced to allow Bethlen to intervene
actively. At the Diet of 1618, Ferdinand's attitude foreboded religious
persecution for the Protestants and curtailment of the Estates' power.
Thus, when the Elector Frederick assumed the crown of Bohemia,
Bethlen realized that the time had come to join forces with him.
Military operations started in September 1619 and were highly
successful. Bethlen's troops advanced easily through the territory of

Habsburg-Hungary and by the end of November he stood at the gates of Vienna. Later he withdrew and eventually an armistice was concluded, during which the Hungarian Protestant estates assembled and on August 25, 1620, elected Bethlen King of Hungary. Bethlen accepted the election, but refused to let himself be crowned with the Holy Crown, which had previously fallen into his hands.

On November 8th, at the battle of the White Hill, Frederick's Czech army was crushed. A man not made to rule, he was abandoned by his western allies (another instance of recurrent eastern European tragedy), and the small forces put at his disposal by Bethlen could not affect the outcome. The unbridled policy of repression then inaugurated by Ferdinand in Bohemia, the persecution of the Protestants, the extinction of national privileges, and the abolition of elective monarchy, made it abundantly clear to Bethlen what Hungary could expect in similar circumstances. With his army undefeated, he continued the struggle against Ferdinand which led eventually to the Treaty of Nicholsburg, concluded on the last day of 1621. This marked a triumph for Bethlen, who at the end of long discussions agreed only to renounce the title of 'King of Hungary' and to return the Holy Crown to Ferdinand. This was almost the sole concession he was forced to make. As far as titles went, he was given those already used by Bocskai, namely 'Prince of Transylvania and of Hungary'; he was also granted the title of a Duke of the German Empire, the principalities of Oppeln and Ratibor and a number of *megye* hitherto belonging to Habsburg-Hungary. More important from the country's point of view were the undertakings given by Ferdinand to respect the clauses of the Treaty of Vienna (1606), and the decisions on religious freedom taken at the Diet of 1608. He also promised to give money for the upkeep of the border fortifications. If we consider that this treaty was signed by Ferdinand on the morrow of crushing the Bohemia revolt, that is, at a moment when his situation had improved beyond measure, the only reason we can find for his accepting such conditions is the desire to gain time until he could free his forces from western obligations, and strike Bethlen with full force. Experience had shown that his available troops were insufficient to cope with that impetuous prince.

Neither of the contracting parties considered the Treaty of Nicholsburg as definitive, and both were ready to attack again as soon as circumstances warranted. On a futile pretext Bethlen reopened hostilities; but realizing the vanity of his campaign, and failing to co-ordinate his effort effectively with that of the other Protestant powers, on May 8, 1624, he concluded a treaty with Ferdinand, signed in Vienna, which was essentially the same as that of Nicholsburg. It was clear that, though on his own ground Bethlen was able to stand up to Ferdinand, he was not strong enough to have his way in extra Hungarian, particularly Bohemian, affairs. The realization of this prompted Bethlen to inaugurate an alternative policy: he asked Ferdinand's daughter in marriage. Had Ferdinand been a more subtle politician he would perhaps have agreed to this suggestion, verging on the impudent. As it was, he refused, and the disappointed suitor turned his attention to the Protestant camp and married Catherine, sister of George William, Elector of Brandenburg. Though the marriage was concluded with the formal assent of Ferdinand, it tied Bethlen more than ever to the Protestant cause.

In 1626 Bethlen made a renewed attack on Ferdinand, an attack which was meant to be simultaneous with an offensive launched by Mansfeld. This ill-fated general had, however, been terribly mishandled by Wallenstein, who came in Mansfeld's wake to face the forces of Bethlen. Neither of the two generals dared to risk an open battle; Bethlen withdrew and Wallenstein did not pursue him. On December 28th yet another peace-treaty between Ferdinand and Bethlen was ratified. Once again the Prince attempted a *rapprochement* with Ferdinand, but met with no response. Once again, in the evening of his life, Bethlen prepared to find allies of suitable strength, who were willing to co-operate in Eastern Europe. He turned to his brother-in-law (husband of his wife's sister), Gustavus Adolphus, King of Sweden.

Bethlen had for some time thought of obtaining the Polish crown, and a Swedish–Russian–Transylvanian alliance, aimed at securing Germany for Gustavus Adolphus and Poland for Bethlen, was gradually taking shape. The plan could not be brought to fruition, because on November 15, 1629, Bethlen died and his successor, George Rákóczi (1630–48), was not a man to face such risks as Bethlen had been ready to take.

At Bethlen's death his widow, Catherine of Brandenburg, had been elected to the throne for a short year (1629–30). Her sympathies with the Habsburgs and with Roman Catholicism caused the Estates to gather round Stephen Bethlen, the late prince's younger brother. But George Rákóczi, the richest man of the eastern parts of the realm, slowly gained ascendancy and, apart from a short conflict in 1636 with Stephen Bethlen, his rule remained uncontested.

George Rákóczi I was a man of integrity. Very cautious, he had no liking for adventures. Thrifty, almost parsimonious, he kept his private finances in order as well as those of Transylvania, and generally speaking maintained Transylvania on the level reached during the reign of Bethlen. In religious matters he was not so open-minded as his predecessor had been. A staunch Protestant, he showed signs of intolerance, which were viewed with antipathy by what was then a steadily growing Catholic community.

During Bethlen's glorious reign, Habsburg-Hungary had also produced a man of outstanding ability: Peter Pázmány, since 1616 Archbishop of Esztergom. Born in a well-to-do Protestant family, he became a Catholic at the age of twelve. Later he joined the Jesuit order and studied abroad for many years in Cracow, Vienna and Rome. On his return in 1597 he was made professor at the University of Graz, and there he stayed for about ten years. He played an important rôle at the Diet of 1608, and during his whole life he remained the principal Hungarian supporter of the Habsburgs. He also became the head of the Hungarian Counter-Reformation. One of the most brilliant prose-writers Hungary has ever produced, and an exceptionally gifted orator, he is an important figure in the history of Hungarian literature. He reorganized the Catholic Church in Hungary, in Vienna he founded a seminary for Hungarian priests, and in Rome a Hungarian College. The University of Budapest traces its origins to the University he founded in 1635 in Nagyszombat. Though a convinced supporter of the Habsburgs, Pázmány never lost sight of Hungary's national interests and exerted his great influence in favour of his countrymen. In religious matters he condemned the excesses of the Counter-Reformation, and tried, successfully, to achieve conversions by persuasion. His *Guide to Divine Truth* (1613) met with no adequate confutation, and his sermons turned the religious tide. The movement of the Counter-Reformation began among the great nobles and steadily gained momentum. The comparative unsuccess of Bethlen's last campaigns finds its cause in the lukewarm reception given him by the re-catholicized nobles of Western Hungary. Towards the end of his reign, Rákóczi found himself defending the rights of a religious minority; an excellent thing from the human point of view, but politically a somewhat thankless task.

The cautiousness so characteristic of Rákóczi's policy prevented him from launching an offensive against Ferdinand. Among the leading statesmen of Western Hungary, Pázmány sympathized with Rákóczi, but the *nádor* Eszterházy was his deadly enemy. The reasons for this enmity were personal rather than political, the *nádor* and the Prince having become rivals in the course of enlarging their respective estates. The western commitments of the Habsburgs remained, however, so heavy that nothing could be done against Rákóczi.

In 1637 Ferdinand died and was followed by Ferdinand III (1637–57), a man of scholarly and artistic inclinations, who, though less intolerant than his father, continued in the main his policies. By 1643, after laborious negotiation, a Swedish–French–Transylvanian alliance was brought into being. In February 1644 Rákóczi attacked. He lacked Bethlen's strategic sense, and his campaign, though not without success, was a sorry spectacle for anyone devoted to the science of war. Negotiations were not on a much higher level, and almost everything depended on co-ordination of effort with the Swedish and the French. Rákóczi expected from his allies more funds and more military help, they expected from him more enthusiasm and efficiency in attack. The Prince argued that the Turks were opposing his plans, and indeed, by that time Habsburg diplomacy had acquired sufficient influence in Constantinople to be able to bring Turkish pressure to bear on Rákóczi, who gradually came to realize that he could achieve nothing by further fighting. Abandoning his allies at Linz on December 16, 1645, he concluded a separate peace-treaty with Ferdinand.

Economically and territorially the Treaty of Linz was in line with the treaties concluded by Bethlen; as far as its religious dispositions were concerned, it presented striking innovations. For the first time the principle of *cujus regio ejus religio* was abandoned, and the religious freedom of the individual recognized. The treaty guaranteed the religious freedom of the *jobbágy*, who henceforth could profess a religion different from that of his lord. Protestant churches were to be returned to their congregations, from whom the privileges of bell-ringing and the use of other paraphernalia of worship were no longer withheld. The Treaty of Linz meant the withdrawal of Hungary from the Thirty Years War. This fact in itself may have seemed advantageous to contemporaries; in reality it was one of those instances—only too numerous in their long history—when Hungarians joined or abandoned an alliance at the wrong moment. Having fought the Habsburgs for twenty-seven years, Transylvania, three years before the final victory, left the camp of the victors. Though mention was made of her in the last-but-one paragraph of the Treaty of Westphalia, as one of the allies of the French, her independence, unlike those of Switzerland and the Netherlands, was not guaranteed.

In the year when the peace of Westphalia was ratified, the Prince of Transylvania died and was succeeded by his son, George Rákóczi II (1648–60), a weak, conceited man, who was soon to jeopardize Transylvania's future. The idea of obtaining the throne of Poland had not been unwelcome to a number of Transylvanian princes. The ambitious George Rákóczi II made the project his own, and in alliance with Charles X of Sweden prepared to attack the Polish King John Casimir. The extremely complex internal situation of Poland was further complicated by the interest shown in her affairs by a number of European countries. George Rákóczi II, blinded by some minor successes achieved against Transylvania's insignificant eastern neighbours, threw himself into the Polish venture. His act was, in itself, unjustified and foolhardy, but the disastrous consequences could have been mitigated had he not omitted to obtain the preliminary agreement of the Turks and of the Transylvanian Estates. The campaign, launched in January 1657, ended six months later in complete disaster. His army prisoner of the Tartars, Rákóczi had to sign a humiliating peace-treaty and returned home only to find that the indignation of the Estates had reached boiling-point. Soon the order arrived from Constantinople to dethrone the disobedient vassal. He was replaced by the harmless Francis Rhédey, the last man to resist Rákóczi should he seek to return to power. The Turks, however, followed a sterner line, attacked Transylvania and stopped military operations only when the Estates declared themselves ready to accept as Prince the Sultan's candidate Barcsai (September 14, 1658). Rákóczi refused to be ousted from his country by the Turks, and, having regained some sympathy among his subjects, who disliked Turkish intervention in their internal affairs, he continued his struggle for his throne against the Turks. He died on the battlefield on May 22, 1660. With him vanished an independent Transylvania. Formally, her existence was to cease only some years later; but she was in fact no longer a free agent in politics.

CHAPTER 20

LIBERATION

FOR some time it had been clear that the military power of the Ottoman Empire had undergone a gradual weakening. George Rákóczi II had been mistaken, however, in thinking that he could ignore the advice of Constantinople, and he had paid with his life for this mistake, which provoked Turkish retaliation on a scale that seemed to belie any unfavourable opinion of their military strength. Repeated Turkish attacks wrought havoc on the flourishing country. Whilst Transylvania was slowly sinking into chaos, and the Tartar soldiery was rapidly destroying the achievements of Bethlen and Rákóczi, a new king, Leopold I (1657–1705), ruled over Western Hungary. During his reign of half a century considerable dangers appeared in every field of the country's life. The complexity of Hungarian history at this epoch is such that only by keeping to the chronological sequence of events concerning one major issue can we hope to give an approximately clear and accurate picture of it. The Turkish wars may well serve our purpose.

Rákóczi's death meant neither respite from Turkish attacks nor a reasonable settlement of the succession. The Turkish protégé, Barcsai, was needlessly executed by John Kemény, who for two short years (1660–2) remained Prince of Transylvania. Kemény's policy was based on expectation of Habsburg support, and it was the inadequacy of this support that caused his fall. The Turkish campaign in 1660 did not stop in Transylvania proper, and, with the Imperial troops neatly arrayed as spectators, the most important town of the Partium, Nagyvárad, fell into Turkish hands. To avoid the repetition of such disaster, Kemény called upon Leopold to send Imperial garrisons to Transylvanian fortresses. The Imperial Commander-in-Chief, the

Italian Count Montecuccoli, was a past master at temporizing. A great military theoretician, he abode by the principle that three things were needed for warfare: money, money and money. Probably because there was no abundance in the Habsburg Empire of the sinews of war, Montecuccoli's main aim was not to win wars, even less to defend the inhabitants of his country, but only to keep his army out of mischief— or better, out of battle. By the time his troops had taken over from Kemény the defence of some fortresses in Northern Transylvania, the Turks had made progress in the south. Montecuccoli made no attempt to meet the enemy and withdrew; and Kemény paid with his life, lost during a battle on January 23, 1662, for his confidence in Habsburg help. His successor, the resourceless Michael Apafi I (1662–90), the last Prince of Transylvania to exercise effective power, was too weak a man to influence decisively the course of events. This was to be dictated by the dynamic grand-vizier, Ahmet Köprülü. In 1663 he launched an attack against Hungary and occupied Érsekujvár, well within the borders of Habsburg-Hungary. Montecuccoli did worse than to watch with folded hands the new Turkish threat: he hampered the organizing of Hungarian national resistance.

The harsh judgment Hungarian historians pass on Montecuccoli is only partly due to their bitterness at the Italian general's reluctance to defend Hungary. His conceptions were not dissimilar to those of the Russians during Napoleon's invasion. But even if we do not blame him for sacrificing Hungary in order to save Vienna (which could have been defended without this sacrifice), he still incurs our censure for paralysing Hungarian efforts that would have served the same purpose. It was a tragedy for the country, as well as for the individual, that Nicholas Zrinyi was denied the opportunity of exerting his exceptional military gifts.

Nicholas Zrinyi (1620–64) was great-grandson of the defender of Szigetvár (cf. p. 172), whose heroic resistance inspired from him an epic poem which secures him an important place in Hungarian literature. Author of several political and military works, Zrinyi was anything but an abstract theoretician. Conscious of the duties imposed upon him by the glorious tradition and the great wealth of his family, he had no other aim than to serve his country. He was only six years old when his father died, and his education was entrusted to Pázmány himself. By birth and education he was a Roman Catholic and a supporter of the Habsburgs.

If he kept his religious convictions, the sight of the mismanagement of the Turkish war tended to alienate him more and more from the dynasty. A bitter personal feud set Montecuccoli and Zrinyi at odds, a phenomenon by no means uncommon among generals with different strategic conceptions. At all events, those of Zrinyi were tested in action. Seething with rage at Montecuccoli's dilatory tactics, he brought his own troops into action and during the winter 1663-4 achieved some important results, particularly the destruction of the long bridge built over the marshes of the Drava through which, for over a century, Turkish troops had been moving into Transdanubia. His attacks provoked vigorous retaliatory action by the Turks. Köprülü attacked Zrinyi's own estates and Montecuccoli was certainly not displeased to see the fall of his antagonist's principal fortress, Zrinyivár. For once, Montecuccoli was right in not engaging the enemy; with his armies kept intact, he could inflict a decisive defeat on the Turks. The battle of St Gotthard (in Hungary) fought on August 1, 1664, ended with the annihilation of the Turkish forces.

Montecuccoli showed no inclination to take advantage of one of his rare victories. Hasty peace negotiations were set on foot and ten days later the Treaty of Vasvár was signed in the camp itself.

This was a strange treaty indeed, for its conditions could not have been more unfavourable for Hungary had the Turks won the battle. Concluded for twenty years, it left in Turkish hands all the occupied territories, including those conquered during this last campaign. Transylvania was to remain under Turkish tutelage, and the Imperial garrisons still occupying some of its fortresses were to be withdrawn. Apafi was to be recognized by Leopold as Prince of Transylvania and, finally, a 'present' of 200,000 talers was to be sent to the Sultan. In short, after having suffered a terrible defeat, the Turks secured terms leaving in their hands the greatest slice of Hungary they had ever possessed. Only madmen or men entirely disinterested in Hungary's fate could have signed—on the Imperial side—such a document, and the country's indignation knew no bounds. The Treaty of Vasvár made it clear that Leopold's government was not only incapable of defending Hungary, but also unwilling to do so.

Zrinyi, disgusted, retired and a few months later lost his life in a hunting accident. Before his death, encouraged by some Frenchmen who had taken part in the fight against the Turks, he toyed with the idea of an alliance with Louis XIV against the Habsburgs. Zrinyi had much sympathy with the great monarch who, as a tribute to services rendered in the defence of Christianity, had sent him a present of 10,000 talers. The idea of a French alliance was later taken up by others, and during the reign of Louis XIV political contacts between Hungary and France were lively.

The outrage committed at Vasvár against Hungary's vital interests was so strongly resented that even the hitherto staunchest supporters of the dynasty felt that an end must be put to the rule over Hungary of a group of men both inefficient and ignorant of the affairs of the country. Though theoretically an absolutist monarch, Leopold I lacked the genius to hold in his own hand all affairs of state. He studied with close application the state documents submitted to him, wrote many letters, held numerous audiences—and did nothing to improve the conditions in Hungary. From 1669 to 1674 the Imperial government was led by Prince Lobkowitz, who copied everything that was wrong in French absolutism, without imitating the great economic and social achievements of Henry IV, Richelieu or Colbert.

Even before Lobkowitz had an opportunity to exert his evil influence, Hungarian dissatisfaction led to a conspiracy which, if we could make abstraction of its tragic end, would lend itself to comic treatment. The plot, carefully fostered by the French ambassador Gremonville, was a nebulous, petty affair, astonishingly childish. The Viennese Court soon got wind of the project or rather of the projects (for these were as many as the conspirators themselves). Several among the conspirators betrayed their companions, and nevertheless continued to play at conspiracy, as if forgetting that their activity was anything but secret. Leopold behaved with remarkable restraint, due partially to the inefficiency of his government, reluctant always to take action. Warnings, however, went unheeded, until in the end some of the ringleaders were arrested and four of them—including Peter Zrinyi, brother of Nicholas —executed (1671). If Leopold had shown restraint in handling the conspiracy in its earlier stages, his final action was undiplomatic and unjust. The defendants were tried by a German tribunal and—though a Hungarian tribunal might not have taken a more lenient view of their activities—this in itself was patently illegal. They were also tried on charges to which they had previously confessed, and for which they had been granted pardons by the Emperor. The trial was a political one, with all the bad implications of this word, and the confiscation of the fortunes of those who had been executed brings more additional unpleasantness to this grim affair.

The conspiracy, named after its instigator, the *nádor* Wesselényi who, however, had already died in 1667, was the first outbreak of Hungarian dissatisfaction. For the following half a century unrest was to become endemic in the country.

The quelling of the Wesselényi conspiracy afforded Vienna an ideal pretext for pressing on with a policy of repression against Protestants, and with the gradual suppression of the Hungarian constitution. The theory made to justify the subjection of Hungary was as simple as the minds of those who conceived it. With the conspiracy, which was tantamount to rebellion, Hungarians had lost their right to be considered as the Emperor's own people, they had been subjected by arms and through this fact had lost all their privileges. Only an 'iron rod' could cope with the rebellious, ungrateful Hungarians; the country must be filled with foreign troops ready to quell any incipient disorder. Whilst religious persecution—some 300 Protestant families were imprisoned—went hand in hand with spoliation, blackmail and military violence, Hungarian reaction was neither intellectually nor morally on a higher level than the Austrian oppression. Following the tragic outcome of the Wesselényi conspiracy, a number of minor conspirators fled to Transylvania, where they were given asylum by Michael Teleki who, in taking advantage of Apafi's weakness, had secured for himself a decisive say in Transylvanian affairs. The refugees showed very little discretion in their general comportment and no consideration towards Transylvania's precarious situation. In 1672 they launched an ill-conceived attack against Habsburg territories, whence they were easily repelled. Their attack provided Leopold with an excuse to suppress the Hungarian constitution, and consequently to abolish the office of the *nádor*. In March 1673 a new governing council was set up in Pozsony, composed of eight members (four German and four Hungarian) under the chairmanship of John Caspar Ampringen, a German whose duty was to ensure that Hungarian opinion, if expressed at the council, should remain in a minority. In fact Ampringen was made dictator of Hungary, a dictator who, curiously, had to execute orders received from Lobkowitz, and who was unable to bring under control the country which, theoretically, was entrusted to his authority.

It must be emphasized that Austrian government of Hungary was not only evil in itself (other governments were not necessarily better), not only deliberately harmful to the country (after all it tried to represent Austrian interests), but also desperately, incredibly inefficient. Red tape, corruption, hypocrisy, a total lack of imagination, were as much responsible for the failure to control Hungary as any local resistance, if not more so.

Perhaps the most odious deeds of the régime were perpetrated against the Protestants, whom Lobkowitz and his successor, the Chancellor Hocher, considered as the hard core of Hungarian resistance. They found a ready tool in Archbishop Kollonich of Wiener-Neustadt, who later became, in Esztergom, a most unworthy successor of Pázmány. His methods were deplored by Buonvisi, the Papal Nuncio himself. In the spring of 1674, at Pozsony, proceedings were instituted against many hundreds of Protestant clergymen accused of political 'crimes'. Some 450 of them had to renounce their functions, and those who refused to desist from exercising them were sent to the galleys, a form of punishment not practised in Hungary. Those who survived the 'death march' to Naples (then under Spanish rule) and the subsequent hardships were handed over in 1676 to the Dutch Admiral de Ruyter.

As German terror increased, more and more men took to the woods. The number of such bands grew steadily, particularly when the government embarked on a mass dismissal of the Hungarian soldiers manning the border fortresses. The nucleus of these irregular bands, called the *kuruc*, found itself in the Partium, wedged between Habsburg Hungary, the Turkish zone and Transylvania proper. Military value, at this stage, the *kuruc* had none. They were a motley crew, not dissimilar to the old *hajdús*, bent on violence and robbery. Their opponents, the pro-Habsburg *labanc*, were of the same sort. A useless, aimless, bloody struggle between the two factions went on unabated.

Leopold had no means to halt *kuruc* activities. Since 1672 the Empire was at war with Louis XIV, and could not spare forces to cope with Hungarian disorder. But the war with the French had also a more positive result in Hungary. Louis XIV had for some time been trying to create difficulties on the eastern borders of the Habsburg Empire, and so he welcomed the *kuruc* activities. His judgment was too sane and his approach to politics too realistic to allow him to offer serious financial help to the unorganized *kuruc* bands. He had more confidence in

Teleki to whom, through his ambassador Béthune and the Prince Apafi, he promised 100,000 talers. Teleki was a mediocre soldier, and soon Imre Thököly, chief of the *kuruc* (then barely twenty years old), became the actual commander of the campaign launched in 1678 against Imperial territory. A pugnacious, reckless and rash young man, he was a good leader and a sly diplomat, but a poor general and was not of the stuff of which really great statesmen are made. His initial successes, due as much to his own gallantry as to the French and Polish aid he was receiving, obtained for him the honour of being elected, on January 8, 1680, Commander-in-Chief of the *kuruc* forces. With the conclusion of the Peace of Nimeguen, Louis XIV lost interest in the Hungarian rebellion, and for a more efficient government than that of Leopold it would have been possible to eradicate the whole source of trouble. Instead of embarking on a counter-offensive Leopold made a sudden *volte-face* and in 1681 convoked the Diet at Sopron.

The Diet, at which the office of *nádor* was once again filled, marked by its very existence a return to more normal government. Some of the dispositions of the Treaty of Vienna (1604, cf. p. 182) and of the Treaty of Linz (1645) were renewed, but religious freedom was recognized only with important qualifications. Difference was made between private and public worship, and, for Protestants, the latter was limited, in Western Hungary, to certain places previously fixed. Perhaps even more important in its consequences was that the religious practices of the *jobbágy* were again made dependent on his lord. The constitutional concessions made by Leopold were more important: the freedom of the country, and the privileges of the nobles, were explicitly recognized, foreign troops were to be withdrawn and the discharge of the Hungarian garrisons of the fortresses was to be stopped. These concessions were tantamount to an admission of the complete failure of Montecuccoli's and Lobkowitz's attempts to suppress the Hungarian nation. Perhaps this was an opportunity to make a fresh start in the relations between Hungary and the dynasty, but it was lost through Thököly's ambition.

Thököly had recently married Ilona Zrinyi, widow of Francis Rákóczi, and had thus added his wife's immense fortune to his own considerable estates. Now he was trying to become Prince of either Transylvania or Hungary, or preferably both. His ambition cleverly fanned by the Turks, grew steadily, and in 1682, jointly with the Turks, he made a successful attack against the Habsburg-held territories. He was made Prince of Hungary by the Turks (he had enough common sense not to accept the title of King), so that for a short period the unfortunate country was torn into four parts: Transylvania, Thököly's 'kingdom', the small portion still in Habsburg hands, and finally the great Turkish zone of occupation. This meant that practically the whole country was, directly or indirectly, in Turkish hands. By their short-sighted idiocy, the Viennese politicians had succeeded in a seemingly impossible task: they had made the Turkish régime appear less odious than that of the Germans. Not that the basic hatred of the Hungarians towards the Turks had changed, but the Habsburg alternative no longer appeared more attractive. It was at this juncture, when Habsburg authority was at its lowest ebb, that the tide suddenly turned.

Encouraged by recent successes, the Turks prepared another full-scale attack against Vienna, the city they had not been able to conquer in 1529. In 1683 a huge Turkish army under the command of Kara Mustafa set out with the avowed aim of attacking Vienna. Leopold, unable to grasp the real significance of the Turkish action, was dreaming of obtaining peace. As so often before only the Pope, Innocent XI, saw clearly both the danger the new Turkish offensive meant for Christendom, and also the possibility of liberating the occupied territories. His indefatigable activities brought about a treaty between Leopold and the Polish King, John Sobiesky; it was his influence that made Louis XIV abstain for a while from continuing his attacks on the Empire; and he also put considerable sums at Leopold's disposal. For two months, from July to September 1683 the Turks besieged Vienna, splendidly defended by Stahremberg. On September 12th the relief forces, under the command of Charles of Lotharingia, comprising the troops of Sobiesky, swept away the Turkish army. Kara Mustafa fled to Belgrade where, on the order of the Sultan, he was strangled.

The victory had an electrifying effect on all concerned, including Leopold, and busy Papal ambassadors, with Buonvisi among them, succeeded in forging a tripartite alliance comprising, besides Austria, Poland and Venice. Leopold in these supreme moments of decision found support and help from his religious convictions, and in the light of opening horizons saw with greater clarity the historical rôle of Hungary and his own relationship with that 'bulwark of Christianity'.

The sixteen years of the campaign which liberated Hungary from the Turkish yoke cannot be adequately treated here. Fortunately,

Montecuccoli was no longer there to hamper operations, which assumed more and more the characteristics of a crusade. The Commander-in-Chief, Charles of Lotharingia, led his troops with courage but not without due caution, and red tape and personal intrigues could neither paralyse his efforts nor dislodge him from his leading position. The year of 1686 was marked by the reconquest of Buda, heroically defended by the Turkish garrison. The besieging army was truly international and comprised Brandenburgian (7,000), Swedish (2,000), Bavarian, Frankish, Italian, English and Scottish soldiers, and also—we should not omit them—sixty craftsmen from Barcelona. After 145 years of Turkish occupation Buda, reduced to smouldering ruins, was once again in Christian hands.

Though Austrians and Hungarians were united in their desire to expel the Turks, this basic unity of purpose did not solve all the outstanding problems. High among these stood the question of Thököly's future and that of Transylvania.

There is little to say of Thököly's personal fate. Immediately after the deliverance of Vienna, Imperial troops, pursuing the Turks, reconquered a number of towns belonging to Thököly's 'kingdom'. The coming years showed fully Thököly's dishonourable and worthless character. Unable to grasp the importance of the change in Imperial policy towards the Turks, he continued to rely on Turkish help and tried to compensate with muddled diplomacy and senseless cruelty for his lack of sound political aims and of military power. On October 15, 1685, in the mistaken belief that his person might represent some bargaining value, the Turks themselves arrested Thököly. Soon released, he became simply a pawn in the losing game played by the Turks. After 1699 he lived in Asia, on a pension granted to him by the Sultan. He died in 1705 at the early age of forty-eight.

The destinies of an independent Transylvania were also fast approaching their end. Not unlike Thököly, neither Apafi nor his chief counsellor Teleki could see that the days of Turkish power in Hungary were numbered. Austrian policy towards Transylvania was also hesitant; the principality had become such a constant factor in eastern European politics that the idea of simply suppressing it and re-incorporating the area in Hungary did not readily present itself. As there was no one in Transylvania able to produce a working project for settling the principality's relations with the dynasty, and still less anyone who could have implemented any decisions taken, the solution of the problem came about by force of circumstances rather than by the will of the parties concerned.

The Transylvanian Estates were thoroughly hostile to the Habsburgs and refused to accept quite reasonable projects of compromise, such as the *Tractatus Hallerianus*, signed in 1686 by Leopold and in the name of Apafi by his counsellor, John Haller. French influence had its part in this refusal, but the success of Buda's reconquest made the Emperor less amenable, and he dispatched Charles of Lotharingia to Transylvania; the country, occupied by Imperial troops, had to assent to the agreement of Balázsfalva (October 27, 1687). This agreement, less favourable than the *Tractatus* which the Estates had refused to ratify, satisfied neither of the signatories. Things were further complicated by the death of Apafi, who was succeeded by his son Michael Apafi II (1690), who never exercised effective power. At the news of Apafi's death the Sultan—still liege lord of Transylvania—produced from the lumber-room Thököly, whom he appointed Prince of Transylvania. In June 1690 Thököly entered Transylvania, and as he was successful in his first battle with the Imperial forces—in which his only rival, Michael Teleki, lost his life—the Estates elected him Prince of Transylvania. A few months later he was driven out by the forces of Louis of Baden, never again to return.

It was Thököly's fate to serve his country in quite unexpected ways. His last Transylvanian adventure—useless as it might seem—produced favourable results. Leopold, quite rightly, felt that it would be unwise to push Transylvania towards extremist solutions, and his *Diploma Leopoldianum*, issued on December 4, 1691, contained a settlement which, in the given circumstances, was surprisingly moderate in its terms. It guaranteed Transylvania's own constitution, religious freedom, and the convocation every year of the Diet. Only Transylvanians were to be appointed as state officials, with the exception of the Commander-in-Chief, who was to be a German, but who was to have no rights of interference in Transylvania's internal affairs. The most important change concerned the Prince himself. Michael Apafi II was replaced by a governor until his coming of age. (In fact, in 1696 he was taken to Vienna, where he later abdicated.) A couple of years later, in 1693, the so-called *Alvincziana resolutio*, by separating the Transylvanian and Hungarian chancelleries and by transferring the seat of the former to Vienna, subordinated the country directly to the Emperor. In fact Transylvania became one of the Emperor's many lands, governed separately from Hungary, though it always remained, legally, part of the territories belonging to the Hungarian Holy Crown. Only a century and a half later, the revolution of 1848 was to effect the reunion of Transylvania with the motherland.

The conquest of Buda had been only a step, though admittedly a very important one, on the road leading to Hungary's complete liberation. In spite of internal dissensions, the Imperial army, since 1688 under the command of the Bavarian Elector Max Emmanuel, was writing the most glorious pages of its history. Its operations were no longer the sterile military deployments so dear to Montecuccoli, but boldly-conducted campaigns, whose aim was no longer to provide a *raison d'être* for generals, but to annihilate the enemy. At the battle of Szalánkemen, fought on August 19, 1691, in which the commanding general Louis of Baden took part in person, 20,000 Turks, among them the grand vizier Mustafa Köprülü, lost their lives.

The French ambassador was present in Köprülü's camp, fortified by French sappers. Since 1688 Louis XIV and the Empire had been at war with each other, and desperate French efforts were made to push the Turks into continuing their war effort. The bridge built at Zenta over the Tisza—another work of French sappers—witnessed on September 4, 1697, a splendid victory by Prince Eugene of Savoy, possibly the best general the Imperial army had ever produced. Pursuing the enemy, Eugene penetrated further south and occupied Sarajevo. The military situation authorized hopes that the Turks would be driven back to Asia. If this did not come about, it was due to the policies of Western Europe. Though the Peace of Ryswick in 1687 put an end to the war with Louis XIV, Leopold's lands were utterly exhausted by the double war effort so long and so brilliantly sustained. As things stood, the peace proposals of the Sultan, transmitted to the Emperor by the British ambassador, Lord Paget, were well received, so much the more that the state of health of Charles II of Spain foreshadowed a fight for the Spanish succession. In the treaty signed at Karlovic (Karlóca) on January 26, 1699, the Turks renounced their claims to Hungary and Transylvania. Only the territory lying between the rivers Maros and Tisza remained under Turkish rule, but even this zone had to be demilitarized. Hungary was liberated from the Turkish yoke.

CHAPTER 21

THE BALANCE-SHEET OF THE
TURKISH OCCUPATION

HOWEVER hardened the historian may be—and the sixteenth and seventeenth centuries, with all the horrors of the Thirty Years War, constitute in this respect a good training—he cannot help being deeply moved when casting up the tragic balance-sheet of the Turkish occupation of Hungary. Perhaps only the Mongol devastations in the Middle East can compare with the utter, senseless, useless ruin Turkish domination brought to Hungary. It in no way diminishes the great military and political achievements of the Ottoman Empire to say that its civilization was much inferior to that of the flourishing Hungary of Matthias. The Turkish occupation not only halted the development of the country for a century and a half, it actually reduced Hungary, in many respects, to a state similar to that in which Árpád's tribe had found it eight centuries earlier.

We can only attempt here to give some of the main headings under which the catastrophic consequences of the occupation can be grouped.

Possibly the principal disaster, from which, directly or indirectly, all the others flowed, was the country's depopulation. This was not caused solely by the constant warfare, for those who died in actual fighting were but a fraction of the total lost. The Ottoman Empire was a slave-power, and Hungarian slaves were a much sought after merchandise. The population was deported by tens of thousands; a constant stream of Hungarian slaves flowed towards the Balkans, Constantinople and further away to Asia Minor and Egypt. The Turks were not particularly cruel, and the treatment meted out to their slaves was, gauged by the standards of the epoch, far from unbearable. But the sufferings to be endured before reaching the haven—if one may use the word—of the slave-market in Constantinople, proved too much even for these hardened men and women. The wastage in transport was tremendous. The manhunts of the Tartars of the Crimea, auxiliaries of the Turkish troops, were particularly dreaded. The result was appalling. The *megye* of Somogy, which numbered 11,000 households at the end of the fifteenth century, had in 1546 only 1,239, and by 1671 the figure had diminished to 106. The township of Nagyszalonta, numbering 384 households in 1552, had none left by 1566. These are merely examples taken at random to illustrate what in fact amounted to an almost complete de-population of the Great Hungarian Plain and the south-western part of Transdanubia. Exodus towards the west or to Transylvania accounts for only a fraction of the population lost.

The disappearance of man had its physical effect on the land. At the close of the Middle Ages Hungary was a comparatively thickly-populated country, and the density of small villages and hamlets was greater than it has been ever since. In previous centuries the great forest of the Hungarian Plain had slowly given way to ploughland, but enough forest remained to ensure a satisfactory humidity. The arid climate of the plain and its poverty in water followed the destruction of the trees, and is a direct consequence of the Turkish occupation, the effects of which were not to be overcome. The once-flourishing country had become a waste, destroyed, uninhabited; and the soldiers or travellers who had to find their way through the roadless, deserted countryside spoke with horror of their experiences. The famous Hungarian *puszta* (a word meaning 'bare, deserted, bleak'), with its undeniable romantic appeal, is not a work of nature; it is the work of the Turks.

Lack of human control allowed the waters to take possession of huge expanses. Streams, rivulets and rivers no longer kept within their banks by man's efforts, joined their waters and created huge marshes, suitable to hide in at the approach of a new group of Tartars, but fit for nothing else. These marshes poisoned the atmosphere: typhoid fever, malaria, dysentery, the much dreaded and ill-defined *morbus Hungaricus*, decimated those who survived the devastations of war.

The vacuum created could never be filled again by Hungarians. Partially, at least, it was filled by others.

In examining, however briefly, the migration of foreign peoples into Hungary, one must answer the preliminary questions of why other populations had sustained smaller losses than the Hungarians in the war against the Turks, and how the immigrants could survive in regions which, as we have just shown, were barely suitable for human habitation.

The answer to the first question is fairly simple. The populations of the Balkans, whence most of the immigrants came, though under Turkish rule for almost two centuries, were not engaged in effective warfare. Their losses, though heavy, cannot be compared to the terrible blood-letting to which Hungary was submitted. The second question finds its answer in the immigrants' modest requirements. The ruins of a village, deserted by the Hungarian survivors of some Turkish raid, were still acceptable dwellings for the immigrants who arrived there in the wake of Turkish troops.

The general direction of this migration was, as could be expected, south to north, and the main ethnic groups it brought to Hungarian territory were Croats, Serbs and Roumanians.

The central part of Hungary's southern border was the main road of penetration for the Serbs, who went as deep into the country as the towns of Kecskemét, Nagykörös and Cegléd. This Serbian penetration was not always peaceful, for Serbs were often found among the auxiliary Turkish troops. Some Serbs engaged in commerce, particularly in cattle trading, others were put in charge of tax-collecting by the Turks and similar highly profitable occupations. These well-to-do Serbs soon reached the cultural level of the Hungarian population with whom, on the whole, they got on well. Croat immigration had started before the Turkish conquest of Hungary, which gave it a further impetus. As early as in 1529 and 1532, Croat settlers penetrated into the depopulated south-western areas, and successive Turkish devastations made it possible for Croats to penetrate so far north as to reach the Danube and thus join the Slavonic populations of North-Western Hungary. A Slavonic belt, in the form of a semicircle reaching from the north to the south and open towards the east, was slowly sealing off the Hungarian populations from the west. The northernmost section of this arc was occupied by the Ruthenians. These, coming from the northern slopes of the Carpathians, grazed their animals on inaccessible mountain pastures, and remained untouched by successive wars which destroyed the Hungarians. Once the fighting was over, the latter were not numerous enough to reconquer lost areas, and the Ruthenians, gradually expanding, penetrated into hitherto uninhabited mountainous regions on the southern slopes of the Carpathians.

In the east, Roumanian immigration took on extraordinary proportions. The internal conditions were such in Moldavia and Valachia, the exploitation by the ruling few so ruthless, that even life in Turkish-occupied Hungary seemed preferable to the oppressed serfs. The Hungarian lords, and the Saxon townships of Transylvania, equally short of manpower, welcomed the new immigrants. Other Roumanians, living on the lower reaches of the Danube, moved towards the Banat and the centre of the Hungarian Plain, and those who had lived, probably for some centuries, in the mountains separating Transylvania from the Hungarian Plain did likewise. In an adjacent region of the *megye* of Bihar, situated in the Plain, 42,000 Hungarians were counted in 1552. Half a century later their place had been taken by 5,000 Roumanians.

Other immigrations, less important, took place, and all contributed to change the ethnic composition of the country, to the detriment of the Hungarians, who for two centuries had shed their blood in their own defence as well as in that of Central and Western Europe. It is impossible to estimate the exact losses in population, for one would have to calculate the losses incurred through the interruption in its natural increase. A few figures may help to indicate the extent of the disaster. At the time of Matthias, Hungary proper had a population of approximately four million, a considerable figure if we accept the estimate that contemporary Europe was populated by some 80 million men. At the beginning of the seventeenth century, in a Europe of 130 million inhabitants, Hungary had but 2·5 million. Before the Turkish invasion approximately 80–85 per cent of the country's population was Hungarian; after the country's liberation this figure was reduced to 45 per cent: Hungarians had become a minority in their own country.

There can be no doubt that the great Hungarian historian Gyula Szekfü was right when he saw in the Turkish occupation the origin of all the subsequent misfortunes of the Hungarian nation.

CHAPTER 22

OUT OF THE FRYING-PAN
INTO THE FIRE

THE road leading to the Peace of Karlovici had not been an easy one, and the quick succession of victories strained to the utmost the physical and moral resources of an exhausted people.

The problem faced by Leopold was of an appalling magnitude. He had not only to reconquer the land but, simultaneously to install his administration. The situation was further complicated by the ill-defined national status of the reconquered territories, and by military, administrative and financial problems, all aggravated by divergencies over constitutional matters. Imperial and Hungarian interests were often opposed, and what seemed to Vienna, engaged on two fronts, a useless squabble about formalities, seemed to the Hungarians, and in fact was, a life-and-death struggle for their continued existence as a nation.

It was fortunate indeed for the nation that Thököly's insurrection had led, in 1681, to the convocation of the Diet and the re-establishment of the Constitution. Though the promises then given were not kept, and no Diets were held, at least theoretically, the country had a constitution and a *nádor*, Paul Eszterházy, who to some extent could counter-balance the absolutist tendencies of the Viennese government. It must be admitted, however, that on the whole the Hungarian Estates showed once again an astonishing irresponsibility.

In 1687 the Diet was convoked and the Government called on the Estates to set up a commission to study the reform of the country's administration. As the Estates declined to do so, the following year, another commission, this time purely foreign, was set up under the chairmanship of Leopold Kollonich. The project, put forward by this avowed enemy of the Hungarians, had something to commend it in social matters, but took no account of Hungary's interests as an independent nation. Kollonich was a man of integrity, but something of a theoretician, who took for granted that decisions taken by a central organ would be effectively carried out by local authorities. This was by no means so, and the actual burden resting on the population was much heavier than that envisaged by the Government which was already very oppressive. The country had been completely abandoned to the plundering, violence, and molestations of undisciplined foreign troops, whose members, from the general down to the trooper, had only one thing in mind: to squeeze out the maximum from the population by any means whatever. The cruelty, the impudence, the greed, the inhumanity of this 'army of liberation' surpassed everything the Turks, as individuals, had ever done, and more than justified Bethlen's and Thököly's pessimistic forebodings of what would happen to Hungary if liberated from the Turks by German troops. Perhaps the most harmful individual was the *Generalkriegskommissär* Carafa. His bestial cruelty and shameless extortions—very often for his own benefit—shocked the Government, though somewhat belatedly, and the Diet of 1687 marks the end of his nefarious activities. Carafa's influence remained strong enough to have an adverse effect on Kollonich's projects, the implementation of which would have threatened discovery to his own malpractices. So in fact Carafa and the Hungarians joined forces against Kollonich's projects, which were shelved. However unfavourable for the Hungarians as a nation, these represented the only serious attempt to cleanse the Augean administration of the reconquered lands and to ease the burden of the common man. The failure of Kollonich's plan entailed the continuation of the anarchy which ultimately was to lead to Rákóczi's rebellion.

The failure of Kollonich's project was not in itself sufficient to administer the reconquered land and the task was entrusted partially to the army, partially to the Hofkammer in Vienna. As the spheres of authority were not clearly defined, a constant tug of war ensued, which diminished even further the benefits the administration could have brought to the population. There was a basic problem to solve: what to do with the reconquered territories. In 1690 a *Commissio neoacquistica* was set up to examine the claims of the former landowners, and to dispose of unclaimed land. Both activities of the Commission gave splendid opportunities for corruption and for anti-Hungarian measures.

In order to acquire possession of the land, the noble had not only to prove (which was not always easy) his right to the land thus claimed; he had also to pay for it, and the sums exacted were often so high that only members of the greater nobility could afford them. The deserted land lent itself to the creation of huge estates, all in one piece, and it is not surprising that those in charge of higher offices, mostly foreigners, but also Hungarians such as the *nádor* Eszterházy, availed themselves of this opportunity. They could do so the more easily as there was a general shortage of applicants, and the Commission found it difficult to find buyers for the deserted lands. Its task was somewhat easier in the towns, but there were simply not enough men to go round, and by using foreign settlers Kollonich tried to achieve a three-fold aim. In fact he was credited with the saying that he intended the Hungarians to become first beggars, then Catholics, and finally Germans. To break the backbone of the nation the Austrian administration tried to plant foreign populations on Hungarian soil, populations which enjoyed special privileges and which were to be trusted allies of the Viennese government against the Hungarians. It was Kollonich who launched the idea, which then for a century or more became an axiom in government circles, that it was essential that the kingdom of Hungary be Germanized so that 'Hungarian blood prone to revolutions and to restlessness be allayed by German blood so as to become faithful and attached towards his natural lord and his hereditary king'.

It was the great tragedy of the Habsburgs that they failed to realize that—in spite of their spirit of independence, or perhaps because of it— the Hungarians were the most reliable and most loyal people within their Empire. It was not the Hungarians but the cherished Slavonic populations which were to become instrumental, in the twentieth century, in the disintegration of the Habsburg Empire.

The first steps towards foreign settlements were taken at the end of the seventeenth century. We have already mentioned the Serb penetration into Hungary which took place during the Turkish occupation. It is probable that many of these Serb settlements—the word is too dignified in fact for the abodes of these primitive, wandering peoples— were wiped out during the wars of liberation. During the penetration into the Balkans of the Imperial army, direct contacts had been established between Austrians and Serbs, and the latter asked for their admittance into Hungarian territories. The idea appealed to Vienna and in the following years efforts were made to secure the allegiance of the Serbs. When the Imperial troops, unable to liberate Serbia from the Turks, had to withdraw from the Balkans, they were followed in their retreat by some 200,000 Serbs who, under the leadership of the Patriarch Chernovitch, entered Hungarian territory. A diploma given to them by Leopold on August 20, 1691, granted or confirmed considerable privileges. This was done on the supposition that the Serbs were refugees, who would eventually return to their former homes in the Balkans. As things turned out, the Balkans remained under Turkish rule, and the Serbs settled in Hungary. At the time of their immigration, great parts of the Hungarian Plain were still occupied by the Turks, and the Serbs found it more prudent to avoid the neighbourhood of their former masters. They were therefore established in the central and northern parts of Transdanubia.

A curious situation arose: the Serbs, evoking the privileges recently granted to them, refused to shoulder the burdens of the local Hungarian populations, particularly that of providing for the billeted troops. They were right from their own point of view, but the privileges had initially been granted for Serbs living in Serbia, and the Serbs, by holding to them in Hungary, separated themselves from the rest of the population. It is not difficult to imagine the Hungarians' resentment against these refugees installed among them.

Fortunately for Hungary the Transdanubian parts of the country were much too civilized for these new emigrants, semi-nomadic herdsmen living in tents or primitive huts half-dug into the ground. They preferred the more deserted regions, and—not without difficulties —they were installed in the south on land belonging to the *megyes*, Bács, Bodrog, Csanád, Csongrád.

The Serb immigrants were designedly kept as a political entity, and in the coming years they were entrusted with the defence of the country's southern borders. The whole southern strip of Hungary, from the Adriatic to Transylvania, was thus given to an alien people whose ethnic, linguistic and religious connections remained with their brethren living beyond the borderline. In fact, an alien people was put in defence of a frontier separating them from their own kin. Even in the wonderland of Austrian administration it must have been realized how unreliable these frontier guards would be in case of a conflict with Hungary's southern neighbours. However, they could be used, and when occasion arose were used, against the Hungarians. The main aim in their installation as a compact national entity, directly dependent on Vienna and organized on a military basis, was to have a trustworthy ally at the back of the untrustworthy Hungarians. The supreme irony of the situation thus created was that the Hungarian state was supposed to provide for the maintenance of its own enemies.

The problem of nationalities, in the modern sense of this word, was unknown in the seventeenth century. Slavs, Hungarians, Roumanians, indiscriminately joined forces with this or the other side in the many conflicts; the armies of Bethlen or of Thököly were mixed. The deliberate policy of the Viennese government, to pit one nationality against another, created the conflict which was to be the cause of so many tragedies in Eastern Europe.

CHAPTER 23

THE RÁKÓCZI REBELLION

THE general misery which, as we have seen, had many causes and affected most strata of the population, engendered a discontent, which was bound sooner or later to provoke an explosion. During the summer of 1697 a rebellion broke out in the Highlands under the leadership of Francis Tokaji. Distinctly social in its aim, and without a head capable of commanding nation-wide support, this movement was quelled fairly easily.

This was not the case with Rákóczi's insurrection, which lasted for eight years and which, eventually, secured a new basis for the relations between nation and dynasty.

Francis Rákóczi II was born on March 27, 1676. Grandson of George Rákóczi II, he was the son of Francis Rákóczi I and Ilona Zrinyi. Both on the paternal and maternal sides he belonged to immensely rich and distinguished families who were, however, traditionally opposed to Habsburg absolutism. His mother, daughter of Peter Zrinyi, executed after the failure of the Wesselényi conspiracy, was a niece of Nicholas Zrinyi, the great general and writer. Francis Rákóczi I, a rather dull man, had also been involved in the Wesselényi conspiracy, but was saved by the intervention of his mother, Sophie Báthory, and by the payment of an enormous ransom. His maternal grandmother, Catherine Frangepan —issue of a most distinguished family—was the sister of Francis Frangepan, executed at the same time as Peter Zrinyi. To complete the picture, after the death of her husband, which occurred when Francis was only a few months old, Ilona Zrinyi married Imre Thököly. At the side of his stepfather the young child soon learned to know the miseries of warfare, and he also took part in the defence of Munkács, maintained by his mother for three years against the Imperial troops. After the capitulation of Munkács, mother and child were soon separated. Ilona Zrinyi left for Turkey to join Thököly, Francis Rákóczi and his elder sister Juliana were left to the care of Leopold, who entrusted them to Kollonich.

It is not difficult to imagine the sort of education the Rákóczi children received from their illustrious tutor. Immense care was taken to make Francis forget his obligations towards his country and to attach him, as far as possible, to the dynasty. Leopold emancipated him at the age of eighteen and he was allowed to make an inspection of his Hungarian estates. Though for security's sake he was kept under constant surveillance, he did not seem to present any real danger to Vienna; by that time he could hardly speak Hungarian! His first visit to his estates was not decisive in Rákóczi's political development. Though deeply moved by the sufferings of his *jobbágys*, which he sought to alleviate, his main concern was to ensure that his activities should not be interpreted in Vienna as directed against the dynasty. In 1695 he married and had a child, who soon after died. Rákóczi was most anxious not to become involved in politics. The people of the Highlands, where most of his estates were situated, looked on him as their natural leader, and Tokaji, head of the rebellion we have already mentioned, tried to offer its leadership to Rákóczi, who, however, felt no inclination to accept it. He literally fled to Vienna to make it perfectly clear that he had no connections with the rebellion. In spite of his extreme wariness, he could not but feel the suspicion with which his movements were followed in Vienna. Irritated, he suggested to the Emperor that he should exchange all his estates for others, situated in Austria or Germany. It is not quite clear why this offer was not accepted by Leopold. Court intrigues and the desire to keep such a 'loyal' subject in Hungary must both have played a part in the decision. It only remained for Rákóczi to return to his estates (1698), and though it would be interesting to follow step by step the evolution of this *revolutionnaire malgré lui*, the scope of our book does not allow us to do so.

During the coming years Rákóczi's efforts were directed towards the reorganization of his estates. Living among Hungarians, he gradually became aware of his responsibilities, and—with the advice of his friend and counsellor Nicholas Bercsényi—reached the conclusion that only an alliance with the French could save Hungary from the Habsburg yoke. In 1700, whilst in Vienna, on the very day on which Charles II of

Spain died, Rákóczi sent a letter to Louis XIV. The Minister of War of this great king, Barbezieux answered his letter, and the correspondence was intercepted by the Austrians. Rákóczi was arrested and would probably have followed his grandfather (whose cell in Wienerneustadt he occupied) to the scaffold, had the devotion of a Prussian officer, the efforts of his wife, and his own temerity not helped him in an escape which still awaits a Dumas to describe it. He fled to Poland, where he was joined by Bercsényi.

At that time the country was full of uprooted men, old soldiers, *kurucs*, followers of Thököly, all very embittered, knowing no other trade than fighting, having no other wish than to be treated as free men. It was one of the Viennese government's bad mistakes that it did not settle these men on the southern border, for thereby their rebellious feelings would have been assuaged, and they would have discharged their duties as frontier guards with more benefit to the country than did the Serbs.

Rákóczi's imprisonment had shown—so it was thought—that he was willing to fight the Habsburgs; his escape stirred the popular imagination. The wretched people, in whose ranks a *jobbágy*, Thomas Esze, was playing an increasingly important rôle, decided to call upon Rákóczi and ask for his leadership in a new insurrection.

Rákóczi had made up his mind to fight the Habsburgs, but was uncertain on the method to adopt. He was more inclined to rely on foreign help (especially French), than to ally himself with the common people in what might easily degenerate into a simple peasant revolt. For a man of his background and education this seemed an almost impossible course to follow. Nevertheless the impossible became true: the richest magnate in the land, the civilized and much-travelled descendant of the Princes of Transylvania, joined with the destitute, the deprived, the peasants, all the down-trodden population in an effort to free their country from foreign exploitation. Rákóczi broke through the inhuman barriers erected by Werböczi on the basis of older class distinctions. For him the nation was no longer the private property of the nobles; he recognized the human dignity of all, their right to lead a life worth living. By doing so, and by doing so without the slightest trace of demagogy, he made the *jobbágys* realize their duties towards their country. Not only Hungarians, but Slovaks, Roumanians, Ruthenians, joined the fight for what they rightly considered their common interest; only the newly-immigrated Serbs remained aloof. Rákóczi's insurrection created a unity unparalleled among similar movements in Hungary. His liberal approach towards class distinctions was far in advance of his time.

In a manifesto issued on May 7, 1703, while he was still in Poland, and signed also by Bercsényi, Rákóczi called on all Hungarians to take up arms against the Habsburgs, whose nefarious activities he circumstantially described. His appeal was well received, particularly by those who had called on him to lead them. But when, a month after having issued his manifesto, Rákóczi entered the country, he found that the bulk of his would-be followers had already been dispersed by Alexander Károlyi, and he was received at the border by an ill-clad, undisciplined little band of some three hundred *jobbágys*.

Vienna, at this stage, failed to recognize the importance of the movement started by Rákóczi, and it was thought that Károlyi's action had nipped it in the bud. As usual the wise men of the Viennese Court were wrong. Soon the *kuruc* forces of Rákóczi gathered strength; by November he had 30,000 men, and one after the other important towns were capitulating and joining the forces of rebellion. The nobles, reluctant at the beginning, having on several occasions fought the *kurucs*, were slow to give their support to Rákóczi. The Prince did his best to enlighten them and also foreign powers on the true character of his movement, and his famous manifesto *Recrudescunt vulnera inclytae gentis Hungariae* did much in this direction. More and more nobles and magnates came to join him, among them Alexander Károlyi himself. By the beginning of 1704 the greater part of the country had joined Rákóczi.

The difficulties facing Rákóczi were enormous, and in trying to overcome them he showed the full measure of his extraordinary genius. Never losing sight of the great issues at stake, he had a keen eye for details and an uncommon reluctance to cause suffering; to measure the extent of his labours one must consider the magnitude of his undertaking, namely the defeat of the Habsburgs with the strength of an impoverished, utterly exhausted and disunited nation.

The *kuruc* army, in spite of all the personal courage of its soldiers and the gallantry of some of its generals, was not capable of securing decisive victories against the Imperial forces. Rákóczi himself was a competent soldier but not a military genius. Hesitant, somewhat slow, he lacked the ruthlessness and the temerity which can sometimes compensate for the lack of power, equipment and organization. He also proved unable to ensure the execution of his orders by field-commanders, and many battles were lost for this reason. At the outset of the campaign his army had been a peasant force, and only from the spring of 1704 onwards did nobles begin to be represented in any numbers in the body of officers. This meant a slight improvement in its intellectual level, but was still not enough. Rákóczi made desperate efforts to improve the efficiency of his army; he made them do regular exercises, provided them with uniforms, and in general took great interest in their well-being as well as in their discipline. In spite of his endeavours strategic blunders were common and the efficiency of his artillery remained very low. It sounds a platitude, but it is worth saying, that the principal cause of Rákóczi's ultimate failure was his inability to defeat the Imperial army.

Efforts to secure foreign help sufficient to force a decision proved unsuccessful. Times had changed since Bethlen lived, and the Habsburgs were on friendly relations with many of their former enemies. Two great powers were likely, however, to have an interest in Rákóczi's rebellion: the Turks, and above all the French.

Thököly was still alive and pinned great hopes to his stepson's activity. As emigrants generally do, he tried to induce the country in which he had taken refuge, Turkey, to intervene against the régime in power in his native land. It was his only hope—as he put it quite candidly himself—to play again a political rôle. More important was the pressure put on the Sultan by the French, who tried to induce the Turks to renew their attacks on the Habsburgs. The French ambassador brought his influence to bear in favour of Rákóczi, but the joint efforts of Imperial, English and Dutch diplomats persuaded the Turks to respect the Treaty of Karlovici and to abstain from helping the rebellion. That this abstention was not complete goes almost without saying, but the help given to Rákóczi was much too insignificant noticeably to influence the final outcome.

The effect western diplomacy had on Rákóczi's insurrection manifested itself in two ways. Louis XIV, whilst providing help to the rebels, encouraged them to continue their fight and to ignore possibilities of compromise. The Dutch and the English, particularly the latter, though theoretically hostile towards an insurrection directed against their Imperial ally, put considerable pressure on Leopold to compound with his unruly subjects. English diplomats (Stepney, Whitworth) were busily engaged in convincing the Austrians that only by making concessions (which would cost their advisers nothing) would they be able to re-establish the internal peace necessary for a victorious pursuit of their common war against the French. The English, as usual, were exasperated by the muddle in which they found their allies, and proposed remedies, excellent in themselves, but too bitter for the patient to swallow.

Vienna sought other means to assuage Rákóczi, who, on his past record, was not believed to be ruthless enough for a revolutionary leader. A lady to whom in his youth he had paid much attention was dispatched to win him over to occupations more pleasurable than warfare, but she failed in her mission and attempts to drive a wedge between Rákóczi and Bercsényi—considered as the more dangerous of the two—were no more successful. Old-fashioned ideas, such as that of assassinating Rákóczi, were toyed with, causing much displeasure to the English ambassador.

The Dutch and the English were—as we have said—Rákóczi's best allies through their ceaseless efforts to persuade Leopold to adopt a conciliatory attitude. In November 1703 Whitworth—replacing the ambassador Stepney during a temporary absence—prophesied that in order to cope with Rákóczi the Emperor would have to make peace with Louis XIV. Under the influence of his report Queen Anne declared herself ready to mediate. Vienna was most reluctant to accept foreign mediation, and endeavours were made to establish contacts with Rákóczi through the intermediary of Hungarians loyal to the court. As these failed, in February 1704 Leopold reluctantly agreed to accept the good offices of Whitworth and of the Dutch ambassador Bruyninx, who in fact got in touch with Bercsényi, still considered the moving spirit of the insurrection.

The Dutch and English diplomats looked with growing sympathy on Rákóczi, and the cruelties of the Imperial troops, who in the spring of 1704 succeeded in reconquering Transdanubia, alienated such English sympathy as survived. The indefatigable Daniel Defoe, whilst in jail, wrote a memorandum suggesting that if the Emperor could not be induced to yield to the demands of the Hungarians, a million pounds be advanced to Rákóczi to help him to set up an independent Hungary and Transylvania, of which he would become king. The ambassador

Stepney was of the opinion that if Rákóczi had the wish to become King
of Hungary, no one could prevent him, but he seemed to have no such
ambitions and was not particularly pleased when the Transylvanian
Estates, gathered on July 5, 1704, elected him Prince of Transylvania.
In fact it was one of Rákóczi's chief difficulties that he could not find a
suitable alternative to a Habsburg king.

The first candidate, the Bavarian Elector Max Emmanuel, could no
longer be considered after the battle of Blenheim (August 13, 1704).
Marlborough's great victory did not diminish the English desire to find
a peaceful solution to the problems raised by Rákóczi, but it made the
Austrians more intransigent and particularly Prince Eugene of Savoy,
who advocated a purely military settlement. It was probably Blenheim
which prompted Louis XIV to pay more heed to Rákóczi, and to
multiply the efforts intended to prevent his abandoning the struggle
against the Habsburgs.

Louis's first ambassador to Rákóczi, Fierville, arrived as early as
February 1704. In April of the same year the French king decided that
the more experienced Des Alleurs should take his place, but owing to
various difficulties (he had to travel by Constantinople) the new
ambassador reached Rákóczi only in 1705. Fierville, though theoretically
a diplomat, was in fact much more a military adviser, and French
officers reached the rebel forces in greater numbers in October 1704.
They proved useful but not numerous enough to force a military
decision in favour of Rákóczi. French financial help was steadily
forthcoming and was of great use to the insurrection.

With Louis XIV supporting more strongly than ever the continuation
of the war, the Dutch and the English redoubled their efforts to make
peace. They foundered on Austrian stubbornness. Stepney had a long
personal discussion with Rákóczi, who explained in great detail the
background and the aims of the revolution. He compared the relation
of Austria and Hungary with the one existing at that epoch between
England and Scotland, and compared Austrian treatment of Hungary
with that meted out to the Irish. Stepney was very favourably impressed
both by Rákóczi's character and by the equity of the cause he represented, and his exasperation against the Austrians, his allies, grew
steadily.

On December 26, 1704, the rebel forces suffered a telling defeat,
telling mainly in so far as it stiffened the Austrian attitude. Leopold's

death, on May 5, 1705, and the accession of his son Joseph I (1705–11) made no real change in the official approach.

The accession of the new king brought to the forefront difficult constitutional problems, since the Hungarians had refused to recognize the Habsburg hereditary claim to the throne of Hungary, and Joseph I had not been elected King of Hungary. To clarify matters Rákóczi convened a general assembly of the Estates (there was some argument about whether this assembly could be called a Diet), which in an atmosphere of general confusion decided to create, following Polish example, a confederation of the Estates, with Rákóczi as its leader. A new title was invented for this office and conferred upon him. This assembly, held at Szécsény, aimed at the re-establishment of the constitution previous to 1687 and in general set conditions whose acceptance would have been tantamount to a complete reversal of Leopold's semi-secular policy.

Rákóczi was as intransigent as the Dynasty, but the latter could better afford such an attitude. Negotiations and fighting went on with alternating success and growing weariness among the rebels. The burden of a lengthy war was too heavy for Hungary, and Rákóczi had great difficulties in keeping up the morale of his supporters. He pinned his hopes on French help; it was the recurrent Hungarian mistake to join with the virtually defeated. Louis XIV himself was in a difficult situation, and his only aim was to create troubles for the Habsburgs. He refused to enter into a formal alliance with the rebels who were, after all, the subjects of Joseph I, as long as they recognized him as their king. His attitude was the principal cause of the decision taken on June 14, 1707, at the Diet of Ónod, to dethrone the Habsburgs and elect Rákóczi Prince of Hungary.

This fateful decision meant the burning of all bridges of possible retreat, and as there was no other alternative before Rákóczi but to continue fighting, Louis XIV saw no reason to go on supporting him, and started negotiations with Joseph I. Rákóczi, deprived of his principal foreign ally, made desperate attempts to find substitutes: Charles XII, Peter the Great, the son of the King of Prussia, were all approached with one plan or another, and so were the English and the Dutch. The plans petered out and mediation was made impossible by Rákóczi's insistence that Transylvania, which in 1707 had been re-conquered by Imperial troops, must remain independent. The long-drawn-out agony of the insurrection began in 1709. Several defections occurred in the Prince's entourage; some of his best lieutenants lost their lives in battle; from 1708 the ravages of the Black Death came to join those of the continuous warfare. It is difficult to understand the reasons which prompted Rákóczi to prolong a struggle which seemed hopeless to most of his contemporaries. As he had shown on several previous occasions that he disregarded his own personal interests, self-deception must be considered the mainspring of his action. He was probably convinced that if he only succeeded in keeping the war going, one of his many schemes would produce a coalition against the Habsburgs and the liberation of Hungary from their yoke. The general state of European politics was, however, not conducive to such a solution. The victory of the Tories in England marked the beginning of a more peaceful era which ultimately led to the conclusion of the Peace of Utrecht, followed by the Peace of Rastadt. In looking back we fully realize how unrealistic Rákóczi's plans were, and how the continuation of the fight would have brought no advantage to the country.

The merit of breaking the deadlock belongs to two Hungarians, one *kuruc* and one *labanc*, who with indefatigable zeal toiled, hampered by their respective masters, to secure peace. It goes almost without saying that, traditionally, both of them are regarded as traitors.

In the autumn of 1710 the Imperial Commander-in-Chief Heister, a cruel and inefficient soldier, whose successes were due exclusively to the even greater inefficiency of the *kuruc* generals, was replaced by a *labanc* Hungarian, John Pálffy. Pálffy's loyalty to the Habsburgs was beyond reproach, and his military capacities far greater than those of his predecessor. With considerable moral courage, instead of forcing a military victory, he made it his aim to work for a peaceful solution. Soon after his appointment he made contact with his old friend, Alexander Károlyi. Rákóczi did not oppose such negotiations, because he hoped from them for respite, but Pálffy, as Commander-in-Chief of the forces supposed to crush the rebels, found himself in an awkward position. An Austrian general was attached to him and after Joseph I's death (April 17, 1711) he was relieved of his post. Thanks to Prince Eugene's intervention he was, however, soon reinstated and a few days later he achieved his great aim—peace.

At the end of February 1711 Rákóczi had gone to Poland to meet Peter the Great, on whom he now pinned all his hopes. Károlyi, who tried to keep him informed of the negotiations, found himself more and more in a quandary, torn as he was between Pálffy, who urged him to accept the peace conditions, and Rákóczi, who without ordering the cessation of the negotiations raised legalistic objections which to Károlyi seemed, quite rightly, misplaced and made without regard for the real situation. Finally, on May 1, 1711, Pálffy and Károlyi—the latter without Rákóczi's consent—signed the Treaty of Szatmár, which put an end to the war which had lost its usefulness.

It must have been a moving sight indeed when, on the day preceding the signing of the treaty, the remaining core of the *kuruc* army, over 10,000 men, were passed in review by Pálffy and Károlyi. Discharged but not disarmed, the men returned to their homes; the war was lost, but at least there was peace and they did not have to capitulate to a foreign army. The 'enemy' Pálffy was as much a patriot as they themselves, and he saw to it that the amnesty given to the *kuruc* was respected. The arguments whether Pálffy and Károlyi were right in acting as they did has been continued ever since. There can be no doubt that most of their contemporaries received the news of peace with immense relief. The simple fact that the troops—not particularly well disciplined—obeyed Károlyi, and that those with Rákóczi in Poland left their much-loved Prince and returned to Hungary, illustrates this point well.

Apart from the fact that it put an end to hostilities, the Peace Treaty of Szatmár contained little to make the Hungarians rejoice. The conditions in it were more severe than those refused by Rákóczi in 1706, and concessions were made on four points only: (1) A general amnesty to everyone, including Rákóczi, if within three weeks he took the oath of allegiance; (2) Religious freedom; (3) Respect for the Constitution as formulated at the Diet of 1687–8; (4) Convocation of a Diet to discuss matters further.

The two main points, which in the past were so strongly made by Rákóczi, i.e. the independence of Transylvania, and foreign guarantees that the treaty would be adhered to, were not mentioned.

Rákóczi found it impossible to accept the peace terms and, having no confidence in Habsburg promises of amnesty, remained abroad, whence he vainly tried to interest foreign powers in Hungary's destinies. From Poland he went to France—landing in England was refused to him at Hull—where he found refuge. In spite of all their differences Rákóczi

had a great respect for Louis XIV, who received the exiled Prince with
due regard. Having spent three years in the court of Louis XIV, he felt
the desire to retire and to lead a life of contemplation and study. Though
for political reasons he went to Turkey in 1717, he never again played
an active political rôle. He died in 1735, an exile, surrounded by a few
faithful men who had followed him in his peregrination.

Rákóczi is perhaps the purest figure in Hungarian history. He lacked
the ruthlessness, the unscrupulousness necessary for a really successful
revolutionary leader. As a monarch he might have ranked among the
greatest. Love of the people, interest in details, and an uncommon
capacity for work were, perhaps, his greatest qualities. His literary work,
particularly his most moving *Confessions*, assure him an important place
in Hungarian literature. A Roman Catholic, he represented, against the
Habsburgs, the interests of Protestantism. At the height of his power as
well as in exile he behaved with a natural dignity that forced the
admiration of all who knew him. In the last twenty years of his life he
found peace in his deep Jansenist piety. This peace was not given to him
easily, his way to God was as much beset with obstacles as had been his
political career. To follow his life is a lesson in true humanity; this is the
reason why we could not resist the temptation to give it a little more
space than strictly necessary in a work as brief as the present one.

PART FIVE

UNDER HABSBURG RULE

CHAPTER 24

STABILIZATION:
CHARLES III, MARIA THERESA

THE Treaty of Szatmár coincided virtually with the accession of Charles III (Emperor Charles VI, 1711–40). A new era was to start in the history of Hungary, an era characterized by constitutional problems which, up to the fall of the Habsburgs, were to use up the greater part of Hungarian energies. During the eighteenth and part of the ninteenth centuries Hungary was not an independent state in so far as it could not exercise many of the rights with which a sovereign country is usually invested. For two centuries the country was to enjoy a relative peace, since the Seven Years War and the French Wars affected it but little, and the short 1848–9 revolution was the only serious breach of peace during a period which could have been one of development on a scale greater than elsewhere in Europe. But peace is not everything, and it was in these relatively calm and uneventful years that Hungary fell behind the West European countries in what was to be their advance to the general prosperity of the late nineteenth century.

Political history was at this period relatively uneventful, therefore, with Hungary having virtually no say in Habsburg policy. It would be preposterous in a short book like this to attempt to deal in detail with the foreign policy of the Habsburgs. Nor can it be our aim to sketch the social or economic history of the Empire of which, reluctantly, Hungary formed a part. Our task will be limited to outlining the special features in which Hungarian history differed from that of the rest of the Empire.

The dominating factor in the period following the Treaty of Szatmár is the constitutional struggle between the nobility, representing the nation, and the King. The struggle took the form of a compromise in which the nobility renounced the rights and advantages of the population as a whole and obtained in return the maintenance of its own privileges. Seldom has a ruling class struck a more shameful bargain. The struggle referred to was, therefore, not national in any real sense of the word, and the fact that the nobility entrenched, and later almost buried, in its anachronistic privileges succeeded in maintaining the continuity of the Hungarian nation, was in fact accidental.

Charles III showed considerable goodwill towards Hungary and under his reign the 'iron rod' policy of the tradition of Basta and Carafa was replaced by a more conciliatory and understanding attitude towards the country's special problems. It is quite clear that—apart from any personal sympathy the King may have felt towards his Hungarian subjects—the Rákóczi rebellion had brought home the lesson that it was easier to come to terms with the Hungarians than to force them to submit by sheer force.

To ensure the collaboration of the nation, the promise made in the Treaty of Szatmár concerning the convocation of Diets was respected. Diets met in 1712–15, 1722–3 and 1728–9, and only the last years of Charles's reign were marked by a deterioration in the relations between king and nation.

An additional reason for Charles's liberal attitude towards Hungary was his preoccupation with the succession. Charles was the last surviving male member of the Habsburgs. A family agreement, concluded in 1703, stipulated that in the absence of direct male descendants the eldest daughter of Joseph should succeed to Charles. Ten years later, on April 19, 1713, Charles promulgated the so-called Pragmatic Sanction which altered the former agreement in such a way as to make the daughters of Charles heir to the throne. The Pragmatic Sanction, to be valid in Hungary, had to be accepted by the Diet, and this was the reason why Charles showed much consideration in his dealings with the Hungarian nobility.

Charles achieved his aim during the memorable Diet of 1722–3, during which the right of the female line to the Hungarian throne was officially recognized. The Pragmatic Sanction was codified in Hungarian constitutional law as a bilateral agreement. The Estates accepted the female succession for the daughters, or their descendants, of Charles III, Joseph I and Leopold II but, unlike the hereditary provinces, stipulated that in the case of these three lines becoming extinct, the right to elect a sovereign would revert to the nation. The hereditary right to the throne did not dispense future Habsburg rulers from the obligation to issue a diploma and take an oath, guaranteeing the Hungarian constitution.

The same Diet also established a 'personal union' between the hereditary provinces and Hungary. Through the person of the King, Hungary on one side, Austria and Bohemia on the other, were united *indivisibiliter et inseparabiliter* in a defensive union. The Diet's wish that a treaty should be concluded directly between the countries concerned was not granted by Charles, who argued that, as an absolute ruler of the hereditary provinces, his word was a sufficient guarantee. The absence of any written document setting out unequivocally the scope and the limitations of the union was to be the cause of prolonged constitutional wrestling, which lasted until 1866, when the relation of the countries concerned was clearly defined.

The reign of Charles III saw a number of important administrative reforms, which affected the life of the country considerably and for a very long period.

Perhaps the most important measure was the creation of a common Austro-Hungarian standing army. The noble *insurrectio*, which had been obsolete for centuries, was to be replaced by a mixed standing army supported by taxes. The need for a strong national army, well trained and disciplined, had been advocated before by men like Zrinyi, and eighteenth-century conditions made its creation even more imperative. The nobility was hostile towards the creation of an army which would mean the end of their privileges. The only reason—or rather, pretext—for their continued exemption from paying taxes was the fictive assumption that the obligation of defending the country rested on them. The bargain finally struck between the King and the Diet is a typical and base example of the general behaviour of the nobility. During the Diets of 1715 and 1722 a standing army was established—and the exemption of the nobles from the payment of taxes maintained. It was the unfortunate *jobbágy* who had to meet the bill. Not only had he to pay the taxes to maintain the army, but military service was now added to his manifold obligations, and as recruiting failed to entice sufficient numbers, he was liable to be forcibly enlisted. For the nobles the situation was highly satisfactory: the existence of a standing army made their *insurrectio* even more outdated and useless than it had been before, and the new system was thus tantamount to a virtual exemption from military service as well as from taxes. The solution was disastrous for the nation. As, theoretically, the noble levy remained the country's national army, the Hungarian recruits were simply incorporated into the regiments of the Empire, under German officers with German as the language of command. The country thus ceased to have an army of its own whilst providing, for more than two centuries, men and money towards the upkeep of the Austrian military power. The damage caused by the sordid class interest of the nobility was incalculable.

With the appearance of an independent state, Hungary was more and more subjected to Austrian rule. Three offices, the so-called *Kormányszék* (*dicasterium*), were the main instruments of royal power: one was the Hungarian Chancellery, sitting in Vienna and acting as an intermediary between King and nation; another was the *Helytartótanács* (*Consilium regium locumtenentiale*), an old-established organ which at this epoch played the part of the chief executive. The seat of this council was in Hungary, in Pozsony and later, in Buda, and its members had no connection with the Diet and were nominated by the King. The activity of the *Helytartótanács* was not only basically unconstitutional, it was also inefficient because the council had little effective power of coercion over the lesser executive state bodies, and the *megyes*, firm strongholds of the nobility, were able to sabotage the execution of decisions taken there. The country's finances were still in the hands of the third office, the *Kamara*, set up by Ferdinand but internally reorganized under Charles. The reorganization did not affect the complete subservience of the *Kamara* to the Viennese *Hofkammer*. Only the war taxes, the so-called *contributio*, remained dependent on the vote of the Diet.

The financial arrangements between Austria and Hungary were—to say the least—unsatisfactory. The notoriously weak finances of the Habsburgs, on the constant verge of bankruptcy, were from 1714, the year of the foundation in Vienna of the *Universal-Bankalität*, largely supported by income derived from Hungary. The deed of foundation of this bank, which in fact administered the major part of the monarchy's income, had not been promulgated in Hungary, so its existence remained *de jure* unknown to the Estates. In fact Hungary's national income was used—without the country's knowledge of it—in a vain attempt to balance the ever-increasing deficit of the Austrian budget.

The religious question, on which the Hungarians themselves failed to come to a settlement, was put to rights with the so-called *Carolina resolutio* in 1731. Drawn up on the lines of the decision taken in 1681 (cf. p. 204), by adding new vexations to the old ones it put the Protestants in a very unfavourable position. Particularly important was that the wording of the official oath to be taken by prospective public servants was unacceptable to Protestants.

During the reign of Charles III the judiciary system had also been reorganized, without bringing any important change in the administration of justice, and the *jobbágy* remained, as before, virtually at the mercy of his lord. The relation between Hungary and Transylvania was also in need of revision, particularly as far as the *Partium*, claimed by the Hungarian as well as by the Transylvanian Estates was concerned. In 1731 Charles weakly cut the disputed territories into two, discontenting thereby both parties for over a century.

Charles's reign was, on the whole, a peaceful one and only two short aggressive wars against the Turks were of concern to Hungary. The first (1716–18), which ended with the Peace of Passarovitz, freed the whole of South-East Hungary, till then in Turkish hands. This meant that Temesvár also became Hungarian, and the whole of historic Hungary was at last liberated from the last remnants of Turkish occupation. During the same campaign—the last to be led in Hungary by the veteran Prince Eugene of Savoy—parts of the northern Balkans, including Belgrade, were also reoccupied. All these territories, with the exception of the Bánát, were lost again in a second war (1736–9), in which Austrian generals—Prince Eugene having died—could once again show their usual inefficiency. It is worth noting that these wars were fought without the participation of the Hungarian nobility.

Thus Charles's last year was overshadowed by a defeat which, together with his many preoccupations, undoubtedly hastened his death. He was succeeded by his daughter, the twenty-three-year-old Maria Theresa (1740–80), the greatest ruler the Habsburg dynasty produced.

The beginnings of Maria Theresa's rule were particularly difficult, since almost everyone capable of mustering some pretext presented himself as a pretender to Charles's throne. In the War of Succession (1740–8) which followed her accession to the throne, Frederick II of Prussia was her principal enemy, and Hungary her principal supporter.

With considerable feminine tact, and taking advantage of her personal charm, the young Queen appealed to the chivalrous feelings of the Hungarian Estates to save her from a desperate situation. In Pozsony on September 11, 1741, the Estates declared themselves ready to give *vitam et sanguinem* for the Queen, and put some 60,000 men, including the *insurrectio* of the nobles, at her disposal. Coming as it did, in a most critical moment, the decision of the Estates had consequences more far-reaching than those on the purely military field. In fact, Hungary saved the Habsburg dynasty, a gesture she had every reason to regret in later years, but which ensured Maria Theresa's goodwill to the nation.

The respite enjoyed by Maria Theresa after the Treaty of Aix-la-Chapelle, which put an end to the War of Succession, was a relatively short one. The so-called Seven Years War with Frederick II (1755–63) was fought with active Hungarian participation and led to a renascence of the Hungarian military virtues. The sterile warfare of the seventeenth and eighteenth centuries, with endless manœuvres and no battles were totally unsuitable to the Hungarian character. The discipline of the Prussian army was not very much more to the liking of Hungarian soldiers who, however, fitted well into the swift, lively wars favoured by Frederick. The renown of Hungarian hussars dates from this epoch.

Hungarian help could not have a decisive influence on the outcome of the war, but it proved to the Queen that Hungarian co-operation could have salutary effects on the monarchy's destiny. Maria Theresa's whole policy was therefore designed not to enforce the submission of Hungary, but rather to make the country a prosperous and happy partner by developing its natural resources and ensuring a better life for its inhabitants. This remarkable woman set out on this difficult task with no desire to antagonize the national feeling of Hungarians; and if at the end of her reign she found herself at loggerheads with the Hungarian Estates, the blame for it must be put on the Hungarian nobility.

To understand the conflict which opposed the Estates, i.e. the nobles, to the Monarch, it is essential to bear in mind that this resistance to the power of an absolute ruler has nothing to do with the constitutional development which in Western Europe led to the disappearance of absolutism. What the Hungarian Estates really represented in eighteenth-century Hungary was medieval feudalism. It was not that the governed were attacking an absolutist ruler, it was an enlightened absolutism that was making desperate efforts to break through a wall of political ideas which seemed almost prehistoric. The Monarch and not the Estates represented progress, and, though the nobility was fighting a losing battle, its desperate rearguard actions to preserve its privileges were successful enough to debar Hungary from the advantages of material progress characteristic of the end of the eighteenth and of the beginning of the nineteenth centuries. This was all the more disastrous because, owing to the Turkish occupation, Hungary was already centuries behind western development.

Not only was the social structure of the country reminiscent of that of Western Europe in, say, the twelfth century, the economic situation was also very much behind the times.

The manner of cultivation was essentially the same as it had been under Charlemagne, a traditional system of rotation, and not even the three-field system, was universal. The greater part of the country, particularly the territories which had been under Turkish occupation, still adhered to the archaic two-field system, and in some sparsely inhabited regions the practice of cultivating one plot until the soil was exhausted and then moving to another plot was still in use. The meagre products of a soil not properly cultivated found little expertise in their further handling. Threshing under the hooves of horses was as wasteful as it was unhygienic, the polluted corn could not stand long-distance transport. The storage of corn was equally primitive. Granaries and barns were practically non-existent, and the corn was stored in caves dug in the ground and sealed off. When these caves were small, as they often were, they were half-filled with corn and covered with straw and earth. Moisture and imperfect sealing caused great wastage. This was less important in the case of huge communal caves, often over thirty feet deep, which were dried out by burning straw. Crops were usually very poor, and a four-fold yield was considered exceptionally good. The soil, after the enforced rest during the Turkish epoch, had been very good, but as no efforts were made to improve it, it soon became exhausted. Manure in plentiful supplies was gathered in heaps or used to fill the potholes of what, with considerable euphemism, could be called the roads. No one thought of using it on soil other than that of vineyards.

Cattle-breeding was, on the whole, on a slightly higher level. It is true that most of the animals were reared in the open, without any other care than that of a solitary herdsman to watch over a herd of some 1,200 to 1,500 animals. The animals died in numbers, and those which survived were of very poor quality. In the western parts of the country the situation was considerably better. Many of the great magnates imported cattle from Switzerland and methodical horse-breeding was also gaining ground.

Maria Theresa's projects to improve the economic conditions of the country, to establish industries and to organize internal consumption and export, failed because of the Estates' stubborn refusal to levy taxes on the nobility. Antagonism came to a crisis during the Diet of 1764. The Queen sought to obtain approval for a number of measures intended to alleviate the burden of the *jobbágy*, and to obtain the commutation into cash payment of the largely fictitious military obligations of the nobility. The highly indignant Estates refused to follow her on this way, thus throwing away their last chance of preventing Hungary from sinking into a purely colonial status. The Queen, vexed by their intractability and reluctant to have recourse to coercion, decided to abide by the opinion of some of her councillors, who for some time had tried to make of Hungary an Austrian colony. As Hungary refused to share the common burden of taxation in proportion to her population, she could not expect—so the argument ran—to enjoy the material benefits bestowed upon the hereditary provinces. The idea was not new, it had been dormant during the inefficient reigns of Leopold and Joseph, but in taking it up Maria Theresa showed far greater abilities in its implementation.

Judicious custom regulations ensured that industrial products from Austria had not to meet with foreign competition in Hungary, whereas Austria received the monopoly of Hungarian exports. Hungarian commerce became tributary to Austrian markets, where the merchandise had to be bought for the prices demanded.

Customs duty on Hungarian raw materials in transit through Austria was so heavy that they could not hold their place in foreign markets. One example may be allowed here to illustrate the cunning refinement of the system. Hungarian gall-nut production had a long-established ready market in Poland. This had to be sacrificed to ensure cheap beef for the Viennese public. The scheme was as follows: beef was subsidized by the heavy prices the Austrian leather industry was compelled to pay for the hides. Compensation to the leather industry was provided by reducing the cost of the gall-nuts indispensable for tanning, imported cheaply from Hungary.

The Estates were too stupid to notice the country's degradation, too indolent to act, too egoistic to be concerned with anything else but their narrow class interest. They lived in a fool's paradise, enjoying their 'liberty' and their privileges without realizing that the gap between western and Hungarian civilization was steadily widening, and that the hope of ever catching up with western prosperity was fading at the same rhythm.

The baroque mentality which prevailed during the earlier and longer part of Maria Theresa's reign contributed in no small measure to the general euphory. Baroque—though present during the seventeenth century—was really flourishing in Hungary during the reign of Maria Theresa, and it was much more than a new style of the visual arts. It was a *Weltanschauung* which, in Hungary, gave a religious, Catholic content to the existing stalemate between absolutism and a feudal constitution. The idea that the country is the realm of the Holy Virgin (*Regnum Marianum*) dates from this epoch, as does the law that the ruler must be a Catholic. The years of peace following the blood-drenched centuries of the Turkish wars filled people with optimism and aroused an interest in national history. The Pyrrhic victory gained by the Estates against the progressive ideas of the Queen awoke in the country an ill-founded self-admiration, stagnation was hailed as a virtue and an end in itself, and the appropriately unearthed saying of an Italian Neo-platonist of the eighteenth century '*Extra Hungariam non est vita, si est vita, non est ita*' became the motto of a society apparently unable to be rejuvenated.

The opposition of the Estates and the general passivity of the country did not prevent Maria Theresa from introducing a number of reforms generally aimed at improving the standard of living of the lower classes of society. The most important among these was undoubtedly the introduction of uniform regulations concerning the contracts relating to socage, the so-called *Urbarium* (1767). The effects of this new regulation were considerable. The *Urbarium* restored freedom of movement to the *jobbágy;* after more than two centuries of quasi-slavery he was henceforward able to offer his services to a lord of his own choice. This freedom entailed the opening of various professions to the *jobbágy*. The *Urbarium* decreed also that in the case of new contracts of socage being drawn up, these must be more favourable to the *jobbágy* than had been the previous ones. The *Urbarium* went as far as it was possible in the peculiar circumstances then prevailing to alleviate the lot of the *jobbágy*, and great care was taken to enforce its execution. This was not always easy, as not only the landlords but, under their influence, even the misguided peasants raised local difficulties.

Maria Theresa did much to improve public education and her reforms extended to all degrees of teaching. She had the University founded by Pázmány in Nagyszombat transferred to Buda, and she founded new chairs. The reform of the University had been made possible by the dissolution in 1772 of the Jesuit order, which had represented a strongly conservative and limited teaching policy. Though secondary teaching remained in the hands of the Catholic teaching orders (e.g. the Piarists) a secular spirit was steadily gaining ground, and the *Ratio Educationis* (1772), which gave a uniform pattern to secondary education, was very much a product of the Enlightenment. Great efforts were also made to create elementary schools in sufficient numbers. All these results were achieved without the help of the Estates, through direct administrative action. The insufficient collaboration of the *megye* hampered the fulfilment of the excellent plans proposed by the *Ratio*, but even so, the reign of Maria Theresa constitutes a decisive step in Hungarian educational policy.

Many other aspects of popular welfare, such as orphanages, homes for the destitute, the problem of beggars, gypsies, etc., received the Queen's attention, and her approach to these has been described as a curious mixture of baroque Catholicism and the ideas of enlightenment. Her attitude could probably be explained also in more simple terms, often disliked by historians: Maria Theresa was a kind-hearted, charitable person. It was not her political self-interest but her sense of charity and justice which prompted her to take sides with the *jobbágy* and try to alleviate his burden. She is perhaps the only 'modern' ruler who has made serious efforts to put into practice the precepts of her religion, to which she was deeply devoted. It was also her basic kindness which made her recoil from the use of extreme measures against the Estates. She preferred to court their goodwill, and during her reign the aristocracy turned more and more towards Vienna. Her Hungarian bodyguard of nobles was to become a seed-bed for writers with whom started the revival of Hungarian literature.

Maria Theresa saw no reason to discard the old form which she knew to be adaptable to new contents. Without antagonizing the nobility unduly, she improved the lot of the *jobbágy*, and the blame for Hungary's degradation into an Austrian colony must be laid at the door of the Estates. These were fairly insensible to the economic subordination of the country which, unaware of the permanent issues at stake, enjoyed half a century of peace, moderate progress, and blissful inactivity. It was a patriarchal, simple life, centred on the family, held together by strict but not ostentatious moral principles. Lord and serf shared a passion for hospitality that was often literally ruinous, and an inclination not to be feverishly active. The economic and social structure of the country set small premium on effort and skill. Only the *jobbágys* worked—and as they could hope for no improvement, they did as little as it was possible. A society without incentive to work hard may, for a while, be pleasant to live in, but it cannot progress and it endorses for future generations a bill which it is itself unwilling to pay. In Hungary's case the last instalment has still to be forthcoming.

CHAPTER 25

ENLIGHTENED DESPOTISM

THE accession of Joseph II (1780–90) brought to an abrupt end the policy of compromise followed since the Treaty of Szatmár. Associated for many years with his mother in the running of state affairs, Joseph had been seething with impatience to put into practice his many ideas on government. It is fortunately rare to see theoreticians of politics with power to implement their theories. Joseph II was one of them, and he tried with a remarkable single-mindedness and a personal honesty beyond reproach to govern his many countries according to what the Enlightenment called reason. He was also an uncompromising Physiocrat, and accordingly considered that landed property was the sole proper object of taxation. As these ideas were in complete disagreement with those of the nobles who owned all the land and who were exempt from taxation, Joseph made an all-out attack on their two constitutional strongholds: the Diet and the *megye*. In order to have his hands free from any contracted obligations, he refused at his accession to issue the Diploma and to have himself crowned. He had the Holy Crown transported to Vienna, to a museum which, according to his opinions, was its place, and considered 'ridiculous' the indignation expressed by the Estates. Hungarians called him 'the king with a hat'. A rationalist *à outrance*, he completely disregarded the traditions and customs of his many countries for which he tried to ensure a uniform happiness of his own brand. But people continued to prefer having candles at the altars, even though they could, admittedly, start a fire, and they disliked the idea of burying their dead without coffins on the grounds that the planks could be used to better purpose.

These petty and stupid measures, which caused widespread bitterness, stand in curious contrast to Joseph's epoch-making decisions on a number of major issues. In 1781 he issued a decree on religious tolerance which put an end to all persecution, direct or indirect, of Protestants. Though a convinced Catholic, he tried to limit Roman influence over the clergy, whom he considered as servants of the state, and paid accordingly. He dissolved a number of religious orders and confiscated their possessions, but he used the funds so obtained to augment the number of the parishes and to erect schools beside the churches. He also regularized mixed marriages. The judicial reforms of Joseph II were intended to speed procedure and to put an end to the lords' jurisdiction over their own *jobbágy*. Great care was taken to ease the burden of the *jobbágy* (even the use of this appellation was banned!) by enforcing the decisions of the *Urbarium* and by exempting them from the personal service due to their lords. Joseph was also ready to demolish the crippling custom duties and to integrate Hungary in a customs union with his other lands, on condition, however, that Hungary should share in the common burden of taxation. As Joseph did not convoke the Diet there was no way of obtaining an agreement to such measures which would not, in any case—it can be assumed—have been given by the Estates.

In 1784 Joseph made German the official language in Hungary, where up to then Latin had been so used. With his total lack of finesse, Joseph stood uncomprehending before the outburst of indignation which followed. He found it more logical to use German than Latin which, so his argument ran, was the language of neither Hungary nor Austria.

To create a solid base to his projects of taxation, Joseph II took a census and started a general survey of the country's whole territory. His activity, watched by the nobles with growing hostility, was completely misunderstood by the primitive Roumanians living in the mountains of Transylvania, who in 1784 revolted and attacked their lords with bestial cruelty. The revolt was suppressed and the leaders Hora and Kloska executed. The whole useless, unorganized outbreak was just a further and tragic warning, which remained unheeded, that the country was not ripe for the reforms which Joseph tried to force upon it.

Whatever mistakes Joseph was guilty of, his reform policy was coherent and governed by strict principles. His foreign policy was inconsistent, and it was a muddled and ill-conceived war with the Turks (1788–9), in which the Austrian armies suffered their customary crushing defeat, which in the end caused the collapse of the whole artificial edifice of Joseph's new state. A successful revolt in Belgium was followed by widespread unrest in other countries, and some Hungarian nobles had already approached Frederick William II of Prussia, offering him the crown. The King, ill and broken, realized his mistakes. On January 28, 1790, he cancelled all his reforms with the exception of those relating to the *Urbarium*, religious tolerance and the parish churches. He died a few weeks later. He was a tragic figure, who saw the failure of everything he had stood for; in his human greatness only one essential ingredient was lacking—understanding for the feelings of others. He paid a heavy price for it, as he had not the satisfaction of witnessing the growth of the ideas which he had implanted in Hungarian soil.

The short reign of Joseph's younger brother, Leopold II (1790-2), was a difficult one, but the new Emperor was a man capable of dealing with complicated situations. An unfinished war with the Turks, revolution in Belgium, seething discontent in Hungary, were the main problems the new King had to cope with, and he set to work with great determination and skill. A peace-treaty hastily concluded with the Turks relieved him of the burden of war, and he could then concentrate on what he considered to be his principal task: keeping hold over Hungary. Considering, quite rightly, that the nobles as the real body politic, were the backbone of any resistance, Leopold embarked on a systematic and artful campaign to undermine their authority. His methods were ruthless, and ample use was made of political pamphleteers and of reports from the secret police—a body which was to play an increasing rôle in Austria. There was also the possibility of inciting the Serbs, permanently discontented by Viennese police (for which they blamed the Hungarians), and of supporting the claims of *jobbágys* and burghers, who were becoming more and more awake to their rights. Leopold played with accomplished art on the many-piped organ of human discontent, and in a very short time did considerable and permanent harm to Hungary. The bad press which Hungary has had until recently in Western and Central Europe has its origin in Leopold's anti-Hungarian propaganda, and in his reign began a rapid worsening of relations between the Hungarian and non-Hungarian populations of the country. Agitation also started among the Saxons and Roumanians of Transylvania.

As usual, the Estates were unable to grasp the really important aspects of the situation. During the rather stormy Diet of 1790-1 they concentrated their efforts on the customary constitutional tug-of-war, reasserting the country's independence, seeking to hinder absolutist practices and to increase the Diet's, i.e. the nobles' influence, and turning a blind eye to the imperative needs for social and economic reform.

The country was in a state of political effervescence which, fanned by news from France, announced the beginning of a new era. It can only be surmised what turn this development would have taken with Leopold II on the throne. The sudden death of this last gifted Habsburg spelt the end of the epoch of enlightened despotism.

CHAPTER 26

NATIONAL REVIVAL

IT cannot be our aim to show the impact of the French Revolution on the Habsburg Empire. Although the ideas of the revolution were to fertilize Hungarian soil, the revolution itself forced the Habsburg rulers to adopt an entirely negative, reactionary attitude, the sole aim of which was the perpetuation of the *status quo*. None of the four Emperors who were still to rule showed any signs of talent. The first of them, Francis I (1792–1835), who succeeded his father Leopold II, was the very embodiment of inactivity. He was both stupid and uncultivated, and his reign not only stopped progress but meant a relapse to the absolutist ideas of Leopold I. In an epoch when new ideas were bursting the old forms, when technical progress was rapidly changing economic and social conditions, Francis I's rule spelt stagnation, immobility, reaction. The King was anything but a tyrant, and as a conscientious, almost indifferent, bureaucrat he was unwilling to follow the often extremist advice of his entourage. He had no hostility towards the Hungarians and showed no reluctance to convoke the Diet. In many aspects his rule was patriarchal, in a primitive way, entirely unsuited to the epoch in which he lived, and very harmful to the countries he governed.

Francis's natural timidity found excellent justification in a conspiracy which was said to have imperilled the institutions of the realm. At the root of this rather hazy affair was an unfrocked monk Ignatius Martinovics, who, after a short spell in the service of the secret police, found it more interesting to form secret societies of his own: the Society of the Reformers, which was to unite the revolutionary elements among the nobility, and the Society of Liberty and Equality, set apart for radical intellectuals. The conspiracy was nipped in the bud. Martinovics, arrested in Vienna, where he was seeking political contacts, was not only ready to give away the names of his real accomplices, but, probably out of vanity, to show the importance of his movement, involved many others whom he knew to sympathize with new ideas. Together with six of his infinitely more estimable companions Martinovics was executed on May 25, 1795, whilst many others, including some important writers such as Kazinczy, were imprisoned.

The Estates, intimidated by the executions as well as by the penetration of revolutionary ideas into Hungary, became a reliable tool in the King's hand, and at successive Diets were ready to lay ever-increasing new burdens, taxes as well as military obligations, upon the *jobbágy*. In the wars with the French, Hungary was taking her full share and many a good Hungarian soldier lost his life in fighting against the ideas which eventually were to liberate his countrymen. In 1809 the noble *insurrectio* drew its rusty sword for the last time, only to suffer a crushing defeat, near Györ, by Napoleon's armies. The nobility, in its own inefficient way, showed its determination to stand by a policy of reaction: the long conflict between the King and the Hungarian Estates seems to have ceased, the once opposing forces, their old energies sapped, lay inert in a torpor of inactivity. Care for the country's future was shouldered by other men, not yet invested with any power, but courageous enough to sound reveille for those who seemed almost to be the dead. These men—all belonging to the nobility —were to atone for the criminal egoism of their own class. With no other arms than their talent, their enthusiasm, their faith in the destiny of their country, and their determination, they set out to catch up with the times, they undertook the Herculean task of making Hungary a place worth living in. Without recourse to violence they made the first half of the ninteenth century one of the most glorious periods of Hungarian history. Their ultimate victory was that of intellect and honesty of purpose; a ray of hope and comfort in the dark picture of human history.

The beginnings of this intellectual renascence in Hungary go back to the time of Maria Theresa, under whose reign the ideas of Enlightenment found their way to Hungary, mainly through certain of the noblemen serving in the Queen's Hungarian Bodyguard. The first interpreter in Hungary of the ideas of Enlightenment was one of these, George

Bessenyei (1746–1811), whose initiative opened new horizons not only for Hungarian literature but also for the country as a whole. One of the most striking features of the Hungarian Enlightenment was its close connection with the hitherto much-neglected vernacular, and it was by transforming the Hungarian language into a vehicle capable of conveying the new ideas of the epoch that the great battle for a reinvigorated country was joined. There could be no question of exerting a direct influence on the broad *jobbágy* masses who were largely illiterate. The bourgeoisie, i.e. the non-noble middle class, was very small indeed, and had little or no influence on the affairs of state. The problem was to awaken the nobility, and this could only be done in Hungarian. First the nobles had to be induced to read, a task not without its difficulties. The greater number of them, virtually buried in the country and satisfied with the *status quo*, showed little inclination to read at all and even less to read about the new ideas. They could, however, be approached through their conservative, anti-German feelings, through works extolling the ancient virtues of the Hungarians. A cultivated minority among the nobles had its interest focused on Vienna, and was in process of becoming denationalized; it had to be convinced that it was worth its while to read in Hungarian. The problem was thus three-fold: to create a Hungarian language adequate to the higher intellectual requirements of the Enlightenment; to induce people to read; and to provide them with literature capable of rousing them from their inactivity and leading them towards much-needed reforms. Rarely, if ever, had a handful of men of letters assumed a greater responsibility; rarely, if ever, were any more successful in their undertaking.

The movement started by Bessenyei gained full momentum under the leadership of Francis Kazinczy (1759–1831). A staunch supporter of the ideas of Enlightenment, Kazinczy, involved in the Martinovics conspiracy, had served a prison sentence of over six years. At his liberation he put all his energies into the service of the Hungarian language and literature. The so-called 'renewal of the language', a movement which he initiated, literally transformed Hungarian and made of it the incomparable tool of poetry that it has remained ever since. By severe criticism Kazinczy improved the taste of the public as well as the general level of literary production. Under his influence literature began to flourish and, in its wake, the nation gained consciousness of its traditional values as well as of the duties imposed on it by a glorious past. The Hungarian language proved its value and a tenacious struggle started to ensure its recognition as the country's official language. On this matter—since no loss of class privileges was involved—the Estates were unanimous; but their resolutions were thwarted by the Viennese Government, fearing, not without reason, that the adoption of Hungarian as the official language of the administration (in replacement of Latin) would weaken its grip on Hungary. In spite of this opposition, the Hungarian language slowly gained ground in successive Diets, its use being gradually extended to more and more branches of the administration. Ultimate victory, however, was delayed until 1844, when, at long last, Hungarian became, without any restriction, the official language of the country. It is possible to ponder profitably on the energy expended in this struggle to obtain what, for most countries, is a fundamental and uncontested right.

The fostering of Hungarian was but one aspect, though probably the most important, of a general drive to develop a national culture. In 1802 Count Francis Széchenyi founded the Hungarian National Museum by a donation of his private collections and his library, and in 1825 the Hungarian Academy came into being, thanks to the generosity of Stephen Széchenyi, his son. Hungarian cultural activities found unexpected support from the *nádor* Joseph, brother of Francis II. Joseph advocated a policy whereby the centre of gravity of the monarchy would have been transferred to Hungary. His views commanded little respect in Vienna, but his activity was, in the cultural sphere, highly beneficial for Hungary and his general comportment secured for the dynasty sympathies there which it would not have otherwise commanded.

The revival of the Hungarian language, and a more vigorous intellectual life, were conducive to a general stocktaking of the country's resources and an increasing realization of her backwardness. It was not long before treatment followed diagnosis, and the nation was fortunate enough to have at its disposal the services of a master-surgeon: Count Stephen Széchenyi. Rightly called 'the greatest of Hungarians' by no lesser a man than Kossuth, Széchenyi made an unparalleled contribution to his country's welfare. He was widely travelled, had spent some time in England, and on his return set himself to the task of planting in Hungarian soil some of the institutions, inventions and even customs which he had found beneficial elsewhere. His extraordinary genius embraced the whole gamut of human activities and few are the fields where he did not leave his imprint.

Széchenyi was particularly interested in improving transport, and Hungarian steamship navigation on the Danube owes its existence to him (1830). To ensure direct navigation down to the Black Sea and thence to Constantinople, Széchenyi made navigable the so-called Iron Gate on the Lower Danube, where he also enlarged the old Roman road built there by Trajan and made it suitable for contemporary transport. Perhaps the greatest single achievement of Széchenyi's was the building of a permanent suspension-bridge over the Danube, and this was also the one he cherished most. Till then a fragile boat-bridge, functioning only in the mild season, had been the sole link between Buda and Pest. In wintertime—unless the Danube was frozen hard enough to allow transport over the ice—the country was virtually cut in two halves. The new suspension-bridge—a splendid piece of civil engineering, built by an Englishman, Adam Clark—was the first important achievement by private enterprise in Hungary and heralded the belated dawn of capitalism. It was also the first serious blow struck at the tax immunity of the nobles: tolls had to be paid by everyone using the bridge. An Act of Parliament was necessary to achieve this! It is impossible to enumerate all the undertakings in which Széchenyi showed an interest. The first steam-mill, the introduction of horse-racing to improve breeding, the founding of a club on the English pattern to become a meeting-place of the Hungarian aristocracy, the introduction of steamship navigation on Lake Balaton, and the controlling of the flow of the River Tisza, the second largest river of Hungary, are but a few examples taken at random from among Széchenyi's achievements.

Széchenyi was no politician. He thought—probably rightly—that the chief evils which bedevilled Hungarian life were of an economic and social nature and that they could be cured within the existing political framework. His first published work: *Hitel* ('Credit', 1830) was like a bombshell for the somnolent, self-deluding aristocracy. In this and subsequent books Széchenyi laid the blame for the country's pitiful state squarely on the shoulders of the nobles. It was useless to blame the government when a medieval social structure paralysed all economic development. The *ösiség*, dating from the time of Louis I, by which a noble's property became inalienable, rendered credit on land security impossible and made the noble the slave rather than the owner of his land. Many of Széchenyi's plans were brought to fruition only by the following generation, but many of his own achievements, such as the suspension-bridge, the control of the Danube and the Tisza, and the creation of the Hungarian Academy, were endowments which have not ceased to bring benefits to the nation. To no one since before the Turkish occupation does Hungary owe more than to him.

CHAPTER 27

THE ERA OF REFORMS

THE spiritual revival of the first half of the nineteenth century took place in a political atmosphere poisoned by the dynasty's opposition to any progress in general, and to Hungarian national aspirations in particular. Reaction, in Hungary, did not wait until the Congress of Vienna sanctified it as the sole acceptable form of government. As early as 1812 Metternich openly reverted to absolutist methods, which were to be employed for fifteen years in governing Hungary. This decision was taken after the Diet of 1811 had refused to satisfy the Government's request to take over almost half of the national (Austro-Hungarian) debt, which remained after the disastrous devaluation of the florin to one-fifth of its former value. The gradual stiffening of national resistance, the *megye's* refusal (or at least temporizing reluctance) to implement Government decisions taken without the approval of a Diet, finally compelled Metternich to return to more constitutional methods, and in September 1825 a Diet was convoked at Pozsony. This Diet, like the following one, which lasted for almost four years (1832–6), brought about no major changes; nor did the accession of Ferdinand V (1835–48). The Government's stubborn opposition alienated more and more sympathies, and the reform movement, which, in Széchenyi's conception, ought to have remained non-political and solely concerned with the spiritual and material welfare of the nation, gradually became on both sides a fairly sterile constitutional struggle, not free from demagogy. Opposition to reforms did not come only from the Viennese Government; many were the conservative nobles who viewed with suspicion any movement which might lead to a loss of their privileges, and who were unable to face the harsh truth that a decisive improvement in internal conditions was impossible within the existing social framework.

A cholera epidemic, which in 1831-2 killed about a quarter of a million people, was followed in the Highlands by brutal and primitive peasant rebellions, set on foot by the belief that the epidemic was caused by the lords and their doctors, who had poisoned the wells! One of the unwelcome consequences of these happenings was a strengthening of the ties between the King and the conservative elements among the Hungarian nobility. Metternich himself was not anti-Hungarian, nor did he object in principle to a gradual and careful adoption of reforms tending to improve material conditions in the country. Reaction in its worst form was embodied in Count Francis Anthony Kollowrat, Metternich's great antagonist, who for twenty years used his not inconsiderable talents to stop any progress and to do as much harm to Hungary as possible.

There was one respect in which the country was particularly vulnerable: the alien settlements within its borders which could be used by a clever and unscrupulous government against the Hungarians themselves. Immigration into Hungary—justified by the vacuum created by the Turkish wars—went on unabated during the eighteenth century. In Transylvania, for example, the number of Roumanians grew from 250,000 to 787,000 between 1700 and 1784. The Saxons, endangered by this flow of Roumanians, were strengthened by new German immigrants, but the Hungarian (and Székely) population, unable to draw on foreign reserves, found itself more and more a minority in its own country. The extremely low cultural standard of the Roumanians represented another unfavourable facet of this mass-immigration. German settlers could have been an asset to the country had their great numbers, and the Government's policy, not prevented their complete integration with the indigenous population. All through the eighteenth century hundreds of thousands of German immigrants settled down in compact blocks mainly in the southern parts of the country. We have also seen how the northern mountainous parts of the country, deserted by their Hungarian populations, had been occupied by different Slavonic peoples. Simultaneously with the Hungarians, and to a great extent under their influence, all these peoples in the first half of the century were developing a national consciousness, initially more allied with than opposed to similar tendencies among the Hungarians. But the embers of nationalist feelings, cleverly but short-sightedly fanned by the Austrians, soon became a fire which menaced—and almost a century later effectively destroyed—the territorial unity of Hungary. Austrian machinations were particularly successful in poisoning the hitherto fairly friendly relations between Hungarians and Croats. Few were the statesmen who, like Nicholas Wesselényi, 'the Széchenyi of Transylvania', realized the danger of nationalist agitation.

In the early 'forties the country was in a state of effervescence. In the ranks of the nobility—it must be borne in mind that the *jobbágy* had still no political rights—agreement existed only on one point: patriotic feeling. As for the ways and means of best serving the country, it was found difficult to conciliate widely-differing points of view. The number of conservatives, who clung desperately to old institutions and tried to prevent any change, was steadily diminishing. The ground lost by them was occupied by the liberals who, from the mid-'thirties on, had become the most progressive party. In their ranks could be found the two greatest Hungarian statesmen of the nineteenth century: Louis Kossuth and Francis Deák. Their influence on public opinion rapidly gained ascendancy and Széchenyi, a solitary towering figure, who refused to tie the country's prosperity to any political party, found himself more and more isolated. Széchenyi still believed that prosperity and the liberation of the *jobbágy* masses could be achieved within the existing constitutional framework. In his view liberty would follow prosperity, whereas the liberals, particularly Kossuth, thought that liberty was a prerequisite for any progress. Széchenyi proposed a programme of toil, of methodical long-term improvement, Kossuth advocated immediate liberation from Austrian tutelage. Széchenyi kept on pointing out the mistakes, the shortcomings, the bad habits of his compatriots, Kossuth put most of the blame on Austria, the cause of all evil, and flattered his countrymen by holding out bright prospects, prospects which had but one flaw, that of being unrealizable. The nonsensical slogan: 'Hungarian, take to the sea!' launched by Kossuth indicates but one of them. Is it necessary to say that the country preferred Kossuth's programme?

In many respects Kossuth's character is difficult to understand. No Hungarian has ever reached a popularity similar to his; he was and still is loved and revered by Hungarians, and the extraordinary power of his personality made a serious impact on the Anglo-Saxon world. He was the greatest orator Hungary has ever produced, and his speeches, when read after more than a century, still have a deeply stirring effect. Yet he brought disaster to his country and, even on the personal level, serious faults can be found in him. His vanity and petty jealousy did much harm to the cause which he served with the devotion, the enthusiasm, the faith of a prophet rather than of a statesman.

Kossuth did not fail to recognize the importance of capitalism, and was particularly interested in the development of industry. But most of his projects lacked the matter-of-fact approach, and he did not possess the stubbornness of Széchenyi to follow plans through and bring them to fruit in spite of opposition. There can be no doubt that Kossuth's basic thesis, that the partnership with Austria was disastrous for Hungary, was essentially right. To think that this partnership could, in a short while, be ended by political agitation was sadly naïve. In pursuit of this chimera, Kossuth was ready, by implication, to sacrifice many improvements within the reach of the nation. The Viennese Government was more and more inclined towards moderate reforms, and, for instance, after the creation of the German *Zollverein*, it advocated the union of the Austrian and Hungarian customs-areas, a step resisted by Kossuth on the ground that a sovereign state—such as Hungary ought to become—should form an independent customs-area. Kossuth was probably right when he emphasized the danger that a customs-union with the huge Germanic world bore for Hungary. His alternative proposals, however, remained vague, spectacular and inefficient, as was the attempted boycott of Austrian manufactured goods.

As so often happens with absolutist régimes, the concessions accorded by Vienna came too late to placate the resentment aroused by earlier intolerance. The radical wing of the opposition gained further ground, and Kossuth, as its leader, succeeded in uniting the two main factions of the malcontents. In vain Széchenyi tried to warn Kossuth of the inevitable catastrophe which would follow his unbridled agitation; his words went unheeded. Széchenyi had lost all influence and his bitter personal attacks on Kossuth were not calculated to improve matters. It was Széchenyi's tragedy that he was unable to court popular favour, and that consequently he had not the means at his disposal to avert the disaster which his prescience foresaw. A general euphory preceded the raising of the curtain on this tragic drama, whose first act brought fulfilment for some of the nation's cherished hopes.

On November 7, 1847, Ferdinand V opened the new Diet in Pozsony. His speech from the throne, delivered in Hungarian, opened the last Diet of the feudal type to be held in Hungary. Within a few months the institutions which for centuries had governed Hungarian life, and hampered its free development, were abolished. Particularly important among the initial proposals were those dealing with the introduction of general taxation, the abolition of the *ösiség*, and the manumission of the *jobbágy* by ending his obligations as laid down in the *Urbarium*. It is to Kossuth's great honour that he succeeded in creating a majority in the Lower House—still entirely composed of nobles—for the abolition of the privileges enjoyed by its own members. No Parliament has ever taken decisions more against the personal interests of those who composed it. Though the Upper House tried to obstruct the implementation of the proposals, and though many members of the Lower House clung desperately to the old privileges, the majority showed a greater sense of responsibility. It would, however, have been in vain for the Estates to agree on reforms which the King was unwilling to ratify; and the Austrian statesmen seemed little inclined to start on a road which, they knew well, would lead to a general liberalization of the régime. External events were to force their hands.

The French Revolution, which in February 1848 led to the fall of Louis Philippe, produced unrest in Austria and on March 14th Metternich had to resign. This statesman, who had been regarded, not without reason, as the principal opponent of progress, was replaced for a short space by Kollowrat, who was in many respects more reactionary than his old opponent, and who was obsessed, as we have already said, by his hatred of the Hungarians. But at this stage his nefarious activities had not yet produced results, and the feeble-minded Ferdinand, made afraid by the collapse of what had been thought unshakable, was ready to grant requests which he had been reluctant even to consider less than a fortnight earlier.

It would be difficult to over-estimate the rôle played by Kossuth during this fateful period. He was more than a politician; he was, as it were, the embodiment of the will of the nation, perhaps less leader than executor, putting into words and translating into actions the deepest and noblest aspirations of his people. His unshakable faith in the cause of justice and the rights of his country, and his love of the people, made him disregard all petty objections which men of lesser calibre could raise. Kossuth, with visionary force and determination, overrode difficulties and objections alike, and with him and through him the Hungarian people could tread a path of their own choosing. But a country which for three centuries had had no independent foreign policy, a people of some thirteen million men of whom only about half a million enjoyed any political rights, was unable to judge the true effects of Kossuth's actions or rightly to assess the balance of forces. No struggle is more hopeless than that against committees and administration, no one is weaker than a genius facing mediocrity. Kossuth and the nation, following or leading him, were running their heads against the rubber wall of Habsburg mediocrity, against a creaking, slow, inefficient, but immensely experienced administrative machine, almost invincible because headless.

During the months which elapsed after the opening of the Diet, Kossuth's political genius reached its zenith. Not only was he able to sway opinion by the extraordinary power of his oratory, he also proved himself an excellent political tactician capable of showing even virtues which he did not possess, such as that of moderation. Foreseeing the impact which French events would have on Austrian policy, on March 3rd he proposed sending an address to the King, to request, among other important measures (such as the abolition of the *jobbágy* status) the nomination of a Hungarian Government and the holding of elections on a national basis. The revolution in Vienna put an end to the temporizing policy of the Austrian Government and Kossuth's memorandum was adopted. He had not asked for more than he had been seeking for some years past, and it could therefore still be hoped that on this basis the King and country would reach an agreement. The news of the Viennese revolution was received in Budapest with great enthusiasm, and on March 15th the inhabitants of the town, their numbers swollen by the presence of peasants there for market-day, staged a manifestation which, though bloodless, is reckoned among the great revolutionary actions of history. The leaders of this movement were mostly young writers, journalists and students with no political experience and even less power. Foremost in their ranks stood the great poet Petöfi.

The events in Pest showed convincingly that a new era was about to begin, and gave the false impression that the Government was unwilling or unable to use force to quell the nationalist movement. This impression was further strengthened by the King's attitude. For all its importance, the manifestation of March 15th in Pest was but peripheral, since the Diet was sitting in Pozsony and the principal negotiations were being carried on between this town and Vienna. On March 16th the

King promised to nominate a Hungarian Government, which, in spite of some obstruction in Vienna, effectively took charge of affairs on April 7th. This, the first modern Hungarian Government, was headed by Louis Batthyány. Kossuth held the portfolio of finance, Széchenyi that of public works. The excellent jurist Francis Deák, who had been for many years one of the mainstays of the opposition, became Minister of Justice.

In Pozsony on April 11th Ferdinand V gave royal assent to a series of laws which transformed Hungary into a modern state. The Diet was to be replaced by a Parliament elected on the representative system. Hitherto the *megyes* had sent their noble representatives to the Diet; now electors were to send men of their own choice to Parliament, which was to have annual sessions. From November 1st the nobles were no longer exempt from taxation and all *corvées* were abolished. The *jobbágy* became owner of the acres he had hitherto tilled and in every respect independent of his former lord, who was to receive due compensation for the loss of his land. *Ősiség* and tithe were abolished; Transylvania and the *Partium* were united with the mother country. A national militia was to be created. Many other important decisions (such as the abolition of the censorship) were taken to ensure that the new independent country should also be a country of free men. Indeed the laws passed by this memorable Diet of 1847–8 achieved more than had ever been hoped for even by the most optimistic of statesmen, and the cautious Széchenyi himself, carried away by the general enthusiasm, hailed unreservedly, and with touching generosity, the achievements of a policy to which he had been steadily opposed. A transformation as deep and as rapid as that which Hungary underwent during these few weeks could not bring a perfect solution for every problem. The new laws were, in some respects, faulty and bore marks of hasty preparation. But the Batthyány Government, composed of extremely able men, could have coped with the problems which thereby arose. But no time was given to the newborn nation to outgrow its early pangs. At the supreme moment of euphory, when the nation, united in hope and in the will to create something noble among men, faced the future with joyous confidence, at this moment, when it seemed that equity could triumph without bloodshed over the forces of reaction, these forces were already gathering strength to turn the wedding-breakfast into a funeral feast, to transform the budding trees of March 1848 into the bleak gallows of October 1849.

CHAPTER 28

THE SWAY OF EXTREMISTS

BATTHYÁNY'S Government, though its members were in general moderate statesmen, was very much under Kossuth's influence. By alternately bullying and cajoling, Kossuth succeeded in directing the course of events towards extremes of which his fellow-ministers secretly disapproved. But even Kossuth did not envisage severing all links with Austria. Indeed, it was one of the shortcomings of the new constitution that the exact nature of the ties with Austria had not been clearly defined, and this led, on both sides, to misunderstandings and mutual accusations of unconstitutional practices. As so often happens in troubled times, subordinates found it difficult to decide whom to obey, and men, seeing the disappearance of the old order, felt reluctant to recognize the new. The change at the helm was considered an excellent opportunity by the different nationalities living in Hungary to put forward their own claims for independence, or at least autonomy. At the instigation of Vienna, these claims were presented to the Hungarian Government which had been unable, during the short time of its existence, to work out a consistent policy concerning these minorities. The lack of such a policy was of small consequence, since on the one hand, the granting of the various claims would inevitably have meant the disintegration of Hungary, and on the other, some of the nationalist leaders, more concerned with the destruction of the new Hungarian state than with the welfare of their own people, would inevitably have rejected any proposal tending to establish peace within the new political framework. The former Habsburg policy of favouring Slavs and Roumanians at the expense of Hungarians now bore its fruit.

Oddly enough the chief threat came from the Croats, a people with whom Hungarians had lived in peace for centuries, and who had given to Hungary leaders such as the Zrinyis. It must be remembered that Croatia had always been a possession of the Hungarian Holy Crown and that it had—theoretically—no other connections with Austria than through its bonds with Hungary. Therefore for Austria there was a danger that the new Hungarian Government, by granting some or all of the Croat claims, would re-establish the old friendly relations between the two peoples. To prevent this Kollowrat had Joseph Jellačić nominated *Ban* of Croatia. Jellačić, a representative of extreme nationalist policy, was *persona grata* with the Habsburgs. He was perfectly aware of what was expected from him. No sooner had he arrived in Zagreb than he introduced martial law, and with the active help of Latour, the Austrian Minister of War, began to prepare an armed attack on Hungary.

Though less menacing, because less well organized, unrest among the Serbs and Roumanians was also rapidly spreading. By the middle of May both groups declared their independence of the Hungarian Government, and with active or passive help from the regiments of the Imperial Army stationed among them began a series of attacks against Hungarian property and lives. Social as well as national motives lay behind these movements, in which the not inconsiderable pro-Hungarian elements were swamped by extremists. In such movements, which, however equitable their ends, are inevitably swayed by mass-hysteria, leadership goes necessarily to the highest bidder, and reasonable men are, by definition, reluctant to contest for it with claims which they know that they cannot fulfil. On Viennese instigation peoples which had not reached political maturity tried to emulate the Hungarian example. But whereas in the one case a thousand-year-old state had sought to regain control of its own affairs, and that by constitutional means, the minorities living on Hungarian soil simply tried by force to carve out for themselves a piece from the country which had, in fact, brought liberation to all its citizens, irrespective of race or language. Kollowrat's policy had liberated a demon which no power was strong enough to conjure back into the bottle.

Everywhere, in Austria as in Hungary and among the turbulent minorities, the real struggle was between moderate and extremist statesmen. With great devotion but less skill, Batthyány tried to avert the catastrophe, and travelling to and fro between Budapest and Austria, endeavoured to achieve the impossible: an agreement with

Jellačić. The *Ban* was obviously preparing action, and as he represented Habsburg rather than Croat interests, it was becoming gradually apparent that no concession made to the Croat nationalist point of view would appease him. Responsible Austrian statesmen were by no means agreed on the desirability of open hostilities within the Imperial boundaries, but, here again, the task of the moderate elements was not made easier by the conduct of the Hungarian Parliament and Government, and particularly by Kossuth's activities, which went far beyond the competence of a Minister of Finance.

Kossuth was convinced that conflict was inevitable, and perhaps at the bottom of his heart he cherished the thought of complete liberation, of a joining together with other peoples longing for freedom. Changeable, unstable, he lacked a clear purpose to which to adhere; his visionary mind made him see possibilities which did not exist but which his art of oratory could conjure before a spellbound audience. The gap between Kossuth and Batthyány widened steadily. The former was more and more convinced that he represented the real people, divorced from a hesitant Government, while the Prime Minister viewed with growing irritation the constant encroachments *ultra vires* of his Minister of Finance. However, their uneasy partnership had to continue for yet a while, as Kossuth had not yet reached the stage of rejecting parliamentary procedure, and Batthyány needed Kossuth's extraordinary gifts.

On September 11th Jellačić, heading an army of some 34,000 men, crossed the River Drava and began his advance towards the capital. It was due to Kossuth that Hungary managed to muster forces large enough to meet this challenge. First, as Minister of Finance he had the task of producing the necessary money, secondly, as a peerless tribune, it fell to his lot to raise a popular army to set against the aggressor. Kossuth excelled in both tasks. Faced with the non-co-operation of the Austrian National Bank, on June 17th he drafted an agreement between the *nádor* (representing the King), the Government and the Commercial Bank for issuing paper money to the value of twelve-and-a-half million florins, guaranteed by a deposit, in gold and silver, of five million florins. He thus counterbalanced to some extent the shortage of money; but the sum was insufficient, and on September 6th—without consulting Batthyány and without seeking the approval of Parliament—Kossuth announced an issue of banknotes of five florins guaranteed by 'the public income of the country'. By this step, highly unorthodox and illegal on the financial and the political level, which was later (also illegally) approved by Parliament, Kossuth laid the foundation of the country's self-defence. Earlier—after a famous speech delivered in Parliament on July 11th—Kossuth had obtained considerable credits for organizing a national army.

The setting up of this army was fraught with difficulties, caused primarily by the King's dilatoriness in countersigning the decrees submitted to him by the Government. His attitude was partially justi-fied by his complete distrust of his Hungarian subjects, who, it must be said, had quite unconstitutionally raised difficulties over helping Austria in her war with Italian revolutionaries. In this they were moved, not only by an understandable reluctance to part with well-trained Hungarian troops at the very moment when an attack against their own country threatened, but also by Kossuth's revolutionary fervour, which inclined him more to help the Italians than to fight against them. The summer and early autumn of 1848 thus passed in a general constitutional confusion, with great financial difficulties and enthusiastic recruiting campaigns. With prodigious energy Kossuth prepared the country for a great ordeal, and in this he was so successful that the ordeal became inevitable. The moderate Batthyány tried in vain to conciliate Austrian and Hungarian extremists. After Kossuth's high-handed financial action Batthyány had tendered his resignation, but one day later he was asked to form the new Government by the *nádor*, the Archduke Stephen, who did his very best to avert a civil war. This happened on September 11th, the day when Jellačić's troops crossed the Drava. Batthyány accepted the charge on condition that the troops of Jellačić be withdrawn and that the Austrian National Bank put at the Government's disposal a sum of one million florins, so as to make unnecessary the illegal issuing of banknotes. Royal consent to form the new Government arrived on the 16th—unaccompanied by any guarantees. In spite of this rebuff Batthyány continued to keep in touch with Vienna, where the *nádor* also used his moderating influence. The Austrian Prime Minister, Wessenberg, was also aware of the harm that could be caused by a civil war raging within the boundaries of the Empire. The joint efforts of men whom no one could accuse of revolutionary or separatist tendencies were not in vain. Count Francis Lamberg, commander of Pozsony, who was well known for his sympathy for the Hungarians was appointed

Commander-in-Chief of all the armed forces stationed in Hungary; it was thought that Jellačić would not dare to continue his advance into a Hungary whose armed forces stood under the command of an officer of undoubted loyalty. But chance so ordained that Batthyány, who went to meet Lamberg, missed him on the way; on arrival in Budapest, therefore, Lamberg was received, not by a friendly Prime Minister, but by a group of hotheads, led by Kossuth (who had just returned from a highly successful recruiting campaign), who were unwilling to see in him anything but another Jellačić. Batthyány was absent, Széchenyi had lost his reason at the sight of the country in turmoil, politics were coming under the influence of the populace. On September 28th Lamberg was murdered by the mob and thus all hope of conciliation faded away.

CHAPTER 29

THE WAR OF INDEPENDENCE,
1848-9

ON the same day that Lamberg was murdered, Jellačić's advance was halted by his first serious encounter with hastily-formed Hungarian troops. The *Bán* withdrew towards Vienna, where a new revolution broke out. The Minister of War, Latour, who had worked in close collaboration with Jellačić, ended his life hanging from a lamp-post and the Court fled to Olmütz. In Austria great emergencies usually produced great men, and in these days when, once again, the Habsburg Empire seemed to be on the eve of dissolution, two men of great determination, the Princes Windischgraetz and Schwarzenberg, came to the fore to save the situation. It took them a year to do so, a year of tragedy and glory for the Hungarian people.

On October 3rd, a few days before the Viennese revolution, the King had at last accepted Batthyány's resignation and, as a reply to Lamberg's assassination, had appointed no other than Jellačić as his successor. At the same time he dissolved Parliament. Its members refused to abide by the King's decree and entrusted a National Defence Committee with the conduct of affairs. Kossuth, as the chairman of this committee, became virtually the ruler of Hungary. With this step even a fiction of legality ceased. The Austrian reaction was quick and no less illegal. On December 2nd Ferdinand V and his younger brother, the heir apparent, Francis Charles, were forced to abdicate in favour of the latter's son Francis Joseph (1848–1916). The reason for this *coup d'état* was fairly simple. Austrian statesmen wanted to see on the throne a ruler not bound by the coronation oath and sufficiently young to be malleable to their own aims. These also were simple and straightforward: the crushing of the Hungarian revolt.

At first this appeared a fairly easy task. Hungary proper was made the target of concentric attacks launched simultaneously by Imperial forces stationed in Transylvania and in the south of Hungary. In the former area the Polish general Bem, on the southern front General Damjanich (himself a Serb) achieved local successes for Hungary against the Austrian attacks, but in the west the main armies under Windischgraetz's command could not be halted by the inexperienced and ill-armed Hungarian troops. On the last day of that fatal year of 1848, on the proposal of Batthyány, a Hungarian delegation approached Windischgraetz, but he refused 'to parley with rebels'. The Government fled to Debrecen and on December 5th Budapest was occupied by Windischgraetz. The situation seemed desperate.

In these critical times the nation rose to great heights of patriotic devotion and courage. Class distinctions, which, barely a year earlier, had divided the population into two so unequal and bitterly opposed camps, seem to have vanished. That this happened, that this could happen, was to Kossuth's credit. Never before, not even under Rákóczi, had the nation's confidence been placed so unreservedly in one man. As had Hunyadi and Rákóczi before him, Kossuth relied on the deep reserves of patriotism in the people at large. Once again the Hungarian peasant proved the backbone of the nation; but it was through Kossuth that he found his way to effective action.

But general enthusiasm is not enough to win a war, particularly if the enemy is so vastly superior in numbers and arms as were the Austrians. From the very first this fact was recognized by a young major, Arthur Görgei.

Like many professional soldiers, Görgei was a patriot but had little sympathy for revolutions. Strict, dry, often caustic in his comments, he was in many respects not unlike Széchenyi. He was able to assess accurately the potentialities of the situation, and showed no inclination to be misled by wishful thinking or demagogy. He took part in the first engagement of the war and distinguished himself in the first victory against the forces of Jellačić. Kossuth's attention was soon drawn to this efficient, well-disciplined soldier, and Görgei was given command of the Hungarian troops facing Windischgraetz. These, as Görgei knew, were totally inadequate for their task. He therefore withdrew, refusing to have his force destroyed in order to please Kossuth, who was bent on immediate successes. From this time onwards relations between the barely thirty-year-old Görgei and Kossuth remained strained and this did considerable harm to the cause they both served. Görgei realized that only a well-disciplined and well-trained force could hope to defeat the Imperial Army, and that, to achieve this, more professional officers were needed. These, however, showed some reluctance to join those who, they had been told, were 'rebels', and to combat an army to which they themselves belonged. Görgei, who could well understand their mentality, did much to put their minds at rest, and at Vác on January 6th, issued a manifesto in which he rigorously defined the conditions under which the army was willing to serve the Government. Görgei declared his faithfulness to the dynasty and to the constitution of April 18th and reiterated his readiness to obey the Government appointed by the King. At the same time he gave warning that the army would not follow those who sought to overthrow the constitutional monarchy by 'inept republican agitation'. This manifesto, hardly proper from a general, had the desired effect of reconciling the officers and thus making continued resistance possible. It had also the effect of further poisoning relations between Görgei and Kossuth.

The result was that Kossuth appointed the untalented Dembinski Commander-in-Chief of the Hungarian army. Under his command, on February 27th, the army suffered a heavy defeat at the hands of Windischgraetz, who felt justified in announcing to the King the death of the Hungarian rebellion. This was blatantly untrue, but it prompted Francis Joseph to proclaim on March 4th a new constitution for the whole Habsburg Empire, under which Hungary was to be incorporated as no more than a province. The decision, to say the least, was premature. In a brilliant campaign during the next month, Görgei—who after some delay had been appointed deputy Commander-in-Chief— succeeded in pushing back the Austrian army as far as Pozsony, and the prodigious Bem, with a handful of soldiers, almost completely cleared Transylvania of foreign troops. It began to seem as if a miracle had been accomplished, as if, against overwhelming odds, the Hungarians had liberated their country from foreign invaders.

Kossuth, pushed by the extremists among his entourage (among whom the Minister of Police, Madarász, played a particularly nefarious rôle) took a momentous but completely useless decision. On April 14, 1849, the Habsburg dynasty was declared dethroned and Kossuth was elected Regent of Hungary. Parliament had ceased to become an expression of the popular will, the absentees had grown more and more numerous, and though few approved this new step, such was Kossuth's influence over his compatriots that no one dared to oppose him openly. It must be emphasized that in one essential point the Hungarian situation differed from the familiar pattern of a revolution degenerating into dictatorship. This was the absence of terror. Though Madarász and some of his companions tried to implant a rule of terror this was so alien to the Hungarian mentality that it could be nipped in the bud. That spectre of the weak, the internal enemy, caused little concern to Kossuth. He had opponents, Széchenyi, Batthyány and Görgei among them, but it never occurred to him to use the guillotine as supreme arbiter in his political disputes. He respected his antagonists as they respected him; errors were committed on both sides, crimes on neither. Kossuth's hands remained clean of blood. For this, if for no other reason, he must rank among the great statesmen of history.

It was not the internal spectre that was to defeat Hungary and the superfluous dethronement of the Habsburgs barely hastened a fate already sealed. Negotiations had been opened between Austria and Russia to secure the latter's help. Francis Joseph went to Warsaw to discuss the nature of Russia's intervention with Tsar Nicholas I, and in June a joint Austrian-Russian offensive was launched against Hungary. Some 152,000 Hungarian *honvéd* (as the soldiers of this war were called), armed with only 450 guns, had to face the 1,200 guns of an enemy some 370,000 strong. The Russian attack came from the north and the east, along almost the same routes used six centuries earlier by the Mongols; the desperate efforts of Görgei and Bem were of no avail. On July 12th Kossuth and what remained of the Government and Parliament fled to Szeged, and then further south to Arad. On August 9th Bem lost the last major battle of the war. A few hours before learning the news, Görgei and Kossuth had spoken together of this possibility. The soldier said that if the battle were lost he would lay down arms, the politician that he would blow out his brains. Some hours afterwards the news of the defeat arrived. Kossuth resigned, handed over his powers to Görgei and fled to Turkey. Görgei had three choices: to follow Kossuth's example, to engage a last hopeless battle with his remaining 30,000 men, or to lay down arms. He took the last course as he had said he would. As a gesture, and with a naïve belief in fair play, Görgei preferred to lay down his arms before the Russians.

On August 13th, at Világos, the last Hungarian army surrendered to the Russian Commander-in-Chief, Pashkievitch.

In spite of all the heroism of the people, the great war was lost, for the politicians had not seen, or would not see, that it was a war impossible to win. And as it was impossible to win, it should have been avoided at all costs. The politicians fled. Madarász became a prosperous farmer in the United States; the soldier Görgei stayed, to be regarded by many as a traitor, responsible for the defeat.

CHAPTER 30

ABSOLUTISM

THE end of the 1848–9 war of independence has many features in common with the surrender which ended Rákóczi's revolution. This time, however, there was no trace of desire on the Austrian side to show restraint or to heal the wounds caused by the strife between peoples who—such was the desire of the Government—were intended to live peacefully within the Empire. A bestial oppression followed the surrender of Világos. Russian intervention only saved Görgei's life. On October 6, 1849, thirteen Hungarian generals were hanged at Arad, whilst Louis Batthyány paid with his life at Budapest for his courageous efforts to maintain peace. Over a hundred patriots were executed in a butchery which roused indignation all over Europe. This was of small help to those executed. In England, perhaps more than elsewhere, feelings ran high among the people. A memorandum to Russell and Palmerston, signed by eighty-three Members of Parliament, could not alter a policy of non-interference favoured by Tories and Whigs alike. Even Cobden, who in November 1849, in a personal letter to Bach, the Austrian Minister of the Interior, appealed to him 'in the name of humanity, to make an end to this renewed terror, which, not content with butchering its victims, must also put to the rack all the better feelings of humanity', even Cobden showed himself cautious when, during Kossuth's visit to England, opportunity came to help the Hungarian cause effectively. The principal instigator of the Austrian reign of terror was the sadist Haynau, already notorious for his cruel exploits in Italy. His fairly short-lived military dictatorship was followed by sixteen years of absolutist rule, tyrannical, inefficient and corrupt. The first and worst ten years of this régime were associated with the name of Alexander Bach, whose super-administration could

have provided material for a hundred Courtelines. 'Organization' was
the word which kept under a magic spell thousands and thousands of
bureaucrats, 'conspiracy' the word which kept busy thousands and
thousands of gendarmes. The much-enduring country turned its back
on an administration which, without contacts with the people and with
no understanding of their problems, produced for its own justification
project after project in an almost complete vacuum. Only an execution,
or a new imprisonment, caused by some real or imaginary conspiracy,
produced stronger reactions by strengthening the passive resistance
which the nation opposed to tyranny. By modern standards this tyranny
was fairly mild, but a century ago it was felt quite unbearable. The
alien minorities in Hungary lost as much as the Hungarians themselves,
for the new system's avowed aim was centralization and Germanization,
with complete disregard of the national point of view.

Whatever its shortcomings may be, an absolute administration is
always capable of doing some good. The Bach system was no exception
to this rule. Problems left unresolved during the war of independence
were now attended to. However reactionary, the Austrian Government
had no desire to return to the pre-1848 feudal conditions which, it will
be remembered, had not been to the liking of Austrian statesmen. As a
customs-union for all the territories belonging to the monarchy had
been declared in 1850, a satisfactory arrangement of compensation for
the losses suffered by the landowners through the abolition of socage and
of the *ösiség* was a common interest. Thus absolutism, though explicitly
rejecting the achievements of the revolution, had in fact to adopt many
of them. The compensation was paid by the State, and was probably
greater than that which would have been awarded by a radical revolutionary Hungarian Government. At the very time that these compen-
sations were being paid out in instalments, the first taxes to be paid by
both nobles and former *jobbágys* were introduced; and the landowning
nobles, deprived of the benefits of socage, and unused to working for
a livelihood, found themselves in great financial difficulties. The
compensation received for the land distributed was in 1880 less than
one-third of its effective value, and only by the end of the century did it
reach some 40 per cent, and the insufficiency of capital made difficult
an up-to-date efficient working of the land. In spite of these and other
difficulties, agricultural productivity grew steadily. The new capitalist
economy proved, as was to be expected, superior to the feudal system in

force until the war of independence. Economic competition now became possible and led on one hand to the formation of latifundia, on the other, and as a corollary of this development, to the growing proletarization of the peasantry. By 1869–70 two and a quarter million landless agricultural workers meant a new problem for the country.

The abolition of serfdom and *ösiség* made large labour forces available to industry, and at the same time made the acquisition of land possible for everyone. The effects of this change on agriculture have already been touched upon. In industry development was on a larger scale. Foremost in expansion was the food industry: mills, sugar factories, distilleries. The construction of railways went on unabated and during the period of absolutism some 2,000 kilometres of track were laid. River transport kept pace, and by 1864 the Danubian Steamship Company owned 134 steamships and 544 tow-boats. The company's shipbuilding yard, employing 1,300 to 1,400 workers, was the greatest industrial works in Budapest.

The volume of trade going through Budapest was considerable, and could compare with that of Antwerp or Bremen. Much of it was in Austrian hands, just as by far the greatest part of industry, mining or transport was financed by Austrian capital. By the middle 'sixties there was a growing tendency to invest Hungarian capital, built up by trade, in industrial undertakings. As wages in Hungary were lower than in Austria, the establishment of new factories was a paying proposition.

It is useless to speculate on the rhythm Hungarian economic development would have taken under different political conditions. It is, however, probable that Hungary's complete incorporation with Austria gave her a chance to catch up with Austrian industrial development. Although Hungarians have in fact strongly resented that, from its inception on modern lines, their country's economy was built up as a corollary to Austria's, this was in principle a sound policy and it produced really unhappy effects only when the links between the two countries were severed. Previously Hungary's economic and nationalist interests had been contradictory, and as usual the Hungarians had paid more attention to politics than to economic and social improvements.

Very slowly the pointer of the political barometer was moving towards 'fair'. The reasons for this were multiple; no oppression lasts for ever, and the Austrians in their *Gemütlichkeit* were far too humane and far too inefficient to be persistently ruthless. The petty red tape tyranny of Bach was killed, one could almost say, by ridicule. Improvement was slow and erratic. The defeat at Solferino induced Francis Joseph to reconsider the internal situation of his lands. A new constitution, granted on October 20, 1860, to all his lands, including Hungary, marked a return to moderate liberalism; and an amendment issued on February 26, 1861, convoked the Hungarian Diet for the purpose of electing members to attend the general Parliament in Vienna. This compromise was, however, unacceptable to Hungary, who stubbornly resisted all attempts to incorporate her in the Habsburg Empire on the same footing as the Emperor's hereditary provinces.

Francis Deák had gradually made himself the virtual leader of the nation, and with great patience and wisdom he paved the way for a reconciliation. His refusal to accept the terms of the 'letters patent of February'; his quiet and dignified readiness to achieve by passive resistance what the war of independence had failed to obtain, namely the recognition of Hungary as an independent state within the Habsburg Empire and as equal partner with Austria, commanded general support. Not unnaturally Kossuth, in exile, strongly disapproved of any compromise. Convinced that partnership with Austria was not viable, in 1862, he produced a project for a Danubian confederacy in which 'Unity, concord, and fraternity would reign between Hungarians, Slavs and Roumanians'. Such sentiments, though highly desirable, might better have been invoked to weld together a confederation within the existing Habsburg framework. History has since shown that, despite its signal weaknesses, the Habsburg monarchy was the only form of government capable of maintaining a measure of concord among the heterogeneous peoples of the Danube valley. Kossuth's plan was unrealizable; and, since wireless had fortunately not yet been invented, *émigré* politicians then found it more difficult than nowadays to poison the atmosphere of their homeland to win support for impossible schemes. In spite of the immense and fully-deserved love the Hungarian people had for Kossuth, public opinion continued strongly in favour of remaining within the monarchy and making peace with the Emperor, who, up to then, had not been crowned King of Hungary.

The Prussian war of 1866 and Austria's defeat improved Hungary's chances and the long-drawn-out, largely unofficial negotiations produced, in 1867, the so-called Compromise, intended to put an end to the centuries-old struggle between the Habsburgs and Hungary: the dual monarchy of the Austro-Hungarian Empire came into being. The labour of preparing the ground for this compromise had been undertaken almost exclusively by Hungarian statesmen. Deák, and, in the later stages, Gyula Andrássy, Prime Minister of the new Hungarian Government, shouldered the heaviest burden of the negotiations. The Empress Elisabeth, a well-known sympathizer with the Hungarian cause, did much to smooth things over, but otherwise Francis Joseph himself was the principal negotiator on the Austrian side.

The Compromise, once achieved, remained for the coming half-century of Francis Joseph's reign the basis of the dual monarchy. The person of the Emperor-King provided the only unalterable link between Austria and Hungary. Both countries had separate parliaments and governments, but the army, foreign affairs and finances were in common. The ministers responsible for these common matters were accountable to a committee chosen from the members of the Austrian and Hungarian parliaments. Hungary's contribution to common expenses was, at first, fixed at 30 per cent of her national income. A series of renewable contracts between Austria and Hungary settled a number of other important questions, such as that of a customs-union, which was established at first for a period of ten years. The Compromise also declared the reunion of Transylvania with the mother-country.

CHAPTER 31

COMPROMISE AND UNEASY
PARTNERSHIP

ALTHOUGH the Compromise left many problems unresolved, it had the merit of giving Hungary a degree of independence which she had not enjoyed since before Mohács. At the same time the dual monarchy involved the renunciation of a number of attributes of national sovereignty, a renunciation which was much more resented in the second half of the nineteenth century than in our own days, when uniformed soldiers of foreign powers are an accepted sight in the streets of many lands, and when national troops are put, by their own governments, under foreign commanders. Though the Supreme Commander of the Austrian and Hungarian troops was, by common consent, the Emperor-King himself, the problem of integrating Hungarian soldiers into the Imperial and Royal army remained a vexed one and caused much resentment on both sides. There were other running sores, and the country as a whole seems to have rubbed salt into them with considerable pleasure. The long period of peace and prosperity which lay ahead was not put to the best possible use. The new independence, obtained by such heavy sacrifices, meant, not a continuation of the democratic and revolutionary tradition of Kossuth and 1848, but rather a relapse into the feudal mire, a return to the outlook of *extra Hungariam non est vita.*

The greatest part of the country's energy was to be spent in the coming half-century in futile constitutional quibbles which found expression in magniloquent patriotic outbursts, in steady obstruction of all constructive policies and, in general, in a growing hostility towards Austria. The country had, rightly or wrongly, accepted the Compromise as the only way out of a terrible impasse. Once it was accepted, the only reasonable policy was to make the best of it and to increase the importance of Hungary within the dual monarchy by greater wealth and better organization. After 1867 the Compromise was the only possible basis for a constructive policy. Francis Joseph held to it with remarkable consistency and absolute honesty; and the successive Hungarian governments had no other alternative than to remain within its terms. Opposition, therefore, unable to put up any acceptable alternative, had to content itself with useless nostalgic reminiscences of '48 and with negative criticisms of the Compromise. It was greatly helped by Kossuth's periodic letters from exile, which, until his death in 1894, caused considerable upheavals in Hungarian public life.

One can forgive Kossuth for seeking to justify himself by a ceaseless repetition of the principles for which he had stood when in power; but it was his so-called followers who, more than anyone, betrayed the democratic ideas which represented the real value of 1848. Blind nationalism alone survived, narrow, stupid and corrupt.

At the root of most evils of the post-1867 period we find the nobles, deprived of their privileges but with their outlook unchanged. Unable to do productive work, or to stand on their own feet against competition as it is encountered in commerce and industry, they swamped the civil service and created a bureaucratic machinery whose main function was to perpetuate itself, as is the case with its like the world over. Prone to nepotism in an unusual degree, they barred the road to office to members of the often Jewish or German bourgeoisie; and the peasantry, lacking education, had no hope whatever of advancement. An iniquitous franchise deprived most of them of the elementary right to vote, and open-vote constituencies gave ample opportunities to put pressure on the electors.

Many members of the ancient nobility continued to farm their own estates, and since agriculture was protected by the customs union with Austria, they made no efforts to increase productivity. The aristocracy which, under Maria Theresa, had been indifferent to commercial treaties as long as its own privileges were respected, was now ready to acquiesce in a semi-colonial status for Hungary, as long as the market for its own agricultural products was protected against more efficient competitors. Some of the greatest estates had remained entailed; towards the turn of the century 4·7 per cent of the country's territory was inalienable property in the hands of a few families. At the same time,

in a country where 72 per cent of the population lived by agriculture,
5·7 per cent only of the arable land was shared by more than half the
peasantry! In other terms, 36 per cent of the population had to live on
under 6 per cent of the arable land. Even less fortunate were the great
masses of farmworkers with no land at all, who were completely
dependent on seasonal work for a livelihood. Their standard of living
was very low, and they provided an almost inexhaustible reserve of
cheap labour, which rendered mechanization superfluous and thus
contributed to a perpetuation of low productivity. The customs-union
with Austria was unfavourable to the creation of industry, which would
have been capable of absorbing the rural proletariat. Efforts to settle the
latter failed through lack of a consistent and courageous policy. Local
outbursts of violence were ascribed to socialist agitators, and strike
movements among harvest-workers were quelled by force.

The lack of any prospect of securing a decent living compelled
hundreds of thousands to seek a new life in America—270,000 in 1898
alone—but the departure of these emigrants could not improve the lot
of those remaining. While Budapest was rapidly becoming one of the
most attractive cities in Europe, while politicians spoke of re-creating a
kingdom as splendid as that of Matthias and dreamt of an Empire of
thirty million Hungarians, emigration was sapping the country's
forces, and infantile mortality stood at 25 per cent.

The movement of the population was not limited to emigration.
While a steady flow of working-class people, stolid Hungarian and
Slovak peasants, left the country unwilling to give them sustenance, a
smaller, but considerable Jewish immigration from the East was creating
a problem which was to have its tragic conclusion half a century later.
Since 1867 the Jews had been fully emancipated in Hungary, which
thus became the promised land for the Jews of Poland. Hungarian
Jewry, just over a quarter of a million strong in 1848, was nearing the
million mark by 1914. Since the public service was a stronghold of the
nobility, Jews entered commerce and industry (despised by the
Hungarian nobles) in large numbers, and also the learned professions.
By 1900 almost half the Hungarian doctors were Jews. Many of these
immigrants had no time to become assimilated, and thus an important
and influential foreign colony was created, not hostile, and in many
respects of value to Hungary, but lacking comprehension of Hungarian
life and ways.

The problem of the 'minorities' (for this epoch the use of the word is no longer anachronistic) also found no solution. Among the Roumanians, Slovaks and Croats it was the extremist leaders who had the greatest following. Moderate, pro-Hungarian politicians receiving little support from the Government, found it increasingly difficult to justify their own attitude towards an official policy which seemed as nationalist as that propounded by their own extremists. In practice the Government was not harder on alien nationalities than on Hungarians. Indeed in many respects the former actually found themselves more favourably placed than the Hungarians. For geographical as well as for political reasons industrial development was—apart from Budapest itself—more important in the territories inhabited by minorities than in those with a Hungarian population, and the electoral law, whilst granting the right of voting to roughly speaking only one in twenty, favoured the non-Hungarian elements. The minorities, powerfully helped either by their brethren beyond the borders (as was the case with Roumanians and Croats), or (like the Slovaks) by an Austrian administration staffed by Czechs, could, and did, spread strong anti-Hungarian propaganda in Western Europe. Ignorant politicians and naïve scholars alike were distressed at the oppression of the minorities, and failed to notice that the treatment they received was not worse than that meted out to Hungarians. They also failed to perceive the obvious, namely that oppression would be infinitely worse under the rule of any of these maltreated national groups.

So oppression there was; but, far from being the product of some totalitarian system, it was the product of liberalism. Because of special historical circumstances, such as the long Turkish occupation, Hungarian political and social evolution had not been continuous, and long-lost liberty, once recovered, was not used with the necessary discernment. In many respects the phenomenon was similar to that observed today in the political life of former colonies. The Government and, indeed, all statesmen, although imbued with liberal principles, never really envisaged tackling at the root the many evils which bedevilled Hungarian life. Their actions were only palliative, and aimed at maintaining order; their oppressive measures were never preventive and were so far justified in that without them, and without the suppression of the underlying causes of unrest, the country would have sunk into anarchy. Many of the mistakes thus committed were common to contemporary Europe; but Hungarian statesmen had the misfortune of having to rule a multinational people, under the critical eyes of European public opinion. Western European statesmen, scandalized by Hungarian refusal to grant autonomy to the minorities, found no fault with colonial policies infinitely worse from the point of view of the indigenous population. There was no discrimination in Hungary against non-Hungarians. The political conceptions prevailing at the turn of the century were simply not suited to the special circumstances in Hungary; the fallacy, then generally accepted, that freedom for all and free competition was the only rule to adhere to, was first belied by internal developments within the Austro-Hungarian Empire. But such was the faith in it, that statesmen all over the world failed to recognize the lesson to be drawn, and ascribed the symptoms to a special Hungarian cause. Today all countries which have to cope with multi-lingual and multinational subjects encounter the same difficulties and are still unable to find an effective remedy, and this in spite of using methods infinitely more efficient and more cruel than the dispatching of the few gendarmes who, before a local election, made a timely appearance in some Hungarian village.

It would be a mistake to draw too dark a picture of conditions prevailing in Hungary between the Compromise and the outbreak of the First World War. The country was taking her fair share in the rather showy prosperity of the period. Industrial development, though insufficient to give work to the millions who could have been made available by a more modernized agriculture, was nevertheless considerable. Besides sugar factories, breweries, tanneries, heavy industry and a textile industry appeared. Though personal initiative was not stifled, state intervention was used more often than in most western countries. Without it Hungarian industry would have been unable to make a satisfactory start. It was moreover nationalization which put an end to the muddle due to the inefficiency of competing private railway companies, and a judicious tariff-reform increased the passenger-traffic from nine million in 1888 to twenty-eight million in 1892. In general, public services (for example, the post) reached a high degree of efficiency, and in many fields small technical innovations put Hungary ahead of western countries.

It was with considerable pride, not only in the nation's past but also in her present, that Hungary celebrated in 1896 the thousandth anniversary of her existence. In a beautiful city, further embellished by buildings of permanent character erected for the Millennium, with relative internal quiet and with no foreign conflicts in sight, the politicians who gathered in Budapest around the aged monarch could honestly think that they had built upon rock. But we have seen that much of this optimism was unjustified, and that below the surface, forces of antagonism were at work, seriously menacing the super-structure.

Early in the twentieth century the hidden discontents were further aggravated by a spiritual crisis. In 1905 the Liberals, who had ruled Hungary for almost forty years, could no longer resist the pressure of irresponsible opposition parties. Whatever their shortcomings had been, the successive Liberal governments stood firm on the only passable road for Hungarian politics, that built on the Compromise. The new generation that had grown up had no memories of the difficulties which this Compromise had solved and saw only through a romantic haze the great dream of complete independence. The levers of politics slipped from the hands of the nobility, and a new, barely Hungarian middle-class gained growing influence over the country's destiny. It was divided into two sharply contrasting sections. The first, of astoundingly low intellectual quality, represented an ultra-nationalism which, without taking any account of the country's resources, preached imperialism. The other faction, much more serious and with a better perception of the social ills, was too abstract, too intelligent, to have a real, effective political following. An irresponsible gutter-press added to the general mental confusion. Criticism, however justified, was decried as high treason by those who had done nothing for the country. It is significant that Andrew Ady—probably the greatest of Hungarian poets—in whom vibrated all the pains and problems of his people, stood under incessant attack because of his supposed anti-patriotism. In the turmoil of ill-digested ideas and demagogy there was no man, no institution capable of providing the necessary antidote. The Catholic Church, whose contacts with Rome had been hampered by the Josephinist tradition in Habsburg policy, fell far short of its rôle. The 'social' encyclicals of Leo XIII had no effect on a higher clergy nomin-ated by the King, very often on political grounds. Divorced from the poor people they were supposed to lead, most members of the higher clergy shared the liberal, *laisser-faire* attitude of their friends, the politicians. A general lowering of public and private morality, a war to the knife in every sphere of public life, helped to create an atmosphere probably not dissimilar to that prevailing before Mohács.

In an epoch when all seemed to have lost their bearings, one man, Count Stephen Tisza, stood almost alone between the country and chaos. Having been Prime Minister in 1903–5, he was called back to power on June 10, 1913. Violent, hot-headed, not always scrupulous in his methods, Tisza—who during his first term as Prime Minister had not hesitated to use force to break the parliamentary obstructions of the opposition—was probably the most hated man in Hungary, but he had something which none of his detractors possessed: a policy with a chance of success. Faithful to the Compromise, Tisza was capable of introducing a number of moderate reforms which might have satisfied the more level-headed members of the opposition, and also of creating social conditions more favourable for the working classes. He further grasped, though not to the full extent, the problem of the minorities. Perhaps above all, he was a man of order, with a strong will to see order prevail in the life of the country. He had little opportunity to show his capacities for peaceful development. On June 28, 1914, the heir apparent, Francis Ferdinand, was assassinated in Sarajevo, and the First World War was about to break out.

CHAPTER 32

THE FIRST WORLD WAR
AND THE REVOLUTION

IT is impossible to examine closely here Hungary's rôle in the 1914–18 war. It was a thankless one. Though the spark that set Europe ablaze was struck near Hungary, it soon became apparent that the Austro-Hungarian Empire and, with greater reason even, Hungary were not among the chief actors in the tragedy. At first Tisza had nothing to gain and neither he nor Hungarian public opinion was roused emotionally by the death of Francis Ferdinand, an avowed enemy of the Hungarians, whose accession to the throne would have meant the renewal of constitutional struggles of the most violent kind. It was the Slavophile policy which Francis Ferdinand had advocated which brought about his death, the dissolution of the Monarchy and the dismemberment of Hungary, which had always opposed these policies.

It was probably the danger of Slavonic imperialism which moved Tisza to acquiesce in the war, which he hoped would remain a simple punitive action against Serbia. Once in it, with his usual realism, Tisza tried to make the best of a bad job. The war silenced the demagogy of the opposition for some time, and a united country followed with anxious eyes the destinies of the Hungarian soldiers engaged, once again, in a foreign war. We have had cause in earlier pages to comment unfavourably on the capabilities of Austrian generals. A study of the First World War is unlikely to bring forth contradictory evidence. All along the northern, eastern and southern fronts of the Central Powers, Hungarian soldiers fought with the courage and quiet stubbornness of the Hungarian peasant; they fought, in most cases, under Austrian or Czech superior officers who cared little for Hungarian lives. While they fought, mostly on foreign soil, profiteering and demagogy throve in their own land. The decline in public morality was accentuated by the stress of war; Tisza was not strong enough to face renewed attacks, and on June 15, 1917, he resigned. On November 21, 1916, Francis Joseph had died. Whatever his shortcomings as a man and a ruler, he was loved and revered by the great majority of his subjects. During his long reign of sixty-eight years his person had come to be identified with the monarchy itself, and his disappearance loosened the bonds uniting the Habsburg Empire. His successor Charles IV (1916–21), the last Habsburg ruler, was for obvious reasons unable to command the same respect and devotion. He was also more hesitant, less authoritative than Francis Joseph, who had learnt to know the transcience of many conceptions, good and bad alike. Charles IV's repeated efforts to conclude peace with the Allies all failed, and his well-meant endeavour to satisfy reasonable demands, with, for example, the reform of the electoral law, came too late to be of any practical use. The desire for peace grew steadily and the fourteen points of President Wilson gave hope of a reasonably just settlement. The centrifugal forces at work against Hungary and against the Austro-Hungarian Empire, would not have sufficed to achieve her dislocation. Pure and simple military defeat was to effect this, but before the final sacrifice a long road of suffering lay ahead of the Hungarian people.

Defeat, in itself inevitable, was greatly hastened by the disruptive forces at work within the country. These were varied in nature and, according to temperament, were geared either to the Bolshevik Revolution or to Wilson's fourteen points, but they were all pacifist and thus hardly conduced to victory. Though defeat had to come in any case, the combatant troops, standing everywhere on enemy soil, were discouraged, if not actively disorganized, from the rear. On their return they found confusion, anarchy, virtual revolution. Those who had suffered the least were the loudest advocates of defeatism.

The war was still going on, with no armistice signed, when Hungarian troops—already in a state of effervescence at the news coming from home—were given orders to return by a new Hungarian Government. Peace, the severance of all links with Austria (with the exception of a common ruler), and land-reform were the principal points of a programme put forward by Count Michael Károlyi who, after having been the president of the Hungarian National Council representing little else than itself, was on October 31, 1918, entrusted with forming a government. The same day Tisza, who had played little or no part in events, was murdered. He was not to be the only victim of pacifism.

None of Károlyi's more distant aims was harmful or dishonest. But they were at that time inopportune and, in any case, he was the last man able to realize them. Weak and changeable, he lacked the true qualities of a leader and was bound to go down in the turmoil of events he had furthered. On November 16th Hungary was declared a 'People's Republic' and on January 11, 1919, Károlyi—by then hardly more than a figure-head—was, by acclamation, elected its President. In the meanwhile negotiations were going on with various self-appointed National Councils set up among the minorities of the country. Forgetting the elementary truth that during negotiations it is well to hold some trump cards, those possessed by the peace-frenzy, intoxicated with Wilsonian fizzy-water, disbanded perfectly well-disciplined troops and watched with folded arms the advance of ill-organized Roumanian and Czech bands towards the centre of the country. Unsympathetic, stiff-lipped French officers watched with distaste the moral and material disintegration of an ex-enemy. In the absence of any resistance the demarcation-lines were constantly re-drawn, steadily reducing what was still allowed to remain Hungarian. On March 21, 1919, Károlyi somewhat unwillingly handed over power to a government of People's Commissars, whose first action was to declare Hungary a Soviet Republic. Communist agitation had been going on virtually unhampered for a considerable time and Károlyi's last step was but the recognition of the real state of affairs. He left behind him complete confusion, into which the Communists—with Béla Kún, the Commissar for Foreign Affairs, as principal moving force—tried to put some order in their own way.

The news of a Hungarian Soviet Republic caused a somewhat belated alarm in Allied circles, and General Smuts was dispatched to Budapest to try negotiations. Kún had been wise enough to refuse a French ultimatum and to start building up an army. He preferred to negotiate as far as possible from strength. The result was immediate and the conditions offered by Smuts were reasonably favourable. 'So what my Government'—writes Károlyi with remarkable modesty in his memoirs—'had not been able to obtain in five months was granted to the Communists after a week, proving that the idea of standing up to the West was not such a bad one.' Kún felt that even the conditions offered by Smuts were unacceptable but his rejection of them proved too dangerous a gamble. A few days later Roumanian troops started an offensive and soon reached the Tisza; the Hungarian Army, disorganized and ill-supplied, offered but little resistance. Kún once again forgot his political theories and called in Aurel Stromfeld, an excellent soldier of the Imperial Army, to organize resistance. Stromfeld set himself to the task, turned against the Czechs, and in less than a month drove them out of the greater part of Northern Hungary. What results the army could achieve, politics were to undo. The policy of the Hungarian Soviets found little popular support; neither the peasants nor the middle classes viewed with pleasure the dictatorship of the proletariat. Only foreign help could have maintained this régime, but the much-awaited international revolution was not to come, and the country, weakened by internal strife, was too tired to start a victorious campaign against the Roumanians. Many by then preferred foreign occupation to Communist rule, and it was to come all too soon. A Hungarian offensive launched on July 20, 1919, failed and the Roumanian counter-attack, which on August 3rd led to the occupation of Budapest, caused the fall of Kún on July 31st. It is almost impossible to give an objective and accurate picture of the 131 days of the Dictatorship of the Proletariat. Accounts given by eye-witnesses are so distorted by political bias that they reflect more the opinions of the narrator than the facts he relates. Terror, as an avowed political instrument, was made ample use of, and the period saw the emergence of the sadist, important among the *dramatis personae* of our century.

The fall of the Communist régime was followed by a brief period of complete chaos, with ephemeral governments, negotiations with allied generals, and acts of savage terrorism. These, known as the 'White Terror', were committed in most cases as simple acts of individual vengeance, and it would be futile to argue whether they were worse or not than the excesses of the Communist régime. They were strongly tainted by anti-semitism. The strong proportion of Jews in the Communist venture (for example thirty-two out of the forty-five Commissars) provides a partial explanation. For a short while the Archduke Joseph—who had been established in Hungary by Charles IV as *homo regius*—ruled as Regent, but on pressure brought by Clemenceau he had to resign. The 'Tiger' was determined to crush every trace of Habsburg power. Archduke Joseph had time to appoint Admiral Nicholas Horthy as Commander-in-Chief of the Hungarian National Army. Horthy showed considerable diplomatic skill in the negotiations which led on November 16th to his entering Budapest at the head of a new National Army. His good manners—he had been *aide-de-camp* to Francis Joseph—and his knowledge of languages had made a good impression on allied, particularly on English negotiators, and his entry into the capital was anything but a military *coup d'état*. His unpolitical past, his military record (he had been the last Commander-in-Chief of the Austro-Hungarian navy) made him an obvious choice, and on March 1, 1920, he was elected Regent of Hungary, with prerogatives similar to that of the King, with the exception of the rights of conferring titles of nobility and ecclesiastic dignities.

While Hungary was indulging in political experiments, the Peace Conference in Paris was busily deciding her fate. It must be said that had she been represented there this would have had no influence upon the proceedings, in which French obstinacy, American ignorance and British indifference were hard at work to wreck the world's future. The first real victim was Hungary, foolish enough to believe the Wilsonian fallacy, and too slow to take to armed resistance. The Treaty of Trianon, signed under duress on June 4, 1920, deprived Hungary of roughly speaking two-thirds of her former territory and population. The new frontiers, though theoretically drawn to correspond to dividing ethnic lines, met in fact the desires of Serbian, Roumanian and Czech statesmen, anxious to secure for their countries as much territory as possible. Thus some 3,300,000 Hungarians—many of them living in compact masses near the new border-lines—were incorporated in the new 'successor-states', where they were to be submitted to persecutions more grievous than their present masters had ever suffered in pre-war Hungary. The treaty left Hungary economically crippled, deprived of the greater part of her industry and raw materials, and with a disorganized transport system. The country's capital resources, estimated in 1910 as totalling £51,794,000 foundation capital and £25,623,000 reserve capital, dwindled by 1921 to £1,824,000 and £1,153,000 respectively. To make things worse, the mutilated country had to provide for all the Hungarian refugees, either expelled from or voluntarily leaving the successor-states. A mutilated, dismembered, disarmed country, surrounded by strong and hostile neighbours, a country without allies, half-forgotten by those who then ruled the world, Hungary had, nevertheless, after almost four hundred years of Habsburg rule, recovered her full independence. We shall now have to examine the use she made of it.

PART SIX

AFTER THE FIRST WORLD WAR

CHAPTER 33

THE HORTHY ERA

THE period between 1920–44 is usually associated with the name of Horthy, and though assessments of his character differ widely, it is generally agreed that he exerted a considerable direct influence on Hungary's destiny. Yet Horthy was anything but a dictator and his powers were only those with which, according to Hungarian constitution, the King was invested. He had to rule through Parliament, but he had the right to convoke, dissolve and adjourn Parliament at his own discretion, and the appointment of the Prime Minister depended entirely on him. Thus, in practice, the influence of the Regent was considerable, but it remained till the end in full keeping with the Hungarian constitution and custom. The historian is entitled to record this undeniable fact and to leave it to political theoreticians to work out the advantages and disadvantages of the system.

Horthy himself was nothing of a theoretician. Conservative by temperament and upbringing he had, as a sailor, little sympathy with disorder and insubordination. The years spent in the immediate entourage of Francis Joseph had left an indelible mark on his character, and as the Head of State he tried in many respects to emulate the old Emperor. Aided by a most capable and charming wife, he bore his high office with dignity and no ostentation. His horizon was limited and his policies, at home and abroad, consisted in holding to well-tried values. He liked the British because they had a good navy and were gentlemen; he disliked the Nazis and the Communists because they did not seem to satisfy either of these requirements. He saw no reason to take away the land from those to whom it belonged, but he was prepared to sanction any policy to improve the lot of the under-privileged classes so long as this did not imply spoliation. He was deadly opposed to

Communism; he disapproved of the theory, and disliked the men who
professed it. The régime of Béla Kún left him with the conviction that
such an episode should never happen again, and in order to prevent the
recurrence he was ready to use what can be called anti-democratic
means. Democracy as an aim in itself meant little to Horthy, but he
never made any attempt to by-pass Parliament or, in general, to use
totalitarian methods. To solve Hungary's internal problems and to
bring the country's prosperity to the level enjoyed by, say, the
Scandinavian states would have needed a genius. This Horthy was not;
but he put an average talent and a more than average honesty unreservedly at the service of Hungary. If his reign ended in disaster, it
was not his fault. No captain could have steered to safety a ship as small
and as exposed as Hungary in the terrible hurricane that blew over
Eastern Europe at the end of the Second World War.

In the initial stages the pattern of Horthy's rule was set not only by
himself but also by Count Stephen Bethlen, who from April 1921 was
Prime Minister of Hungary for a decade. Bethlen's basic political ideas
were very near to those of Horthy and, without any revolutionary or
spectacular measures, order and stability slowly returned to the
country. Two ill-conceived attempts by Charles IV to regain the throne
of Hungary ended in his losing it altogether. On direct orders from the
Entente, the dethronement—the third and the last—of the House of
Habsburg was enacted by Parliament on December 3, 1921. Charles
was taken as a prisoner on a British man-of-war down the Danube and
thence to Madeira, where he soon after died. The danger of disorder
from the Legitimist side was thus reduced, and Bethlen steered a
cautious course between the extremists of right and left, among whom
the adventurers of the White Terror and their companions were by far
the most dangerous.

Budget deficits, unavoidable in the terrible economic circumstances
due to the Treaty of Trianon, grew steadily and resulted in an inflation
which—though not as disastrous as in post-war Germany—was still
crippling. Bethlen succeeded in obtaining considerable foreign loans,
which led to a monetary stabilization, and in July 1925 to the introduction of a new currency, the *pengö*. The country's economic recovery
was such that foreign capital was readily invested in industry and real-
estate. Industrial and farm production were rising rapidly and foreign
trade was flourishing. The depression which started in 1929 put an end

to Hungarian prosperity, demonstrating, once again, that no less in the economic than in the political field a small country is at the mercy of the great powers. The failure of the Österreichische Creditanstalt, in May 1931, precipitated Hungary into an economic crisis which was to last for two years. Bethlen, unable to find a solution to these problems, resigned and was followed first by Count Gyula Károlyi (1931–2), cousin of Michael, then by Gyula Gömbös (1932–6), Kálmán Darányi (1936–8) and Béla Imrédy (1938–9).

The economic crisis was slowly overcome and in home affairs matters did not change much under Károlyi and Gömbös. The latter, whom Horthy himself described as 'colourful', was in many respects a somewhat ridiculous personage, less harmful than fame had made him. A great admirer of the totalitarian methods of Hitler and Mussolini, he died in time (October 1936) to avoid the agonizing choice between patriotic and ideological calls which he would have had to make in later days. The emergence of Hitler was for Hungary, as indeed for the whole world, of the greatest importance. The short-sightedness of western politicians, particularly the French, was to drive Hungary into his fold.

In foreign affairs Hungary had, and could have, only one aim: the recovery of some of her lost territories. The aim was obvious; it had nothing imperialistic about it, and only peaceful means were thought of to achieve it. Though no responsible western statesman could consider the Treaty of Trianon as satisfactory, nothing was done to change it, and many perfectly justified Hungarian complaints were lost in the muddy marshes of the League of Nations. The French remained in eastern European matters under the influence of their Czech and Roumanian friends, and continued to show little or no sympathy for Hungary; the British, mildly sympathetic, could do little. The first European statesman to realize the value of a stronger Hungary was Mussolini; on April 5, 1927, he and Bethlen signed a treaty of friendship —the first Hungary was able to make with an ex-enemy state. Relations with traditional friends, Turks and Poles, were also cordial; those with Austria and Germany were acceptable.

Gömbös hit upon the bright idea to gear his foreign policy to the Rome–Berlin 'axis'—a word which he himself coined; and with feverish and far-from-foolish activity he did much to bring the Italian and German points of view closer, especially so far as Austria was concerned. He also concluded a trade-agreement with Germany which, though of great immediate help to Hungary's strained economy, had the effect of interlocking the two countries' production to an extent which made Hungary dependent on German economy. Another unfavourable effect of Gömbös's term of office was the infiltration of Nazi ideology, which found more and more adepts among the German-speaking population (6·9 per cent in 1920), and among the diehards of anti-semitism. A number of more or less crazy sham Führers also appeared, who were looked upon by the public with a derision mingled with contempt. The Horthy régime was too benign to stamp them out.

The *Anschluss* in March 1938 created an entirely new situation. Not only was the Reich now on the borders of Hungary, but it had become apparent that the world was ready to let aggression go unpunished. The Agreement of Munich was to confirm this. The Agreement, whilst creating a new situation in world politics, made it possible for Hungary to recover some of the lost territories which she had never ceased to claim. The so-called first Vienna Award (November 2, 1938) returned to Hungary part of the Highlands lying immediately across her borders, with a population of some 800,000. The award, signed by Ciano and Ribbentrop, satisfied no one. In March 1939, when Hitler seized Czechoslovakia, Hungarian troops—encountering no resistance—reoccupied Ruthenia, which before the Treaty of Trianon had belonged for some nine centuries to Hungary. This action also served to establish a common frontier between Poland and Hungary, both countries hoping to join their efforts to resist German imperialism in Eastern Europe.

The world was on the threshold of a new war, which Hungary had every reason to dread. Before beginning the last chapter of what can still be considered Hungarian *history*, it may be useful to glance at the balance-sheet of the Horthy era. This could be more favourable but, then, this can be said of balance-sheets of governments the world over. The main shortcomings were to be found as everywhere in Europe during that period, in the social field. Governments, and that of Horthy was no exception to the rule, were quite unable to decide in favour of a complete break with liberal methods. The sight of the Front Populaire in France, and of the Spanish Civil War, was not likely to induce a man like Horthy to try his hand at socialist experiments. With half-measures it was impossible to eradicate all the old injustices of Hungary's social structure, but much had been done to improve the standard of living of the people. By 1939 a forty-eight-hour week, holidays with pay, national insurance, etc., had been introduced, and the life of the industrial workers was, by European pre-war standards, quite acceptable. Agricultural labourers were less favoured, but even there some improvement had been made, and clearly the tendency was one of further amelioration. The middle classes enjoyed, on the whole, a pleasant life. Housing conditions were good, food was plentiful and of good quality, life was gay, arts and sports were flourishing. The foreigners who came in ever-growing numbers to visit Hungary and particularly Budapest, glittering with floodlit buildings, with streets thronged with elegant men and beautiful women, a city of incomparable swimming-pools and glorious gardens, could hardly believe what difficult social problems remained still unsolved.

Cultural life—so sensitive a barometer—was more pulsating than ever before. The music of Bartók, Kodály, Dohnányi, and the splendid successes of Hungarian sportsmen, did probably more than anything else to create in the world at large some interest in Hungary. Never before had Hungary had such a number of fine writers and poets; many among them, such as the novelist Sigismund Móricz or the poet Attila József, made no secret of their criticisms of the régime. In fact freedom of expression was almost complete. Personal attacks against the Regent's person were dealt with as constituting *lèse-majesté*. The Communist Party, as such, was forbidden, but many men known as Communists (among others the poet József) went undisturbed as long as they did not take part in any open, seditious activity. The absence of any 'Secret Police' of the Gestapo type is to be emphasized. The forming of political parties was not hampered, but 'private arrangements' always ensured a comfortable majority for the Prime Minister's party. Within certain limits—decided in the lobbies of political life—the electors could express their preference for a party or a man of their choice. In practice, the system was not vastly different from present-day British procedure, where the elector usually has the choice between two candidates put up by party-committees in the composition of which he has no say. The choice was greater in Hungary, the collusion on major issues between parties, perhaps, more widespread.

Politics are in general distasteful and they were made particularly displeasing in Hungary by the infiltration of Nazi ideology. The Hungarian propensity to create secret societies (known to everyone who cares to be informed), coupled with a less honourable and more dangerous willingness to indulge in personal intrigues, made Hungary an ideal field of activity for political adventurers of the lowest type. To these the Hungarian Nazis belonged, and among them Szálasi was to play the most evil rôle. That a criminal madman of his type should have been able to find a reasonably large number of followers speaks ill for Hungarian political discernment. The liberality of the régime made the proliferation of political movements possible, and there was no Secret Police to nip these in the bud. Horthy himself was too much of a Head of State and too little of a politician to be aware of all that went on. Though perfectly capable of taking decisions, he was not always well informed, and his choice of collaborators was more than once unfortunate.

The choice of Imrédy as Prime Minister is an instance of his ill-judgment, though no one could foresee that a brilliant financial expert known to be pro-British, should, once in power, turn into a pro-Nazi of the first magnitude. The recovery during his premiership, thanks to German help, of some of the lost territories enabled Imrédy to introduce some anti-Jewish legislation, fairly mild by German standards, but repulsive and cruel by any other. Public opinion forced him to resign and on February 16, 1939, he was followed in office by Count Pál Teleki, a man of the utmost moral rectitude.

With the outbreak of the war Hungary's situation became extremely precarious. A German victory, as everyone was agreed, would have meant purely and simply the absorption of Hungary by the new German Reich. This was so obvious that all who believed that the Allies would succumb to the German assault found it realistic policy to ensure the friendship of their future ruler. Neither Horthy nor Teleki was among these. Convinced that the maritime powers (Horthy was a sailor) would eventually have the upper hand, they were determined to keep Hungary out of the conflict, keep her out at all costs, even at the cost of concessions which they found repugnant. The example of Poland—not to mention that of Czechoslavakia—was there to show the effectiveness of western help to eastern allies, so that, understandably, Hungarian politicians had to take care not to overstrain German patience.

In 1939 Hungary flatly refused to have anything to do with the attack on Poland and gave shelter and refuge to scores of Polish refugees. The fall of France did not make Hungary change her attitude, though it strengthened the hand of those who wished to attach the destiny of Hungary to that of the victorious Reich.

On June 26, 1940, the Soviet Union sent Roumania an ultimatum, which was followed immediately by the annexation of Bukovina and Bessarabia. This prompted Hungary to press her territorial claims, outstanding since Trianon. The Axis Powers, supremely annoyed by the turmoil created by these renewed claims, decided to intervene in the Roumanian–Hungarian dispute, and the so-called Second Vienna Award returned to Hungary some 43,500 square kilometres of her former territory with a population of approximately 2·5 millions. The solution, though it partially repaired an old injustice, dissatisfied everyone. The cause of Roumanian dissatisfaction was plausible, the Hungarians were angry that the Germans did not help them more, the Nazis were furious that their hand had been forced and that trouble was brewing at their back.

The protraction of the war made Hungary's *nonbelligeranza* more and more difficult, and in April 1941 she became the unwilling accomplice of Germany's wanton attack on Yugoslavia. Teleki, unable to prevent German transit through Hungarian territory, committed suicide and Horthy, much against his better self, reoccupied some of the territories formerly belonging to Hungary.

Teleki's successor, Bárdossy, felt less reluctance to co-operate with Germany, and yielded to German pressure by declaring war against the U.S.S.R. This took place on June 27, 1941. The British, though showing some understanding of Hungary's difficult situation, answered on December 6th by a declaration of war on Hungary. The attack on Pearl Harbour seemed to have dealt a decisive blow to Allied hopes and this prompted Bárdossy to declare war on the U.S.A., without consulting the Regent or Parliament.

On March 10th Horthy succeeded in getting rid of Bárdossy and nominated Nicholas Kállay as his successor. Kállay tried with great skill to maintain the country's independence. Though he gained time and probably saved many—mainly Jewish—lives through his temporizing policy, he was doomed to fail. On March 17, 1943, Horthy, who had been asked to pay a visit to Hitler, left the country. During his absence Hungary was occupied by German forces and on his return the Regent was forced to appoint another government. The new Prime Minister, Sztójay, was a willing tool in German hands and the unfortunate country was to feel the full weight of Nazi methods, assiduously emulated by the scum which constituted the Hungarian Nazi movement. The tragic deportation of Jews began, some 450,000 in all, most of whom were to perish in Auschwitz. It took some time for Horthy to get over the shock created by the new situation—one must not forget that he was seventy-six years of age—and to find means to intervene effectively in the conduct of affairs. That he could do so at all was because the Germans were anxious to keep up a semblance of legality, and Sztójay was unable to render harmless all the supporters of the Regent.

Horthy's activity was as much concerned with short-term tasks—such as stopping the Jewish deportations, in which he succeeded—as with the principal problem of getting Hungary out of the whole ghastly business Contacts with Allied, particularly British, circles had been established even under the premiership of Kállay, but negotiations were, on the whole, fruitless since, from the Allied point of view, the question was of secondary importance only. In July 1944 Horthy made it known to Hitler that, unless he was able to ensure an effective defence of Hungary against Russian attack, he would have to ask for a separate armistice. At the end of August, in the confusion created in German circles by the new, pro-Soviet volte-face of Roumania (who after the Second Vienna Award found it more prudent to make friends with the Germans) Horthy was able to oust Sztójay and appoint a new Prime Minister, General Lakatos. As Horthy, and most of the Hungarian politicians, had no sympathy with the Soviets, and as the Anglo-Americans refused to have dealings with them, the decision to ask for an armistice was not easily taken. In the meanwhile the Gestapo arrested the most trusted men of Horthy's entourage one by one, including his own son. On October 15th Horthy made a broadcast speech in which he announced that Hungary was asking for an armistice. It was too late. The state machinery had been sabotaged and his decision had little more effect than to make things even more confused. Horthy, arrested, was carried away to Germany and Szálasi reached what he was always waiting for, supreme power, bringing in his wake robbers, murderers and sadists.

Fortunately for the country, disorganization had reached such proportions that mass murders, on the efficient German scale, could not be carried out. Time as well was lacking. On Christmas Eve 1944 the Russian army reached Budapest. The day before, under Soviet protection, a new, provisional Hungarian government had been formed at Debrecen. In the west of the country fighting went on until April; in Budapest and the rest of the country a new life had earlier begun.

However tempting it is to follow the transformation of Hungary into a People's Democracy, the events of the subsequent years are still too recent to be seen in perspective, and there is not sufficient source-material available on which to base an objective historical judgment. Hungary's history since 1945 has not been uneventful, and the tragic days of autumn 1956 have left their imprint on the minds of all; but it is still too soon for the historian to replace the reporter in recounting them. It is necessary therefore to leave Hungary at what is undoubtedly the beginning of a new chapter in the history of this much-torn country.

A SELECT LIST OF DATES

896(?)	The Conquest of Hungary
955	Battle at Lechfeld, end of the 'Adventures'
1000–1038	St Stephen I
1038–1041	Peter (for the first time)
1041–1044	Samuel Aba
1044–1046	Peter (for the second time)
1047–1060	Andrew I
1060–1063	Béla I
1063–1074	Salomon
1074–1077	Géza I
1077–1095	St Ladislas I
1091	The Conquest of Croatia
1095–1116	Coloman ·
1116–1131	Stephen II
1131–1141	Béla II the Blind
1141–1161	Géza II
1161–1172	Stephen III
1162–1163	Ladislas II (anti-King)
1163–1165	Stephen IV (anti-King)
1172–1196	Béla III
1196–1204	Imre
1204–1205	Ladislas III
1205–1235	Andrew II
1217–1218	Andrew's Crusade
1222	The Golden Bull
1235–1270	Béla IV
1241–1242	The Mongol invasion
1270–1272	Stephen V
1272–1290	Ladislas IV, the Coman
1278	Battle of Marchfeld
1290–1301	Andrew III, the last Árpád
1308–1342	Robert Charles I of Anjou
1342–1382	Louis I, the Great, of Anjou
1347–1350	Italian campaigns

1351	The promulgation of laws resulting in the social division of the country
1366	First battle against the Turks
1367	Foundation of the first Hungarian University
1370	Louis I crowned King of Poland
1385–1387	Maria of Anjou
1387–1437	Sigismund of Luxemburg
1396	Sigismund defeated by the Turks at Nicopolis
1410	Sigismund Holy Roman Emperor
1437	Peasant revolt of Anthony Budai Nagy
1437–1439	Albert of Habsburg
1440–1444	Vladislas I
1440	Battle of Varna
1446–1452	John Hunyadi, Regent
1452–1458	Ladislas V
1456	Hunyadi's victory at Belgrade
1458–1490	Matthias Hunyadi
1473	The first book printed in Hungary
1485	Occupation of Vienna
1490–1516	Vladislas II
1514	Dózsa's peasant rebellion
1515	Vladislas's matrimonial agreement with the Habsburgs
1516–1526	Louis II
1526	The battle of Mohács
1526–1564	Ferdinand I
1526–1541	John Zápolyai, 'national' king
1538	The Treaty of Várad between Ferdinand I and Zápolyai
1541	The Turks occupy Buda
1541–1551	Izabel rules the Eastern Kingdom
1551	Martinuzzi murdered—For fifteen years Transylvania and the motherland are united
1556–1571	John Sigismund rules the Eastern Kingdom
1564–1576	Maximilian I
1566	The fall of Szigetvár
1571–1576	Stephen Báthori, Prince of Transylvania
1576–1581	Christopher Báthori in charge of Transylvania
1578–1608	Rudolf
1581–1597	Sigismund Báthori, Prince of Transylvania

1591–1606	Fifteen Years War
1595	Turkish victory of Mezökeresztes
1604–1606	The Bocskai rebellion
1606	Treaty of Vienna between Bocskai and the Habsburgs; Treaty of Zsitvatorok with the Turks
1606–1608	Sigismund Rákóczi, Prince of Transylvania
1608–1613	Gabriel Báthori, Prince of Transylvania
1608–1619	Matthias II
1613–1629	Gabriel Bethlen, Prince of Transylvania
1619–1637	Ferdinand II
1621	Treaty of Nicholsburg between Bethlen and Ferdinand II
1630–1648	George Rákóczi, Prince of Transylvania
1635	University of Nagyszombat founded by Cardinal Pázmány
1637–1657	Ferdinand III
1645	Treaty of Linz between Rákóczi and Ferdinand
1648–1660	George Rákóczi II, Prince of Transylvania
1657–1705	Leopold I
1660–1662	John Kemény, Prince of Transylvania
1662–1690	Michael Apafi I, Prince of Transylvania
1664	Treaty of Vasvár with the Turks
1666–1671	The Wesselényi conspiracy
1674	Protestant clergymen sent to the galleys
1678–1682	The Thököly rebellion
1686	The reconquest of Buda
1699	Peace of Karlovici—Hungary liberated
1703–1711	The Rákóczi rebellion
1705–1711	Joseph I
1711–1740	Charles III
1722	The Pragmatic Sanction—Hungary accepts the female succession
1736–1739	War with the Turks
1740–1780	Maria Theresa
1767	The *Urbarium*. The review of contracts relating to socage
1772	*Ratio Educationis*
1780–1790	Joseph II
1784	Roumanian peasant revolt
1790–1792	Leopold II
1792–1835	Francis I

1795	Martinovics and other conspirators executed
1801	Kazinczy leaves the prison
1802	Count Francis Széchenyi founds the National Museum
1825	Foundation of the Hungarian Academy
1830	Beginnings of steamship navigation on the Danube
1831–1832	Cholera epidemic
1835–1848	Ferdinand V
1842	Laying of the foundation-stone of the Suspension Bridge
1847–1848	Important reforms voted by the Diet
1848–1849	War of Independence
1848–1916	Francis Joseph
1867	The Compromise
1896	Millenary celebrations
1914–1918	First World War
1916–1918	Charles IV
1918–1919	People's Republic—Soviet Republic
1920–1944	Nicholas Horthy, Regent
1920	Treaty of Trianon
1921	Dethronement of the Habsburgs
1925	Introduction of a new currency, the *Pengö*
1927	Italo-Hungarian Treaty of Friendship
1938	First Vienna Award
1939	Reoccupation of Ruthenia
1940	Second Vienna Award
1941	Attack on Yugoslavia—War with the U.S.S.R., Great Britain the U.S.A.
1943	Germany occupies Hungary
1944	Horthy abducted to Germany—Soviet troops enter Hungary

INDEX

[The names of the kings of Hungary are not included.]

DATE DUE

NOV 30			
Dec 15			